BETHEL *and* AURORA

AMS PRESS

NEW YORK

Dr. William Keil, founder and leader of the colony.

BETHEL *and* AURORA

AN
EXPERIMENT IN COMMUNISM
AS PRACTICAL CHRISTIANITY

WITH
SOME ACCOUNT OF
PAST AND PRESENT VENTURES
IN COLLECTIVE LIVING

By
ROBERT J. HENDRICKS

"*From every man according to his capacity to every man according to his needs.*"

The PRESS *of the* PIONEERS
New York
1933

Reprinted from the edition of 1933, New York

First AMS edition published 1971

Manufactured in the United States of America

International Standard Book Number: 0-404-08428-1

Library of Congress Catalog Card Number: 75-134380

AMS PRESS INC.
NEW YORK, N.Y.   10003

Land of the Empire Builders,
Land of the Golden West,
Conquered and held by freemen,
Fairest and the best,
Onward and upward ever,
Forward and on, and on,
Hail to thee, Land of Heroes,
My Oregon.

Land of the rose and sunshine,
Land of the summer's breeze,
Laden with health and vigor,
Fresh from the Western seas,
Blest by blood of martyrs,
Land of the setting sun,
Hail to thee, Land of Promise,
My Oregon.

————

DEDICATED

TO MY WIFE

CONTENTS

ILLUSTRATIONS

AN APPRECIATION

*T*HE *true story of the successful Aurora cooperative
colony, spiced, as this narrative is, with revealing imaginary conversations and incidents, introduces a new figure
in American history. Dr. William Keil had rare qualities of
leadership. He was a dictator, but his unquestioned control
rested upon confidence and and love, and not upon force.*

*And for some readers, the book will have even greater
significance. In this modern world, when ideals are submerged and overwhelmed in the mighty flood of materialism, it is well to be reminded that sentiment still persists
and still maintains an existence. In every generation, there
are those who cling to their ideals, and who believe in the
healing virtues of loving kindness and gentle tolerance. Always, there have been, and always there will be, some who
will keep the lamp burning, no matter how dark the night
may seem.*

*So, when the world has grown tired of coarse and ignoble
vulgarity, truth and brotherly love will gain wider recognition, even if not universally accepted.—*

CHARLES H. CAREY, President,
Oregon Historical Society.

FOREWORD

A FEW families near the then struggling town of Pittsburgh, Pennsylvania, in 1844 went to the wilderness of Missouri and began building Bethel, founded upon the principle of property and labor in common. They adopted a constitution. They brought into community use money, livestock, machinery, implements and tools to the value of $30,802.75. Most came empty handed. They held together under their original leader slightly more than thirty-three years. In that time they built four towns; they sent five covered wagon companies across the plains, and about a hundred members by way of Panama. They paid back in money the original amounts contributed, and they had left to divide among themselves about 23,500 acres of land and the mills, shops, stores and other personal property of three towns, worth at present day prices about three million dollars.

They paid their taxes, but they did not add one cent to the burdens of government with a single person sent to jail or even arrested, or committed to a public institution of any kind. Of course they had no paupers, or money from poor funds. There was never a divorce or separation; no lawsuits; no quarrels or even disputes not settled amicably among themselves. They suffered no fire loss in their larger colony at Aurora, Oregon.

Their leader was Dr. William Keil, whom they trusted. He was their guide in things spiritual and temporal; a benign autocrat with iron will and firm purpose; honest, wise, kind, just—though claiming no autocratic powers, but rather assuming the offices of a faithful servant to all his people.

Coming into the community at the beginning were two profound scholars, graduates of German universities. They studied the ideals of social history, the ambitious speculations of the leaders of thought from Pythagoras and Plato and Jesus and Paul and all the rest, who dreamed of the perfect society for the world's people in their upward march from the dark beginnings of the race. The triumvirate of speculative thought arrived at this eternally true and absolutely essential basis for harmonious colony life: "From every man according to his capacity to every man according to his needs."

The Golden Rule of the Sermon on the Mount they observed; but they went a step further, to the Diamond Rule of communal life: "Be kindly affectioned one to another with brotherly love; in honor preferring one another," as given by Paul to the church of Rome: a complementary and binding rule the observance of which is alike required, to give the stamp of permanence to such a society.

Under the guidance of Dr. Keil, the colony covered wagon train sang its way across in 1855, when perhaps fifty thousand turned back or feared to start, owing to the menace of the hostile red tribes; the first and only cavalcade of "boat canoes" that was led by a plains hearse—and the last of its kind and under like circumstances the world will or can see.

This makes a story worthy of an epic by a genius of Homeric mold, forms an epoch in the winning of the West in the days when the perils and barriers of prairie, plain and mountain seemed insurmountable.

Such are a few of the high lights of an interesting experiment in Communism as practical Christianity, the most successful the world has witnessed, considering the space of time it endured and that it had no peculiarity of religious belief, or dress, or living conditions, or social relations, in any way different from that practiced by its neighbors, other than the one fact that its property was held in common and the fruits of its labors flowed to a common treasury.

Observing in letter and spirit the rules of the Keil colony, starting with its present assets and liabilities, a community any where in the United States would become at once solvent and self contained, and soon prosperous—without violating a precept of American loyalty or patriotism. And this would hold true for any country with a like system of laws.

R. J. H.

Salem, Oregon, July 15, 1933.

BETHEL *and* AURORA

CHAPTER 1

PARTING OF THE WAYS

SMALL things change mighty events. Battles have hung on the quarter of the wind, on the weather, on a word. Wars have started from a wink, from the raising of an eyebrow. It has been said the map of Europe would have been different with an inch added to the length of Cleopatra's nose. A shower shifted the tide of victory at Waterloo. Lives of individuals are tuned to high success or turned to dismal failure by an impulse.

John A. Roebling, destined to give to the world a new idea in the building of bridges, was born at Mülhausen, Prussia, June 16, 1806. Soon after graduating from the polytechnic school at Berlin he came to America, and in 1831 entered on the practice of his profession in Western Pennsylvania. He established in Pittsburgh a manufactory of wire rope, and in May, 1845, completed his first important structure, a suspended aqueduct across the Allegheny River. This was followed by the Monongahela suspension bridge at Pittsburgh and several suspended aqueducts on the Delaware and Hudson Canal. Removing his wire manufactory to Trenton, New Jersey, he began in 1851 the erection at Niagara Falls of a long span wire suspension bridge with double roadway for railway and carriage uses, which was completed in 1855. Owing to novel design the most eminent engineers regarded this bridge as foredoomed to failure, but with its complete success suspension bridges rapidly multiplied and the use of wire ropes instead of chain cables became all but universal.

In 1867, Mr. Roebling was the builder of a still more

remarkable suspension bridge over the Ohio River at Cincinnati, with a clear span of 1056 feet. This added to his
reputation, and his design for the great bridge spanning
the East River between New York and Brooklyn was
adopted. While aiding in laying out the towers for the
bridge, Roebling received an accidental injury which resulted in his death at Brooklyn from tetanus on July 22,
1869. The bridge was completed by his son, Washington
Augustus Roebling, who had joined his father in building
the Pittsburgh suspension bridge across the Allegheny.

Soon after the arrival in America of the young engineer
from Germany, he was a visitor at the farm home of Andrew Giesy, thirteen miles west of the town of Pittsburgh.
The Giesy land now forms a part of the fashionable resi-
dential district of Sewickley, Pennsylvania. Young Roebling there met Helena Giesy, beautiful daughter of the
household. Occasional visits grew into frequent calls, and
first favorable impressions blossomed into mutual devotion,
followed by ardent love and the pledges to which such
affairs of the heart have led since the race was young.

Success followed the hard work and close application
of the struggling young engineer. The genius which Edi-
son once defined as ninety-five per cent hard work and
the inspiration which another has said comes principally
from perspiration were pointing the way to a future bright
with promise. Marriage vows were exchanged. The day
for the nuptials was set. The wedding trousseau was ordered. This was in 1843. John A. Roebling was thirty-
seven, Helena Giesy was twenty-eight. They were old
enough to know their minds. Their hearts were ripe for the
mutual love they felt. They were well matched, suited to
each other in native tongue and temperament. They both
spoke German and had learned English. Andrew Giesy and

his wife and older children had come from near Berne, Switzerland.

But there was a halt in the wedding preparations. There had appeared in that vicinity a young German preacher with a new interpretation of the Christian religion and what it means in the life of the world. He was Dr. William Keil, born in Prussia March 6, 1812. He had learned the trade of tailor in Germany, and marrying had come to New York City where he opened a merchant tailoring shop and prospered. But he had imbibed the zeal of the reformer, and he was restless in an ambition to do a great work in the world. Against the wishes of his good wife, who urged him to let well enough alone, he disposed of his business and turned his face westward. He was then thirty-one. As was but natural, the exponent of the new doctrine commenced work among the people who understood his language, for up to that time the late comer had acquired only a smattering or working knowledge of English.

He preached the gospel of unselfishness, which was proclaimed by him to be the very essence of love. "Love one another" he held to be the words of fundamental truth, the corner stone of the entire structure of Christianity, and in time, if not from the beginning, his interpretation of these words was made in so broad and liberal a sense as to require a community of goods and effects.

Dr. Keil had broken with the Lutheran church and joined with the Methodists, but had finally come to oppose every sectarian creed, having convinced himself that the implication of lessons of the New Testament was against all sects.

Dr. Keil was made welcome in the Giesy home. From that temporary shelter, he fared forth and preached his gospel of love and unselfishness, and soon he had a following. By the intense earnestness of his fiery zeal, he won zealous adherents, willing and ready to follow his leadership.

He was by nature a leader. Few have repeated themselves in their sons in the world's long history. Nature in most cases seems to break the mold, as it were, after the first cast. It was to be said of him nearly a half century after his death, by a lifelong follower:

"Dr. Keil was a natural born leader, who was deeply impressed that he was serving God, and the people obeyed him as if he were a father. This was due both to the originality of his ideas, and to his strongly vital temperament. In person he was a very powerful, heavy-set man. He was above medium height, and weighed considerably over two hundred pounds, being in form and figure like most all leaders of men, such as D. L. Moody and others. He had an upright bearing, a most open countenance, but with positive features, and even a bold and searching eye and direct gaze. In all matters he was a leader."

Many have spoken of his searching eyes. One of the men until recently living who was a follower of Dr. Keil from his own childhood, and to the day of the leader's death, said lately that "the old doctor," as he was familiarly known in his closing years, "could inspire courage and confidence, and obedience to his wishes, in any one by the piercing look of his eyes, as if he were gazing into the innermost recesses of the heart and searching the very soul of his listener."

FIFTEEN children were born into the family of Andrew and Barbara Giesy. Coming from their native Switzerland to America seeking larger opportunities, they had settled on newly opened land in Western Pennsylvania. One boy, Rudolph, had died in infancy. There was another Rudolph among the younger children, whose activities were to be singularly helpful in community life.

Adolph Sutro, designer and constructor of the famous Sutro tunnel, built to drain and ventilate the mines of the celebrated Comstock Lode in Nevada, pioneer millionaire of San Francisco, the philanthropist who gave the city by the Golden Gate a great library and park, was a relative of the Giesys.

Andrew and Barbara Giesy and all their ten sons and four daughters joined at once or later in supporting the activities of Dr. Keil. Among the sons four, Andrew, Christian, Samuel and Henry, became preachers—were active in carrying on the campaign of speaking and teaching. Andrew and Christian, near in age to Dr. Keil, and Henry, one of the younger brothers, were soon on fire with the enthusiasm of new converts. They gave effective aid in expounding the new doctrine and gaining adherents to the movement they were convinced would lead to better ways of living and higher ideals of serving their fellow men.

Helena hoped she might bring Mr. Roebling to embrace the teaching of her brothers and the man they had accepted as their leader. There is doubt as to whether Dr. Keil had in his first plans visioned anything more definite

than the preaching of what he had come to believe the true
Christian religion, under the fatherhood of God and the
brotherhood of man; not as a vague theory or according to
a hypothesis expressed in empty words, but in spirit and
in truth, literally, an all powerful and all seeing and all
knowing Father, a Father with the attributes of an earthly
father infinitely magnified and extended, and a brotherhood embracing all the race. The intensity of his idealism
attracted the curious. Soon there was opposition. Some who
came to hear the new preacher were displeased with his
teaching.

Living in the neighborhood at that time were a few
former members of the Rapp colony at Economy, Pennsylvania, not far distant. When "Count" Leon had led
away about a third of the Rapp colonists, these had been
among the seceding members. They had followed "Count"
Leon because he had promised them greater freedom, better living conditions and larger opportunities. The Rappists had become celibates after a religious revival, though
at first they married and gave in marriage. Husbands in
the Rapp colony had given up their wives and wives had
given up their husbands, and afterward to the end of their
community life they practiced celibacy. The seceders coun-
tenanced marriage. "Graf" ("Count") Leon had an in-
gratiating way. He was suave, plausible. The seceders
formed a new colony at Philippsburg, Pennsylvania, ten
miles below Economy. Though the Rappists had paid the
seceders $105,000 in three installments within twelve
months, they did not prosper under the adventurer's control, and the property, which had been in common, like
that of the Rappists, was divided and the members scattered. (By right name, the German adventurer was Bernhard Müller, who had assumed the title of Graf or Count
Maximilian de Leon. He had absconded with a few of his

followers in a boat to Alexandria, Louisiana, on the Red River, where this singular character perished of cholera in 1833.)

It became noised about that the new preacher wished to form a colony with the property of the members held in common. There were many conflicting rumors concerning the strange beliefs of Dr. Keil and his followers. There was persecution. Some of his meetings were broken up. Scenes were enacted like the ones that attended the first gatherings of the Salvation Army in the towns and cities of the United States. As "the blood of the martyrs is the seed of the church," and intolerance at all times and everywhere has largely defeated its own ends, there resulted a closer bond between the Keil followers and their leader, and between the members themselves.

At more than one meeting, eggs were thrown at the speaker, spattering his clothing, and vegetables were hurled from the hands of hangers-on. But the preacher serenely pursued his work, only occasionally halting his regular discourse to mildly condemn these outrages against free speech and free assembly and the right of any man to worship God according to the dictates of his own conscience for which cause the Pilgrim Fathers braved the perils of the sea and faced the dangers of hostile savages that they might establish new homes and raise up a civil society dedicated to these primary rights of a government of and by and for the people.

Dr. Keil's life was threatened by mob violence, but he calmly went his way. It was not long till the young men who followed him were ready to defend his right to expound his doctrines. They came armed, but when the leader learned of this he counseled patience. He told them God would protect them and him and show the scoffers and disturbers the error of their course.

" 'I will render vengeance to mine enemies,' " he told his followers, "was the spirit of the old dispensation, and those who thought they were God's chosen people hated their enemies and adopted as their rule an eye for an eye and a tooth for a tooth—and had to establish six cities of refuge to prevent miscarriages under that cruel law of retaliation; but the new dispensation taken from the Sermon on the Mount is this: 'Love your enemies, do good to them that hate you, and pray for them that despitefully use you, and persecute you,' so we must carry our law of love even to the point of including those who place themselves in the position of enemies."

This was a difficult precept for the young men. They were reluctant to follow it, but Dr. Keil did; and he firmly demanded its strict observance in letter and spirit; and he had the satisfaction of seeing several who came to scoff remaining to pray, and soon numbered these with his congregation. In cases where the use of halls and school houses was refused, the meetings were held in homes. A small number of the seceding members of the Rapp colony were early among his company. Their counsel was for a new trial of Communism under his leadership, in a place where there would be none to dispute or hinder the working out of the experiments in which they had been participants.

CHAPTER 3

THE wedding day of John A. Roebling and Helena Giesy approached. He was rising in his chosen profession and prospering in his business. She was torn between the love of the man to whom she was betrothed and loyalty to her family. In tender entreaty she pleaded with him to join the movement that was gathering strength under the preaching and teaching of Dr. Keil and her brothers, for by this time it was determined that they should go further west, where land might be had for the taking or at low prices, and where they could worship as they pleased, away from persecution and the sneers of intolerance. More especially were they resolved to free themselves from the influences of sectarian doctrines. They desired to follow the man who had convinced them concerning the right way of life.

This was the time of testing for Helena Giesy. Happiness was hers for the choosing, with protection, companionship and love in the home that was planned. Hardship surely lay the other way, but it was in her belief the path of duty. It held her by the blood bonds of filial gratitude and the devotion she felt for her brothers and sisters. It was a hard choice. She had come in life's journey to the forks of the road. Pioneering in a strange country, following an experiment that led she knew not whither, loomed in the direction one road led, toward the setting sun. The promises of happy wedlock and the comradeship of the man she had learned to respect and honor and had come to love devotedly beckoned and appealed for the near way.

There was a last meeting the details of which the members of her family were not privileged to know, nor were they ever divulged. They were buried with the man and the woman who were the actors in the drama of the parting of the ways.

Sadly but firmly Helena Giesy turned her tearful face westward. Young Roebling had made up his mind to remain with his business and his work. He could not bring himself to the breaking point of following the fortunes of the people who were bound to cast their future with the Argonauts of the new dream. She could not force herself to stay. She had finally refused the offer of marriage to the man to whom she had pledged herself for time and eternity. She had declared she would never wed another. She had room in her great heart for but one such love. She faithfully kept the promise for herself, not asking and not wishing for a mutual pledge. Helena Giesy never married. She became one of the saints of the community at Bethel and at Aurora, serene, lovely in spirit, devoted in service, free from self pity. She retained her singular beauty throughout her useful life, even in mature age, up to the very last.

In the private cemetery at Aurora, near what was once the park for the community, in its time the most charming spot of its kind in Oregon, there is a marble shaft marking a well kept grave. On its white surface is lettered this inscription: "Helena Giesy. Born 14 December, 1815. Died 29 May, 1890."

Near by rests the leader of the colony at Bethel and Aurora, with a headstone no more pretentious, engraved: "Dr. Wm. Keil. Born 6 March, 1812. Died 30 December 1877."

In that little cemetery sleep other members of the Keil family, and a few of the leaders in helpfulness whose unselfish service in life brought them the honor of a place in this hallowed retreat, according to the verdict of the people among whom they spent their days.

Helena Giesy graced the frequent festive occasions in the colony life. She was the repository of many a secret whispered into her ear in confidence. She was as a fond mother of all the children, though denied any of her very own. She seemed everywhere at once on the great occasions of colony life. She was the good angel of the first large covered wagon train that brought part of the colony people from Bethel, across over 2000 miles of prairie, plain and mountain wilderness.

She carried her own secret nor ever complained. It was as if her pure heart, denied by a combination of circumstances its first great longing, opened in a prodigality of outpouring love for all the people she had made it her supreme choice to serve.

There will be found in these pages, under the title, "What Might Have Been," further words concerning the genius of the Brooklyn bridge, John A. Roebling.

CHAPTER 4

DR. KEIL and a few of his followers went to Missouri in 1844. They took up four sections of government land in Shelby County and added more by purchase until they had four thousand acres there and thirteen hundred acres some sixty miles away, in Adair County. They began the building of the town of Bethel. As fast as they could dispose of their property in Pennsylvania, others came. Still more were added from Missouri, Ohio, Iowa and elsewhere. A few came from Germany. There was at least one Jewish family. They built homes for the first comers with families, in order of precedence and need. As soon as roofs had been provided for these, provision made for the single men and women, and shops and stores opened for the beginnings of their trade, they finished a church and a school house. They erected a saw mill and a woolen mill, and plied their mechanical industries. Thus thriftily they built a prosperous town.

On the tract in Adair County, there was already a small saw mill, at the point they named Nineveh, on the Sheridan River, using the water power there—the main reason for the location. Finding this seasonally insufficient, they added a steam plant, and they maintained at Nineveh a bustling village with shops to supply their own needs and accommodate outsiders for the colony's profit. They erected there a grist mill and ground good flour that gained a wide reputation and brought a fine custom for a capacity output. Also, their Nineveh shop making boots and shoes enjoyed like favor and a profitable patronage, with a con-

siderable force of expert workmen under the direction of
Charles Becke, Sr., related by marriage to Dr. Keil, and
afterward patriarchal head of the upstanding family at
Aurora bearing that name.

The colonists aimed to grow or make everything they
themselves required, and by supplying their neighbors and
more remote customers from their factories and shops and
stores, they steadily developed a status of sure and expanding prosperity.

As for their own wants, there was always enough, nor
was there ever any rationing or stinting, and no books were
ever kept in supplying the necessaries of life, though in the
beginning they endured the ordinary hardships of the
pioneer; but with hard work they made progress from the
first.

The members of the community were all considered as
one big family. The family purse belonged to all. There
was a common treasury. The things each one needed, in
clothing, boots or shoes, hats or food and all other articles
of whatever kind for home or farm or shop or mill, was his
or hers for the taking or asking; and no one abused his or
her privileges. This was true from the beginning to the
end, from 1844 to the last day but one of 1877, when Dr.
Keil died; over a third of a century, and up to the final
dissolution of the colony, which was decreed in 1881.

The original colonists went to Missouri to establish a
Christian community. Most of these first comers were willing to leave the ordering of everything to Dr. Keil. At
one of the early meetings the form of their contract was
discussed. There were differences of opinion. Several tenta-
tive plans were suggested.

"I am willing to put in all the money and property I
have, and I want no receipt or contract—as for me and
mine, we ask only the word of Dr. Keil that he will guide

and protect us; we want that, but we wish only that," spoke up one of the leading men—and the sentiment was generally approved by those present.

The meeting was in the nature of a religious revival, such as stirred men and women more deeply, perhaps, than has been done or was possible in the past half century.

These people had run against something of the same form of intolerance and persecution that drove the passengers in the *Mayflower* out to the open sea in search of a new home, the hardships and dangers of which they were more than willing to risk for themselves and their families. It was even more intense than the spirit of the covered wagon caravans that was soon to stir the restless urge of pioneering. It was much more profound than the glamor of the days of 1849 that was aroused by the lure of gold. It ran deeper. It recked not of profits and thought little or nothing of riches as measured by the possession of this world's goods. Born of the love of God, it grew in the passion for putting into force the precepts of the brotherhood of man.

"Love one another," admonished Dr. Keil, and his followers were ever resolved to practice what he preached.

CHAPTER 5

LITTLE OR NOTHING

A MAJORITY of Dr. Keil's first adherents would ha been satisfied to trust him with all they possesse asking no receipt and demanding only his word that h would pilot them, but he would not have it that way. He would lead them, but also he would share with them his little all in money, and his services to the uttermost.

As one of the first acts of the beginning, a book was opened at Bethel in which was kept an "alphabetical list of the names of persons who conduced any money or stock to the original fund with which the Bethel community was first founded, with the respective amounts set opposite their names." (The quoted words made up the book heading.)

Sixty-one persons in all brought in money or livestock or both, or tools or machinery or implements counted in value as money, as the livestock was also valued. The largest single sum was $2713. There were only nine other amounts of $1000 or above; seventeen were below $100. One "conduced" $5 and another $6. Dr. Keil himself was credited with $81.94. Christopher W. Wolff, concerning whom there will be much to say in the following pages, brought $127.39. One of the former members of the Rapp and "Count" Leon communities contributed $630.28. Most brought nothing, excepting themselves and their wives and children and their willingness to work hard and serve faithfully.

The total of money and stock and machinery and implements and tools was $30,802.75. That was the entire original capital destined to grow through diligent labor to

a large total, in ten years to a value for land and improvements above $100,000, as values now go, several times $100,000. And eventually all the first "conduced" money and stock was to be returned (in money) to those who gave it, without interest, unless it had already been so refunded.

The contract or constitution of the society was very simple, written in German. The original is preserved by a friend of the writer. The date of its adoption was August 30th, 1844, soon after the beginnings were made at Bethel. Translated into English, it reads:

RULES OF THE CHRISTIAN COMMUNITY

Having united ourselves into a Christian society we have drawn up the following rules for a faithful observance and have unanimously adopted them:

1. Every member must lay all he possesses into a common treasury and labor for the common welfare of the society during three years, in order to establish the beginning of the common welfare, so that each one might come to his own during these three years.

2. This society must not rest on anything else than the love of God, so that every opportunity for selfish gain be excluded. But our diligence and activity must be as an open fountain in order to do good to the poor, that by our means we might be of benefit not only to the brethren that are with us at present, but also to the poor in the future. To this end also shall serve those of the poor who are strong. Therefore a common treasury is attainable, wherein all diligence and activity on the part of each member is shown in abundance, and this must be the source from which we must draw continuously.

3. If one or another brother should leave us during these three years, we cannot promise to any one a large requital, because the purpose of this society is not to lay up treasures, but to administer continuously help to the poor, and in this we base ourselves on the Word of God: "Having therefore food and raiment let us be con-

tent." But should one or another brother be no longer willing to remain with us, the Word of God also says: "You shall not let your brother go away from you empty." Thus, in this matter also, we shall find a way to deal with the brother, that we might abide in love.

4. Although we cannot promise much to any one at the beginning, nevertheless to the single brother who leaves the society shall be given, from the society, yearly twenty dollars and to the single sister twelve dollars, provided she is eighteen years old, and this applies to such as live with their parents as well as those who live outside their families. In regard to the fathers (men who have families) who leave us, it shall be granted for them, for their wives and their children, under age, the sum of forty dollars, for each year, as a compensation.

5. Should a brother who has brought in property leave us, then one-fourth of this will be refunded to him, and within three years the other three-fourths, that is every year one-fourth, without interest. The house or land is left to the society with all its belongings; the same with the craftsman in town.

6. In case some one should marry within these three years and make a claim for a house or land, this shall not be conceded to him, until all other families which have already been with us are taken care of, after which they shall in their turn be also taken care of. This society, moreover, does not allow them to marry with such as do not believe in our teaching. This, however, does not mean that no one shall marry with a person of the outside world, because if such a person is or will be a believer in the Word he is welcomed by us.

7. Twelve men from among us must be elected who will look after the welfare of the society in all things; every single community having the right to choose two men, to whom it must bestow its full confidence, so that when a person wishes to give money for the good of the society it will be handed and entrusted to their care. These twelve men also have the right for the good of the society and for the advancement of the same, from time to time, to draw up rules which are suitable to circumstances, so that we may always be enabled to abide in love and peace. Amen.

This "constitution" was never more than a "scrap of paper." The real compact was an implied one, written on the tablets of the hearts of the people who built Bethel (meaning the house of God), its only provision being a general one that all would follow the leadership of Dr. Keil, their chief preacher and their sole arbiter in things both spiritual and temporal. He was their benevolent autocrat, by tacit and common consent. His word was law. None other was needed, fundamental or by legislative or initiative enactment. Nor any enforcing officers. Nor divorce courts, jails, asylums, almshouses. As a matter of course, they took care of all their own, in health or sickness or old age, and every disagreement was settled by Dr. Keil. The land titles were in his name, personally or through the chosen trustees, who were in most cases his echoed voice and his right hand rather than independent overseers of the activities and industries of the colony people. The government was like that of a large and loving family. There were no hard and fast rules. All worked long hours at first and denied themselves much, and they labored diligently thereafter, but no one was driven, and by natural selection, as it seemed, each took the task to which he was best suited, whether hard or easy.

No regard was paid to the three year period mentioned in their written "constitution." For over thirty years, few of the newly admitted members or the younger people knew there was a constitution. The community steadily prospered. They accumulated a surplus. Their numbers increased by births and from outside accessions, till about a thousand members were at Bethel in the early fifties.

Then came the epochal emigration bound to the Oregon Country, which began to assume large proportions in the late forties. Many members of the "covered wagon" trains were from Missouri. The colony people made their own wagons, of the best materials, honestly built. A considerable number of the Bethel wagons had crossed the plains to the promised land beyond the Rockies and the Blue Mountains and the Cascades. These wagons were of a style peculiarly their own, and their sturdiness gained such favor as to make the demand for them the capacity of the Bethel shops, after their fame had gone forth among the outfitting caravans along the Missouri River.

Naturally there arose a desire among some of the members to go to the Oregon Country. The blood of the pioneers was in their veins. It had carried them across the Atlantic on sailing vessels; to the first settlements in Pennsylvania; to the new land in the wilderness of Missouri. It was decided to send out a scouting party, like that of the Children of Israel in their wilderness wanderings, of which Joshua of old was the chief optimist, according to the sacred record. So eight men and one woman were commissioned, and in 1853 they traveled across the plains, a very small part of the 50,000 or more people who completed the journey from Missouri River starting places to points west of the Rocky Mountains that year in the covered wagon caravans that made almost a continuous procession of white topped caravels of the desert up the Platte Valley in the early months, after the spring grass was in sufficient abundance for their cattle and horses and mules. The "spies" from Bethel were Joseph and Adam Knight, Adam Scheule, Michael Schaefer, John and Hans Stauffer, John Ginger and Mr. and Mrs. Christian Giesy. This party, among whom Christian Giesy was the leading spirit and most nearly and ably represented the ideals of Dr. Keil, made the long journey without more than the usual hardships. At The Dalles of the Columbia River, they negotiated a crossing to the north side.

They arrived at old Fort Vancouver in time to see Ulysses S. Grant, then regimental quartermaster attached to the United States regular troops near the fort of the Hud-

son's Bay Company, so long in charge of Dr. John Mc-
Loughlin, called the first Governor of Oregon. The death
of Colonel Bliss of the Adjutant General's department on
July 5, 1853, promoted Grant to the captaincy of a company then stationed at Humboldt Bay, California. But notice did not reach him till in September, and he was on the
point of leaving for his new command. After this strange
pawn of fortune had commanded the victorious forces in
the greatest armed struggle in history up to that time, had
served eight years as President of the United States and
completed his trip around the world, he told in his Memoirs, that were finished on his death bed, about his service at Vancouver, when his pay and that of his fellow officers was so low, and the cost of living so high, that they
decided in 1852 on growing potatoes the following year,
and Grant bought at a low price from an immigrant a team
of horses worn out on the plains. He held the plow and his
fellow officers planted the potatoes, and the promise of an
abundant crop was in the early spring more encouraging
than they could have wished. General Grant wrote:

"Luckily for us the Columbia River rose to a great height
from the melting of the snows in the mountains in June,
and overflowed and killed most of our crop. This saved
digging it up, for everybody on the Pacific Coast seemed to
have come to the conclusion at the same time that agriculture would be profitable. In 1853 more than three-
fourths of the potatoes raised were permitted to rot in the
ground or had to be thrown away. The only potatoes sold
were to our mess."

The Bethel colony spies went from Fort Vancouver to
the lower Willapa Valley, reaching that little explored
country by way of Olympia, then a crude village, now the
capital of the State of Washington.

While they were searching out a location for their settlement, they fell in with Ezra Meeker, who had crossed the plains the year before and was then also seeking a place for his future home in the Puget Sound region, of which he had heard favorable reports after wintering on the south side of the Columbia River, near Portland. Mr. Meeker gave them what information he could. He was then twenty-three, and he lived to be nearly ninety-eight, after spending a singularly busy life and becoming the chief protagonist of the importance of preserving the historical values of the Old Oregon Trail, which, with other pioneering enterprises, made him one of the most widely known and best loved men in the United States. Mr. Meeker built his pioneer cabin on McNeil Island, where the federal penitentiary is now located.

The Bethel spies made as their choice for the location of the colony home the densely timbered district on the Willapa River a short distance above the head of Willapa Bay, which is a part of Shoalwater Bay, the first inland body of water on the Pacific Ocean north of the Columbia River's mouth. They took up claims there and began preparing for the colonists who were to follow by building homes of logs and clearing land for crops.

They were led to their choice partly by the magnificent growth of timber and the fertility of the soil. The abundance of fish in the streams helped. The clams and native oysters in the mud flats inveigled them. As it was later expressed, "God Almighty set His table twice every twenty-four hours" with the recurrence of low tide. The small native oysters had a flavor more pleasing to their taste than the large bivalves of the same family found along the Eastern coasts. Many who have followed them have been free to express the same gastronomic preference. There were clams of various types, in wonderful supply, and also crabs, to say nothing of sea fish, all ready and free for the taking. It was before the day of fishing licenses or regulations.

These early comers were led to the knowledge of the great supply of clams and the abundance of the oyster beds by the habit of the crows, which had a trick of swooping down and taking them in their bills, carrying them up into the air and dropping them onto rocks below, thus breaking them open. Wise old crows. It made easy living for them; the art that must have had its origin in the coastal crow race a million years before and been handed down to these ebon partakers of "oysters on the half shell" to the wonderment of the new comers.

They found also a wealth of native berries and much wild game, from quails to deer and elk. It seemed a land especially prepared for and inviting to a settlement of pioneers, with a variety of fare far beyond the manna for the hosts led by Moses, with only a special supply of quails to break the monotony. Unlike the report of the committee of the Israelites of old in the wilderness, the favorable message of the Bethel spies was unanimous. And it was enthusiastic.

Though the pioneer settlers in their western wilderness were surrounded by Indians, they had been received with no unfriendly tokens by these first Americans, but rather with signs of welcome, albeit mixed with curiosity.

Reports went back to Bethel by the painfully slow mails of the progress being made at the Willapa settlement, and after a winter and spring of unremitting toil in the erection of houses, and clearing land and planting crops, Joseph and Adam Knight returned across the country by way of San Francisco to report in person, remaining at Bethel till the coming of the second large wagon train in 1863 to join the main body of their people who were then establishing themselves at Aurora.

The remaining seven of the forerunners worked away diligently and made good progress in preparing for the first colony covered wagon train scheduled for the fall of 1855. They had no trouble with their Indian neighbors, but the curiosity of the tribesmen shown in their frequent visits appealed to the caution of Christian Giesy, and soon after the departure of the Knights he counseled with his companions.

"Forewarned is forearmed," he said. "We are not sure what effect the coming of the large company of our people will have upon our red brothers. They may take fright over the possible loss of their lands and their rights. We must next build a house that shall be our fort. We will make it in seeming a dwelling, but it must be large enough to accommodate our own people by crowding."

So it was agreed, and they went about the task of erecting what was to be called "the fort." It was built with logs, much like the United States Army forts of the early days in the West; the outposts of civilization—similar to the one at Fort Sheridan on the Grand Ronde Indian reservation, which a few years ago was removed some distance to Dayton, Yamhill county, Oregon, where it now stands as a memorial, housing historic relics. But the Willapa "fort" was much larger than this one, where, as a young second lieutenant, Philip Sheridan was in command, little dreaming then of the not distant day when he would be the chief cavalry leader of the Union forces in the struggle over slavery and secession, as he often in his horseback excursions threaded the pioneer trails accompanied by Frances, beautiful Rogue River Indian girl, graceful as a gazelle, slender as a fawn. He had just passed his twenty-fifth year when he took charge at Fort Sheridan. He was only thirty-three when he made his famous ride, celebrated in heroic verse, from Winchester to Cedar Creek.

After the families arrived at Willapa, the caution of Christian Giesy in proposing the erection of "the fort" was appreciated. There were several rumors of intended attacks by the Indians; a number of occasions upon which they were all gathered into the big log house for days and nights on end, with pickets stationed on the outside and the men and boys sleeping with their guns and axes, ready for the threatened coming of the tribesmen.

But they suffered no harm or other inconvenience further than bad scares and sleepless night vigils, and the frequent feeding of the Indians who came prowling about. Long afterward one of these attached himself to the household of Rudolph Giesy in the colony at Aurora, as a sort of "friendly Indian," performing a little work and enjoying much good food at the sumptuous boards of the kindly colonists, but never admitted to membership in good standing of the community. They called him "Friday." He had no other name, so far as they knew. Friday would not have understood the principles of the community. But he was faithful in his way, as became the name and the character—after the companion of Robinson Crusoe. Friday lived out his days in the colony and was gathered to his tribal fathers there.

Rudolph Giesy was the member of that family spoken of in a former chapter, who was given the name of the son who died in Pennsylvania. He never married, but the household over which he presided was generally a numerous one. It occupied a large log house, baronial in its appointments, and under its friendly roof many came upon their first arrival at Aurora, remaining there till new houses could be prepared for them, or other dispositions made. That was the case with Prof. Finck, the music master, when he came with his motherless children from Bethel, and with others prominent in the annals of the community. That house still stands, little altered, and was famous as the home of the Mueckes, prominent in the hop and asparagus industries long after the dissolution of the colony.

The Willapa section had been in Oregon Territory up to the third month of the year when the first colonists settled there. General Joseph Lane, hero of the Mexican War, first Governor of Oregon, proclaimed the territory March 3, 1849. From part of the area of what was originally known as the Oregon Country, Washington was made a territory March 2, 1853, and Idaho March 3, 1863. The part west of the Rockies in Montana and Wyoming went into those territories May 26, 1864, and July 25, 1868, respectively.

A strange quirk of fortune (shall we say destiny?) placed in the hands of Horace Greeley the Oregon proxy in the Chicago convention of 1860 which nominated Abraham Lincoln for the Presidency—the proxy of Leander Holmes, sent to Mr. Greeley on the advice of Jesse Applegate, chief of Oregon pioneers. He was the Jesse Wingate of "The Covered Wagon" of Emerson Hough. But that is another story.

CHAPTER 6

ACTIVE preparations began at Bethel for the trip to the Oregon Country, to establish a new home for as many as desired to go—or rather as many as could get away—for most members hoped to be favored by selection for the journey. Plans were made to send out the first party in 1855, starting as soon as winter had passed and there was sufficient grass on the western prairies beyond the Missouri River to sustain their stock.

Ruth Baker had come with her parents, Hiram and Mary, of Pennsylvania Dutch (German) stock, to the colony from Western Pennsylvania early in the year after the first settlement, a girl of ten, eldest of a family of five. Next in age was Hannah, less than two years her junior, followed by Ethan, Beulah and Joseph, the last named a babe in arms. The Bakers had suffered from poverty and the parents were allured to colony life by the promise of security from worry and want. The father had no fixed trade, and the wolf was constantly at the door, with no steady wages and the usual ups and downs of sickness that brought the doctor with his bills, and the proverbial ill luck and distress that all too commonly dog the footsteps of the poor. Thus their domestic ship wallowed in the doldrums on a sea of indecision, getting nowhere in all their planning to provide even the bare necessaries of existence, much less making any provisions for the future, for the sunset time when they should be too old for the drudgeries of a drab and comfortless finish of their earthly journeying—thoughts they found, as so many millions before them, harrowing to their very souls and destructive of all buoyancy and every vestige of that resiliency they shared with one another in the first days of their lives together. In this plight the Bakers were found by that zealous prophet and protagonist of the community life, in which all should be for every one and every one should be for all in mutual service and hope and helpfulness, that same Christian Giesy who, even as the plans for the westward trek were being made, was in the Oregon Country preparing for a still better home, the full fruition of which he was not himself destined to see and share. Under his spell of enthusiasm, the Bakers, empty handed, but provided with the means of getting to Bethel by the help of Christian Giesy eked out by the sale of their scant furniture, were soon in the community home in Missouri.

Being found to have a bent and liking for mechanical work, Hiram Baker drifted by the law of natural selection from one shop to another, but came before long to be a fixture in the harness and saddlery shop, while Mary Baker helped at odd times in glove making, which was carried on as one of the principal first sources of revenue by the Bethelites, there being a ready sale for the fine and honest product they turned out, and she was soon an expert at the trade. The children were in the colony school. The Bakers were happy and well content, with hearts singing all the days from sheer satisfaction and gratitude for their release from soul destroying worry. They were wont to make comparisons. When little Joseph was born in Pennsylvania they had no food in their home, not a crust. Neighbors came to congratulate them, and they smiled and were too proud to tell of their dire want.

"It was like giving three cheers to a starving man," Hiram Baker told his Bethel brothers and reminded his wife.

"Yes, it was like a man in a stout boat praying for a

drowning woman instead of throwing her a rope," contributed Mary Baker. "I am overjoyed," she added, "when I realize that we now own all the broad colony acres here and are full partners in every industry, in so far as we need to be in having a roof over our heads and every want supplied, by right and without question, though we brought nothing but ourselves and our children; came with empty hands and remain with full hearts. The cup of my joy literally runs over, fills beyond the brimming point when I think the doctor's services are ours, and the druggist's, too, and there will be nurses and neighborliness and kind attention to the end of our days. We are millionaires in our own right, and as good as the best; changed in a twinkling from hungry paupers."

Another family brought in through the efforts of Christian Giesy on one of his missionary trips in the South was that of the Cushmans, alike empty handed, who came from among the mountain whites of Tennessee—Levi and Rhoda Cushman and two sturdy boys of the lank type of which Abraham Lincoln of the same mountain white stock was a sample. The Cushman boys were Amos and Asa, followed by a troop of younger children, Sarah, Naomi, Martha, Felix and Lot. Amos was aged twelve when he came to Bethel in the late spring of the same year the Bakers arrived, and Asa was two years younger. Their brothers and sisters trailed along in age in the order just named, Lot being the baby of the family.

Though among their neighbors Bethel was generally known as Dutchtown, as was the new colony in the far away land to be also, its people were not all German, and some of the grownups among the men and women spoke both languages and the children generally had at least a working knowledge of English, though the school was taught in German.

A singular coincidence in the Baker and Cushman families was that the parents in both cases bore Bible names, and they had given to their children monikers taken from the Book, each having a meaning, as all names once had. Christian Giesy had noted this fact, and it perhaps had a bearing on his insistence in urging both the Bakers and the Cushmans to join the colony forces, and especially the latter family.

Levi Cushman was "handy" with the saw and the axe, which he had used since boyhood, and he was given work at the saw mills, though in his mountain home there had been no such mills. He was transferred often to work in the furniture making shop, from which came the supply for colony use and for sale. Before long he was proficient, and the products of this department became famous both in Missouri and Oregon. Samples are sought to this day, and high prices paid for them.

Amos and Asa Cushman at once became school and playmates of Ruth and Hannah Baker. The Cushman boys knew no German on their arrival, and they found the Baker girls useful teachers, for they had acquired both languages at once from their babyhood without knowing when they learned either. Through association more than by the lessons in the school, Amos and Asa within three months had a working knowledge of the German tongue, though they had far to go in correct pronunciation.

Amos Cushman was tall and strong for his age, and at fourteen could do a man's work on the farm or as helper in the various shops. At eighteen he was the physical superior of the average man in a community made up mostly of the robust type and with few weaklings. He had a restless disposition and went often with the teams to the market towns, delivering the surplus products of the thrifty colonists, for with their directed and united labor they became prosperous and always had something to sell from their farms and gardens and their mills and shops.

They had accumulated property to the value, even in those days, of over $100,000, including 4000 acres of good land in Shelby County and 1300 acres at Nineveh in the adjoining county of Adair. They had added at Nineveh a tannery and blacksmith and wagon making shops. At Bethel, in Shelby County, they had stores and numerous shops and the first saw and flouring mills, outside of the larger cities, run by steam in the State of Missouri. These were housed in a spacious brick building. They made the brick. They had a woolen mill and even a distillery at Bethel. It was the Golden Rule distillery—strange name, in the light of later events and opinions. The colonists made "good whiskey," as it was commonly termed in those days, but they themselves drank none of it, or very little. They never at any time drank to excess, nor was there ever in the colony days a saloon, though most families made wine of grapes and their garden fruits, like currants, and generally offered it to their guests in their homes.

They marketed their whiskey in towns as far away as Quincy, Illinois, forty-eight miles distant, where it was sold as low as 25 cents a gallon. They made the barrels, and they did the transporting, by ox and mule and horse teams, and it was all profit, for they grew their own corn and wheat and rye. They had enclosed in one field at Bethel 1100 acres of land.

Amos Cushman was soon given the responsibility of driving some of the teams with the colony products to the market towns, because he was expert with the work animals, self reliant in all matters, and spoke English with better facility than most members of the colony. He was reliable and shrewd in getting on with the business part of his responsibilities. He "feared neither man nor devil" in what was then a more or less turbulent country. Missouri was a border state, negro slaves were kept, and party feeling was high and fierce. Salmon Brown, youthful son of old John Brown of Osawatomie, was employed at the New Market station of the mother of a girl who became a member of the Bethel and Aurora colony—and he went to Oregon and lived neighbor to her there, in Salem, long after the tragic events at Harper's Ferry had taken a high place in the history of the armed conflict over slavery, when the song, beginning, "John Brown's body lies a-mouldering in the grave, But his soul goes marching on," had for many years ceased to stir the deeps of a nation of brothers at deadly grips.

Rubbing shoulders with the outside world gave young Amos Cushman a taste of freedom from the quiet routine of colony life. It added to the restlessness of his spirit, to what the Germans call his wanderlust. He had his pick of the saddle animals and sat a horse like a centaur. He could outride the best of the men of the colony in that day when horseback riding was an art and was practiced by young and old, men and women. The colony life would not have kept him long after he became a teamster, excepting for his growing attachment for Ruth Baker, his helpful companion and keeper of his confidences. He told her of experiences on his excursions to "the world," as the members called life outside of their community.

He returned from one of his trips to Quincy with a new secret for Ruth. He had been offered employment by a merchant of that town who was a buyer of colony products and a seller of some of the supplies the colony people bought, which were not many, for they were largely self contained. They had been still more so in the first years, when they worked hard in getting their homes and church and school and stores and shops and mills built and in fencing and improving their lands, which were unbroken and virgin soil, a considerable portion covered with timber. The logs for their saw mills came from their own timber, drawn by ox teams.

Ruth was all sympathy for the restless boy, for though he was man size in stature, man strong in body and man reliant in self assertiveness, he was yet in seeming just a boy to her, as he had been since their first meeting.

"Would you part from your people, your father and mother and blood brothers and sisters and your bond brothers and sisters of the community and the sure future you have with them and go to the world and risk the loss of all this, and leave us all behind who are so bound to you by such strong ties of love?" she pleaded.

"But think of the wages and the promotion and the savings," he urged. "I would be my own man. I am not afraid of the future." And he waxed eloquent with a word picture of the ways of the big world on the outside, where one might build up for his very own a fortune and surround himself with every comfort. It was worth the risk, he reasoned. If misfortune came, he could try again. Finally he avowed his undying love.

"It is for you," he urged, "more than for myself. I have wanted to say all this for a long time. You must have felt it. I want you. I want all the care of you, all the pride in you. Perhaps Dr. Keil and the rest are right. Maybe I am selfish, but it is something I cannot help. It may be atavism, running in the blood, back to the cave man when my distant ancestors fought for their own with little or no regard to others. But I want you and you only for myself and myself only." So he pleaded and all but prevailed, ending his argument with embraces and kisses that were longer and more fervent than the shy and stolen ones of their first youthful days together.

But Ruth had come thus far on her way, under the preaching by Dr. Keil of the law of love, to regard the colony life as infinitely better than that of the world, with its selfishness and strife and often lack of tender care for the aged, the sick and the weak and poor. Between sobs with tears she urged her case for the right way as she saw it. They did not forget that day, though no promise was given or taken.

But Amos believed in his secret soul that he could win his spurs in the big world and then bring Ruth to his manner of thinking and finally claim her for his very own. She went away sorrowful, conjuring arguments for use in convincing him in good time of his sin of selfishness, which, as she believed, if persisted in, would surely lead him from the right ways of life.

The mind of Amos was fixed upon going. He would risk it, believing in his boyish exuberance that he would win. With misgivings, the colony people outfitted the young man for his excursion into the world, and gave him money, according to their rule, "You shall not let your brother go away from you empty." On the next trip of the teamsters to Quincy an extra driver was taken along, and after goodbyes were said and tears were mingled with laughter and jesting, Amos went to the big town.

News came back through the teamsters of his progress, he heard from them how things fared in the colony, and letters were in the same manner passed between him and Ruth. He came on a visit after three months, and much was made over him, with favorite dishes in the Cushman home for which colony life was famous there as it was to be in Oregon. There was music by the band and orchestra trained by Prof. Finck, the old songs were sung, and there was a special mention in the Sunday sermon by Dr. Keil. There were walks and talks and horseback rides with Ruth.

She taught in the colony school now, and had a class in the
Sunday school. She was more beautiful than ever, in her
blossoming into full womanhood, with a mingling of the
German type of the Bavarian, akin to the Latin races, inherited from her mother, and the American strain on her
father's side that gave her grace and elegance of figure.
She was worthy of the blood of all the races that coursed
in her veins. Good she was, and altogether lovely. There
were again tender partings as Amos went away. But no
change had come in their decisions.

Word came back that Amos Cushman had been hurt in
the handling of a crate of goods that had fallen and badly
crushed him. It was said there was fear of internal injuries.
The mother and father were hurried to Quincy. They
hoped to bring him home. But the doctor interposed his
veto and said the patient would be unable to go for a long,
long time.

The weeks wore on. Expenses piled up. The colony people paid the bills and brought him back as soon as he could
be moved. Weak and homesick and broken in body and
morale, after his long struggle, Amos was overjoyed to be
with his blood and bond brothers again, with tender nursing and expert and thoughtful care such as no other circumstances could give. This was all his as a matter of course;
as a duty, written on the tablets of the hearts of all members of the community. Rights were little regarded in the
life of this colony. Duties were paramount. They were
never shirked, in thought or deed.

As Amos was nursed back to health and won his way to
full strength and vigor, he had time to think of the comparisons between colony life and that lived in the outside
world.

He harked back to the familiar words of Hiram Baker,
Ruth's father, "It was like giving three cheers to a starving

man," which he had used and repeated many times in telling about the state in which Christian Giesy had found the Baker family in Pennsylvania and expressing his gratitude for present blessings. There were confidences between Amos and Ruth touching all these things. He was subdued. But his restless spirit had not been entirely tamed, even by the comparisons and the memory of his trying experiences. He reasoned that it was a matter of accident; it might have been avoided. When he was fully himself in vigor again, plans were well under way for the far western journey to the new colony home.

He rode to Quincy on his favorite colony mount to visit his employer and his friends there. He met one of the store's customers who was making plans for the trip to the Oregon Country the following spring; he was offered a chance to go with his covered wagon train. Visions of independence came in full form again. He was for accepting the proffered place, that would lead to free land for the taking and a home outside of colony life.

Hesitatingly, ashamed almost of his words, he talked to Ruth of the offer when he returned to Bethel. But she had news for him. She told him their family had been chosen to go with the first large company in the spring, which Dr. Keil himself would lead, to make the beginnings of the Oregon settlement, or rather to further the work being done by the spies sent to view the promised land who were already busy preparing for their coming.

That was a coveted and signal honor. The services of Hiram Baker would be useful in keeping the harness and saddles in order on the long journey and in setting up the shop for these trades in the new town planned in the Oregon Country. They would require gloves on the plains and in the hard work of getting their new footing, as had been the case at Bethel, and Mary Baker was needed in this work. As for Ruth herself, she was twenty now and would have another birthday on the plains, and as she had helped in teaching at Bethel, she would be the teacher of the plains school, for in all the American communistic colonies, in which Bethel was no exception, nor was the new settlement to be, there was always school. Not three or six or nine months, as in the districts of the sparse or less sparse settlements or the towns and cities, but for the whole year. There was always teaching. Amos understood this. And the great covered wagon emigration trains, too, that had crossed the plains every year since 1843 generally had included teachers, with school sessions by the evening camp fires.

"Amos, you must go, too," Ruth argued, "for your family will be taken also. It is already understood. Your father will be needed in the saw mill and in the making of furniture. Homes must be built, and there must be furniture for them," she went on like a special pleader.

"This makes a situation that is hard for me," he said, "especially on your account. But I have more than half promised to go with the other train, and the man, Eldon Bradford, said he would count on me, and would not make the same offer to another. He will think I am yellow and chicken-hearted. There are many others here who want to go. My going would deprive some one of them of a coveted opportunity. In that much, it would be selfish of me, seeing I have another chance to get to the Oregon Country, and at the same time earn wages on the trip."

"Amos," answered Ruth, "do you remember the sermon of Dr. Keil when he took Hobab the Midianite for his text? I remember it well. Hobab was the brother-in-law of Moses. 'Come thou with us and we will do thee good, for the Lord hath spoken good concerning Israel,' said Moses to Hobab as the hosts of the Israelites started on their wilderness journey. But Hobab was not interested.

He said he would depart to his own land and his kindred. 'Leave us not, I pray thee: forasmuch as thou knowest how we are to encamp in the wilderness, and thou mayest be to us instead of eyes,' pleaded Moses. And thus Hobab was won over. He was a sheik of his Arabic tribe, and he knew the country. HE COULD SERVE. This was service above self.

"And so it must be with you, Amos," pleaded Ruth. "Not for your gain, but for our good. You shall be our Hobab; to us instead of eyes. You will be needed, along with your own people, and our people; all of us. You are strong, resourceful, a good rider. You speak better English than most of our people, and I am sure you can learn Indian, or at least make them understand.

"It is the place of the strong to protect the weak. You have never been known to shirk a duty. You may save lives. There are Indians, perhaps hostile tribes, to encounter. There are dangerous rivers to cross. I do not plead for myself. I am not fearful. Dr. Keil has said we will put our trust in God and fear no evil and all will be well, and I have faith and am unafraid. I am counting the days. I want to go. On this account, too, I believe you will be safer with us than with the independent Bradford wagon train. That fact, as you must know, Amos, makes my heart put words of pleading on my tongue."

Amos understood.

"I would be more craven than any Bradford could picture me," he said, "if I disregarded your appeal, and I hope to measure up to your estimate of me," and they sealed the compact with a loving embrace and a rain of kisses fervent enough for remembrance not only on the plains pilgrimage but throughout all their days, whatever fortunes they might meet or share.

Of course Amos would go with the colony train, and

he rode away at once to inform Mr. Bradford that he could not accept his offer, and as he went and came on his errand he thought of the companionship he would have with Ruth on the long journey, and made plans in his mind for her safety and their diversion.

He would do his duty and bide his time. The dangers of the plains did not give him the least concern. He could make further plans and decisions in the new home in the Oregon country, inside or outside of colony life.

So Amos Cushman was soon in the thick of the preparations for the epochal trek. He grew hourly more eager for the time of starting. The free air of the prairies and plains and mountains would be as sweet incense to his nostrils, and all the hardships would but whet his appetite for new adventures. He would see Ruth all the way and his chief concern would be to guard and protect her, with the rest.

CHAPTER 7

IDEALS OF COMMUNITY LIFE

Men look to the East for the dawning things, for the light of the rising sun,
But they look to the West, the crimson West, for the things that are done, are
  done.
The eastward sun is a new-made hope from the dark of the night distilled;
But the westward sun is a sunset sun, the sun of a hope fulfilled!
So out of the East they have always come, the cradle that saw the birth
Of all the heartwarm hopes of men and all the powers of earth—
For out of the East arose a Christ, and out of the East has gleamed
The dearest dream and the clearest dream that ever a prophet dreamed.
And into the waiting West they go with the dreamchild of the East,
And find the hopes they hoped of old are an hundred fold increased.
For there in the East they dream the dreams of the things they hope to do,
But here in the West, the crimson West, the dreams of the East come true.
—Anonymous.

CHRISTOPHER W. WOLFF, a graduate of the University of Göttingen and a highly educated man, was a' member of the Bethel Colony. He was among the first to join and to contribute his little all. He was to become the teacher of Henry T. Finck, the first student from Oregon to enter Harvard. But more of this later. He was to lead the second large wagon train across the plains. He was to become the keeper of the community store in the new colony home. Wolff had been a minister, and on some occasions preached to the colony people at Bethel, and later in Oregon. He believed sincerely in the ideals of community living, was a strong and able advocate of the doctrine of the holding of property in common. He was known as Prof. Wolff at Bethel, as he was to be at Aurora.

As the workmen in the shops went on making the wagons and preparing the outfits for the journey to the

Oregon Country, Prof. Wolff and Dr. Keil discussed the plans for the better and greater things to be done in their dreamed of new home in the land more than 2000 miles across the prairies and plains and desert wastes and over the mountain ranges.

Dr. Keil had read little but the Bible. But he had read the Bible much, and committed many passages of the Book. He had come to firmly hold the fundamental truth of Christianity to be, "Love one another," and he now sincerely interpreted this in so broad and liberal a sense as required a community of goods and effects. He held that the very essence of love was unselfishness, and his sermons were filled with warnings against what he called the cardinal sin of selfishness. He often quoted the words of Luke in Acts 2:44-45 and 4:32-34-35: "And all that believed were together, and had all things common; and sold their possessions and goods, and parted them to all men, as every man had need. And the multitude of them that believed were of one heart and one soul; neither said any of them that ought of the things which he possessed was his own; but they had all things common. Neither was there any among them that lacked; . . . distribution was made unto every man ACCORDING AS HE HAD NEED."

These words in the charter of the first Christian church, according to Dr. Keil's clear faith, have had singular power over men in all ages since they were written. They have been the fundamental doctrine of most communistic societies that have been formed and have achieved success in the United States. In that sense, every one of these societies has been a church. The Bethel colony was essentially a house of God, true to its name,—a church.

But Prof. Wolff had read widely. While Dr. Keil had imbibed in his home land something of the unrest and the Christian zeal of the German mystics and pietists of the sixteenth and seventeenth centuries, protesting against the dogmatism of the sectarian beliefs, he had not studied the doctrines of the German and French Socialists, but Prof. Wolff had. Wolff had while a student in Germany been inspired by some of the fervor of Baboeuf and Cabet and Saint-Simon and Fourier and Louis Blanc and Proudhon and of the school of French Socialists and Communists that followed them. He had gathered, too, some of the rising tide of democracy and socialism in Germany, given voice by the teachings and writings of Rodbertus, Karl Marx, Ferdinand Lassalle and others. He had come into contact with the ideals of Christian socialism—holding that the Gospel is the good news to the poor—the announcement of the advent of the kingdom in which the humble shall be lifted up and the disinherited shall possess the earth.

There was never any question of the sincerity of Dr. Keil. No one who knew him doubted his honesty. Differences of opinion have arisen regarding his ambitions. It has been suggested that he considered at this period the planting of colonies throughout the Oregon Country, and perhaps later all along the way from Missouri westward. Some of his former followers say he had in mind in the beginning in Pennsylvania only a Christian community, where people of one faith might worship together as they wished, without the interference of carping or intolerant neighbors. If that was the limit of his first ambition, his vision had broadened. It had burgeoned into Bethel. It was about to blossom into Aurora, with greater room for growth.

Professor Wolff, with his knowledge of history and his study of the socialistic ideals of French, German and English thinkers, had without question been a factor in shaping the bent of Dr. Keil's mind. In those countries men had dreamed the dreams of the things they hoped to do, but here in the West the dreams of Europe's communistic dreamers had come true, or they were in the way of coming true, or at least being put into action. None of them took root in Europe in actual practice with signal success, unless the dreams of Saint-Simon be noted as an exception. Some of them had no trial at all in the lands of their birth.

Dr. Keil was a practical idealist. If his head was in the clouds, he kept his feet on the ground. He was not reckless of consequences in anything he undertook. He counted the cost; looked before he leaped. He did not allow his enthusiasm to run away with his judgment. But it is certain that he had been impressed by his many talks with Prof. Wolff. How far this led in the way of ambitions to head a wide-spread and general movement, in shaping the course of large events in the way he thought was right and for the good of humanity, there is no way of knowing.

But that was a time of pioneering. The country was in the making, in many particulars. The setting was "different." The United States was "half slave and half free." Cross currents were running that have not been witnessed since. Under the direction of a great organizer, there might be a different story to tell. Witness the Mormons under Brigham Young.

The talks of Professor Wolff and Dr. Keil were intimate. They were soul searching. They ranged over the whole social history of the world. The beginnings at Bethel had been modest in size and unpretentious in scope; but they had been singularly successful in their way. In material gains and physical well being, they were remarkable, considering the opportunities in the pioneer days of that section. The time was opportune for such an experiment. The community spirit was in the air in America.

CHAPTER 8

BROOK FARM AND OTHERS

THE Shakers had been establishing successful communities in the eastern part of the United States since 1794 and in the western section of the country since 1808. Charles Nordhoff in 1874 found 18 societies of Shakers, with 58 Shaker communities or "families," all in a more or less prosperous condition, scattered over seven states, containing an aggregate of 2415 souls and owning real estate amounting to about 100,000 acres; 50,000 acres being in their own home farms. The Rappist community was established in 1805, the Zoarites in 1817, the Eben-Ezers or Amana communists in 1842-1844.

The Harmony Society of the Rappists was established by George Rapp, a German born in Wurtemberg, who had drawn his people from his home land, and had started his colony 25 miles north of Pittsburgh, in the valley of the Connoquenessing, on 5000 acres of land. In 1814 to 1815, the whole colony had moved to a purchase of 30,000 acres of land in Posey County, Indiana, on the Wabash, having sold 6000 acres of land and the manufacturing plants, homes and other improvements for $100,000. They built up a town on the Wabash, called New Harmony, and increased to 700 to 800 in number. But in 1824 the Rappists moved once more. They sold the Wabash property and improvements to Robert Owen, the English Communist, for $150,000, and Owen settled on it his New Lanark colony. Then the Rappists bought their property at Economy, Pennsylvania, and in 1825 moved to their new and final home.

In 1831 came a German adventurer, Bernhard Müller, who had assumed the title of Graf or Count Maximilian de Leon, and had gathered a following of Germans whom he imposed with himself on the Harmonists at Economy, on the pretense that he was a believer with them in religious matters.

But Count Leon began, after having become a part of the Harmonist community, advocating a different life, including marriage and greater freedom of individual action—for the Harmonists had become, as has already been said, celibate in their living, though they at first married and gave in marriage, and were turned to the celibate idea after a great religious revival. So there grew up at once a division among the Rappists. It was decided to take a vote. The result was 500 for Rapp and 250 for Count Leon. The Rappists at Economy, as heretofore mentioned, paid the seceders $105,000, in three installments, in one year, and Count Leon and his followers removed to Phillipsburg, a village 10 miles below Economy, and on the other side of the river, where they acquired 800 acres of land, and set up a society on community principles, but permitted marriage. Their efforts fell far short of success, and Count Leon absconded to Louisiana and in 1833 perished with the cholera.

After the departure of Count Leon, the members of the community at Phillipsburg divided the property and closed community life. But the ideas back of this way of living were disseminated very generally in the United States. In 1841, Brook Farm had its beginnings, at West Roxbury, Massachusetts, "to insure a more natural union between intellectual and manual labor than now exists; to combine the thinker and the worker, as far as possible, in the same individual; to guarantee the highest mental freedom, by providing all with labor adapted to their tastes and talents, and securing to them the fruits of their industry; to do away with the necessity of menial services by opening the benefits of education and the profits of labor to all; and thus to prepare a society of liberal, intelligent and cultivated persons, whose relations with each other would permit a more wholesome and simple life than can be led amidst the pressure of our competitive institutions.

"To accomplish these objects," George Ripley wrote to Ralph Waldo Emerson in a letter of November 9, 1840, "we propose to take a small tract of land which under skillful husbandry, uniting the garden and the farm, will be adequate to the subsistence of the families; and to connect with this a school or college, in which the most complete instruction shall be given, from the first rudiments to the highest culture."

So Brook Farm was started, in April of the following year, headed by George Ripley, assisted by his wife, and to this association or community came Nathaniel Hawthorne, Mr. and Mrs. Minot Pratt, Charles A. Dana, and other teachers and literary leaders of that day, supported in one way and another, in sympathy if not with more than mere solicitude, by Horace Greeley, Ralph Waldo Emerson, Theodore Parker, Margaret Fuller, George William Curtis, Dr. Channing, Albert Brisbane, and many others. Brook Farm, in fact, had the moral backing of the whole school of transcendentalists, a term used to designate a numerous cult of forward looking thinkers of the New England States, with the intellectually elect of Boston the central group.

Fourierism had been brought to America about 1840, and soon found numerous advocates, including many names of which America is proud. At first Brook Farm was not called a phalanx, although from the start it combined many of the features of Fourierism, but it shortly fell in line and became a Fourieristic experiment. The erection of a phalanstery was undertaken at Brook Farm, the better to work out the ideas of Charles Fourier, who believed that one successful phalanx, embracing completely the elaborate program of his Utopian dream, would lead to the speedy reorganization of the *whole of human society*. He believed this might come about within the space of ten years. But the phalanstery of Brook Farm was burned on the eve of its completion. The Brook Farmers had not taken the precaution to carry fire insurance, and the destruction of the great building, which was to be used to perfect the ideal community life, was the beginning of the end of the experiment of the Brook Farmers.

Fourierism was in the air in the early forties, in the United States, and it is corroborative of the progress this dream of universal unity was making, particularly in the City of New York, that the Society Library, a highly conservative institution, should have opened its room in 1844 to lectures by Godwin, Greeley and W. H. Channing, on the merits of the scheme. In the fall of 1846, when about 200,000 Americans are said to have acknowledged the name of Fourierists, there was opened a battle royal between the pens of Horace Greeley and Henry J. Raymond, formerly on Greeley's staff, and then writing for Colonel James Watson Webb's *Courier and Enquirer*. It was occasioned by a letter written by Albert Brisbane on his return from Europe in 1846, to the *Courier and Enquirer*, but printed in the *Tribune*, Mr. Greeley's powerful newspaper. For six months, and in twenty-four articles, afterward gathered into book form, raged this spirited and able controversy. After that notable newspaper debate, though Greeley no longer waved the banner of Fourierism, he did not relinquish his efforts for social amelioration. As late as 1868 he reaffirmed a faith in Association (as represented by the Brook Farm ideals), but rejected Communism as at war with one of the strongest and most universal instincts.

There was held at Skanateales, New York, on October 14 and 15, 1843, a meeting "in the interest of a reorganization of the social system by a community of property and interest throughout the country." On December 26 and 27, 1843, there was a convention in Boston of the "friends of social reform" in New England and elsewhere. This convention lasted over from the closing week in December into the first week in January, and marked, in W. H. Channing's words, "an era in the history of New England." It proved to be a veritable love-feast of the communistic associations at Northampton, Hopedale and Brook Farm; the drift of the convention as a whole was Fourierward. Not forgetting his former strictures, Channing said that it at least seemed to him that Charles Fourier had "given us the clew out of our scientific labyrinth and revealed the means of living the law of love." The resolutions of the convention indorsed Fourier and hoped to see a "test of the actual workings of his principles."

After the failure of the Brook Farm experiment, the tide of Fourierism began to ebb. But two vestiges were left on seemingly sure foundations—the North American Phalanx at Red Bank, New Jersey, which lasted fourteen years, and of which Greeley said "if it could not live, there was no hope for any other," and the Wisconsin or Ceresco Phalanx. These two went in the end.

CHAPTER 9

A DEVELOPING DREAM

THE discussions at Bethel went on as the preparations for the westward migration proceeded. There was another member of the community who was a finished German scholar. He was Charles Ruge, principal teacher of the school. He participated in these discursive reasonings. When Nordhoff visited the Aurora colony in 1874 he described the school teacher as an old man bearing a remarkable resemblance to Horace Greeley. This was Professor Ruge.

These three, Dr. Keil, Professor Wolff and Professor Ruge, made a sort of triumvirate of study and teaching. They reviewed the whole range of social history, and the trustees and other leaders of the community often joined in their discussional councils. Professor Wolff described the communities of Buddhist and Christian monks and the villages of the Essenes in Judea as the forerunners of such communal groups in America as the Bethel experiment had become, and the proposed improved branch in the far West near the Pacific ought to be.

He told of Plato's Republic. That prize pupil of Socrates in Athens four hundred years before the birth of Christ, dreamed of a better state of society, as every thinker in all the ages of man must have done. Such dreams differentiate the human race from the lower animals. They mark civilization's rising tide of sympathy and brotherhood above the savage. They answer THE FIRST RECORDED SOCIAL QUESTION OF HISTORY, asked at the gates of the Garden of Eden of the God of Creation Himself, and

48

Christopher W. Wolff, chief of the triumvirate of speculative thought and study at Bethel and Aurora; teacher of the higher branches; the man who trained Henry T. Finck, first student at Harvard from Oregon.

an affirmative reply required from the earliest born son of earth's original parents, "AM I MY BROTHER'S KEEPER?"

Socrates had drunk the hemlock, condemned to die because he could not trust the mob and would not beg pardon of the "democracy" of that city state, most of the people of whom were slaves, and whose supreme court was made up by alphabetical rote from the citizens without respect to learning or ignorance, and the decisions of which body were swayed by what we in this day would call soap-box orators or in Wolff's time were designated as stump-speakers.

Plato, pupil and lover of Socrates with such deep feeling that history has carried its name down to the present as Platonic love, leaving Athens because he feared its type of democracy might condemn him, too, because of his sympathy for the dead philosopher and his lack of sympathy with the mob, wandered for twelve years over the then known world, visiting all the seats of learning and studying their ideas and systems.

At forty years of age he returned and began to formulate the dream of his Republic. Plato held that democracy means perfect EQUALITY OF OPPORTUNITY, especially in education. So he planned his imaginary Republic, his Utopia, on the idea of a ruling class having everything in common—including wives and husbands—starting his race of guardians or governors from children taken from all classes and weeded out by tests of knowledge and fitness, from youth to mature manhood and womanhood. These most wise and learned of the citizens were to be the guardians of the state. But the two other classes, the soldiers and the workers, were to live as before, having nothing in common.

Thus Plato's Republic provided educational election to public office. It was to be a democracy of the schools—

a hundred fold more honest and more effective than a democracy of the polls. There was to be no caste, no inheritance of position or privilege. It was to be a government of the wisest and most fit.

"FRIENDS SHOULD HAVE ALL THINGS IN COMMON," Pythagoras had declared a hundred years before.

Plato's guardians of the state were to have no property, nor private houses. They were to have common meals and live together, like soldiers in a camp. They alone of all the citizens were not to touch silver or gold, nor to be under the same roof with them, nor wear them, nor drink from them.

"And this shall be their salvation and the salvation of the state. But should they acquire homes or lands or moneys of their own, they will become housekeepers and husbandmen instead of guardians; enemies and tyrants instead of allies of the other citizens; hating and being hated, plotting and being plotted against, they will pass their life in much greater terror of internal than external enemies; and the hour of ruin both to themselves and the state will be at hand."

Their sole reward shall be honor and the sense of service to the group. They shall dedicate themselves solely to the maintenance of freedom in the state. They shall be legislature and executive and court in one; even the laws shall not bind them to a dogma in the face of altered circumstances; the rule of the guardians shall be a flexible intelligence unbound by precedent.

(For the sake of the continuity, the main story is resumed, and, that the thoughtful reader may get a full picture of the discussions at Bethel of the historic ideals of social justice that led to the conclusions of the leaders there, that part of the theme is carried over as originally arranged. [See page 277.]

CHAPTER 10

OFF TO THE OREGON COUNTRY

THE time of departure for the Oregon Country was at hand. In the midst of the bustle of preparation, Willie, son of Dr. Keil, named for his father, fell ill. He was a favorite among the members of the community, an active, robust, bright, good natured youngster of nineteen. He had for over two years taken great interest in the plans and was now engrossed with the preparations for the start; talked of it in his wakeful hours, dreamed about it at night. His whole heart was set on the big adventure. Willie pictured in his mind the part he would play; in his youthful zeal fancied to himself a long holiday. He had for several years seen many a covered wagon roll out from the Bethel shops, gay with new paint and fit for the hard usage it would have. He had witnessed the passing of covered wagon caravans on the way west with their drivers and families indulging in song and jest and with hilarious exhibitions of high spirits in the beginnings of hegiras the drab and dismal and tragic endings of many of which he never heard or as much as imagined. What boy of the eager 'teen age cannot picture the dismay Willie Keil felt when he was attacked by the malaria that was the dread and scourge of that section in its early settlement?

"Please, father, do not leave me behind," he begged, when it was evident that he could not be strong enough for ordinary travel by the time fixed for the start.

"Whoa, Buck! Gee, Billy! Get up there, Jim! Haw, you Jack! Steady, Blackey! Go to it, Brindle!" the youth shouted in his delirium to the visioned three yoke ox team he dreamed he was driving. He had helped break to the yoke in their calfhood these familiar animals, had himself given them their names, and, as was not unusual in the long ages when oxen were the chief means of traction, they were in affection like members of the family.

Willie held his fond father's hand and pleaded to be taken. The promise was given. He would not be left behind. Willie would be in the lead wagon, heading the train. He would be first in starting, the earliest arrival in the new colony home. His pony would be taken along, too, so that he might help with the stock, as he had talked and hoped. He must compose himself and be quiet and rely on his father's word, that he knew was never broken. Dr. Keil felt that the bracing air of the plains would soon restore his son to health. So a light wagon to accommodate a bed was fashioned in the shops, especially adapted for its purpose, and a sturdy span of young mules, bearing the names of Queen and Kate, fitted with stout harness. The outfit was a plains ambulance. Everthing was ready.

Saturday, May 19th, four days before the time fixed for the departure, Willie Keil died. Then general grief mingled with fears that the preliminary arrangements for the funeral and the burial ceremonies would delay the time of starting, with the already unusual bustle incident to making all things ready.

But there was no funeral, nor any postponement beyond the following Wednesday long arranged for in the customarily meticulous planning. The shop foremen were given rush orders to change the plains ambulance to a plains hearse. His father had promised Willie that he should go; that he would lead the train and be the first to arrive in the beautiful land by the sundown sea. So it must be. In community precept and practice a promise given was a performance assured. Instead of a bed there was a coffin lined with lead and this container for the body filled up with alcohol—

And it was the strangest if not the only hearse that ever crossed the plains.

It led the first and only covered wagon funeral train among all the plodding caravans which made that hard journey of over two thousand weary miles.

And such a funeral procession will never, can never be duplicated in a like setting, a similarly weird progress, an equal environmental awsomeness, in this changed and changing world. It is all the more eerie, unique and strange because of its absolute, historical accuracy, a verification of the trite tradition that truth is stranger than fiction.

Thus, on the morning of departure, Wednesday, May 23, 1855, there was brought onto Bethel's main street, which nearly all the buildings faced, a passing strange exhibit, the plains hearse. This novel equipage was placed first in the wagon train that was receiving its final burdens of supplies for the long heralded signal of setting out.

The last piece of luggage was packed. The drivers were ready; the band of loose stock lined up at the rear of the procession. But the colony people always sang; there was constant music. And in this epochal departure there was to be no exception. Dr. Keil had been very busy. With all his duties, however, he had found time to compose and set to meter a song that was to be used at the far off graveside of his son; the first opening of mother earth there to receive a member of the colony or any representative of the white race. It had been given patient practice by the whole body of the colony people under the direction of the music master, Prof. Finck, in the hurried hours of making all things ready for the train's start. "Das Grab ist tief und stille," ran the title line. The song was the prearranged signal.

As the wagon train was ready to move away, accompanied by all the colony people at Bethel, there was sounded the strain of a song the beautiful words and solemn music of which were to be heard in every funeral service throughout the community's life, and long after:

> "Das Grab ist tief und stille
> Und schauderhaft sein Rand;
> Es deckt mit tiefer Hülle
> Ein unbekanntes Land.
>
> Das Lied der Nachtigallen
> Tönt nicht in seinem Schosz,
> Der Freundschafts Rosen fallen
> Nur auf des Hügel's Moos.
>
> Doch sonst an keinem Orte,
> Wohnt die ersehnte Ruh'.
> Nur durch die dunkle Pforte,
> Geht man der Heimat zu.
>
> Das arme Herz hienieden,
> Von manchem Sturm bewegt,
> Erlangt den wahren Frieden,
> Nur wo es nicht mer schlägt."

The strange and impressive procession moved slowly out of the town and the leading bier pointed westward, accompanied by the entire population. Farewells were spoken and embraces exchanged, as the last strains of music accompanying the words of the funeral song died away.

"Auf wiedersehen!" shouted a chorus of voices in the last salutations, for all expected to see one another again in the Oregon home. Those who were to stay at Bethel accompanied the caravan to exchange final greetings until one by one they dropped out of line and turned back Bethelward, as the procession proceeded at the slow and steady pace of the oxen, followed by the loose stock.

These were driven under the direction of Amos Cushman, on a splendid bay horse, with Ruth Baker keeping with or near him on a white pony, and Asa Cushman and Hannah Baker, next in age of the two families, riding sure footed mules that were a near blue in color. They were shortly named the Uncle Sam quartet, with their red, white and blue mounts representing the Stars and Stripes. It seemed like a holiday jaunt to these four, who thought little of the dangers or the days of weariness ahead.

The wagons and harness and saddles and supplies required on the journey, almost to the last item, had been grown and made, and milled, fashioned and prepared on the land and in the shops at Bethel, with the exception of the guns and ammunition needed to aid them in provisioning the company with game on the westward way.

This first large train of the colonists contained thirty-five wagons, drawn by mules and oxen and horses—mostly oxen, as being best adapted to maintain themselves on the grass of the plains. In the company were about 250 men, women and children. Extra saddle animals were provided, and cows for the milk supply, or in case of need to take the places of oxen that might not be equal to their tasks, or might die on the way.

The caravan moved steadily westward over the pioneer Missouri excuses for wagon roads. Without unusual incident, St. Joseph was reached, the Missouri River crossed by ferry, and six miles west camp was made. They were at the borders of civilization, entering the Indian country. By June 7th they had come into sight of the Iowa Indian mission and passing that point, headed straight into the land of adventure and danger, but unafraid, under the leadership of the man they trusted.

"It was at this mission," Dr. Keil told his people as a short halt was made, "that Richardson, the courier sent from Fort Hall by W. H. Gray to overtake Jason Lee, stopped long enough to secure word that the man he sought had already passed; then the lone rider sped on to the Pawnee mission near Westport—the Westport Landing of our time (now Thirty-ninth street in Kansas City, Missouri), and late at night on the first day of September, 1838, the dusty horseman handed to the man he sought an oilskin packet of letters, one of which was encased in black, bearing the tidings of the death of Mrs. Lee and their new born baby boy—first white woman and child for whom burial ground was opened in the Oregon Country.

"The fateful message under the black seal," continued the leader, "was started the day of Mrs. Lee's death, June 26th, from the Williamette mission; thence to Dr. McLoughlin at Fort Vancouver; from there to Dr. Marcus Whitman at Waiilatpu; thence to Fort Hall, and on across the Rockies and over the plains, three halts in sixty days—remarkable speed for that time. We will not make the record of the lone rider, but we may hope for better progress than the average of the covered wagon trains with women and children.

"Under the hospitable roof of his brother missionary, Rev. Thomas Johnson (who made history in that day, and gave his name to a Kansas county), the pivotally placed pioneer of the pioneers was found at his devotions by the travel worn courier, preparing to retire for the night," continued Dr. Keil. "Bowed down with grief and momentarily stunned into inaction on receipt of the sad news, Lee did not turn back from his work, the least faltering in which might have lost the whole Oregon Country to the United States, and the rest of the territory west of the Rockies, too. Without the early settlers in the Oregon Country the Mexican War would not have been fought, gold would not have been so soon discovered in California, and the arc of our Republic might not have been extended from the snows of the Rockies to the sands of the Pacific.

"After a sleepless night of agony and tears," Dr. Keil concluded, "Jason Lee plunged into the feverish activities of a speaking tour; thundered forth the clarion call of a challenging message to Christian zeal and American patriotism; pleaded with prophetic earnestness and statesmanlike vision for the saving and the settlement of the Oregon Country; brought in quick and eager response the Lausanne, Mayflower of the Pacific. His station already had the first medical missionary ever sent to a foreign field."

The Iowa Indian mission station, which served also the Kickapoo tribe, was something over thirty miles out of St. Joseph.

"The Dorion woman of the Hunt party of the Astors was a member of the Iowa tribe," concluded Dr. Keil.

(A daughter of this Indian woman of destiny by a later husband was the second wife of George Gay, then the richest man in what is now Oregon, and builder of the first brick dwelling west of the Rockies and north of the California line (still standing), where Lieutenant William Peel, third son of Sir Robert Peel, was entertained in 1845, while making for his illustrious father the investigation that resulted in more than century long and hoped for permanent peace instead of a third war between Great Britain and the United States, and the report of which led directly and quickly to the treaty ratified June 15, 1846, settling the boundary question and terminating the hazy tenure of joint occupancy by the two nations.)

Some forty miles beyond the Iowa mission the colonists

were obliged for the first time to lock one wheel of their wagons to get down long hills. Twenty miles further on they forded the Big Blue River and made their camp on its western banks, where there was good grass and the women did some washing while the men fished and caught enough for a refreshing meal.

CHAPTER 11

"MUSIC HATH CHARMS"

AT THE camping place on the Big Blue, Dr. Keil held a conference with his people. Amos Cushman, Hobab of the wilderness wagon train, who was to his people "instead of eyes," had been warned at St. Joseph, at the Iowa mission, and many times by stragglers of the returning host, that they were taking their lives in their hands; that they were entering dangerous territory.

"I'm not afeared for myself, but I am scared stiff about trusting my wimmen folks and our young ones to the red devils," said a man who had started from Ohio, to Amos. That was the general attitude, alibi and excuse. The return of the warned host had grown to a panic.

"The Indian tribes are combining against the white nation to hold back the westward tide of immigration that has been swelling for a dozen years," spoke a booted and spurred cavalryman to Amos.

"The Arapahoe and Cheyenne warriors are just ahead; and they are in a bond of defensive fellowship with the Sioux chiefs of the plains—and the Sioux think they own the buffaloes. On beyond are the Utahs and the Snakes, the Nez Perces and so-called Flatheads, the Cayuses and the Walla Wallas, and the rest. They are all in a league; have laid aside their ancient grudges; quit killing one another long enough to stop the covered wagons and save their game and their lands."

"Shall we turn back?" asked Dr. Keil of his people. He told them thousands were turning back and many other thousands were refusing to start, on account of the warnings—many thousands who had assembled in the accustomed camps at Westport and Independence and other points east of the Missouri and Kaw (Kansas) rivers. The question was up for decision.

(Here should be quoted from a recent letter of George H. Himes, secretary of the Oregon Pioneer Association, these words: "I have to say this: that a number of people —an unknown number—were arranging to cross in 1855, but few really started, because of the threatening attitude of the Indians. . . . I have no information concerning the 1856 immigration; as a matter of fact I do not believe there was any aside from those who came by water, because hostilities continued almost the entire year in western Oregon and Washington, and even continued into eastern Washington and Oregon more or less in 1857 and 1858.")

"I will not lead my people into danger and possible destruction against the advice or wish of any one of them; it is not too late to turn back, as you see so many others doing. The way is open. The Iowas and Kickapoos behind us are so far friendly, as you yourselves have witnessed." Thus spoke Dr. Keil.

No one made a move of turning. There was no sign of fear. The leader asked for expressions.

"As for myself and my people, we are willing to trust the decision to Dr. Keil," spoke up Hiram Baker. Words of the same import were uttered by Levi Cushman, and all the heads of the families and most of the younger members gave similar signs of confidence and trust.

Dr. Keil said he read in his Bible, in the book of Numbers, sixth chapter, thirty-first verse, these words: "Be strong and of good courage, fear not, nor be afraid of them; for the Lord thy God, he it is that doth go with thee: he will not fail thee, nor forsake thee."

"As for myself and my precious charge, I rely on these

words, spoken on a similar occasion by the Almighty to his
people, who trusted the promise and went on, and all was
well with them," said the leader.

The bugle order was blown to break camp, and the leading bier pulled out, followed by the rest of the wagons,
and behind them the loose stock kept in order by the
Uncle Sam quartet of outriders, and as the formation was
completed and the wagon train pushed on, music of the violin and guitar, the clarinet and flute, the zither and the
drums, and the other instruments carried by the colonists
took up Luther's Hymn, "Ein' feste Burg ist unser Gott,"
and all the voices down the long line joined in the song
that rang out over the prairies in a concord of sweet sounds
never before heard or echoed there. Even the drivers of
the oxen and the outriders of the Uncle Sam quartet chimed
in, and the steady treading teams and the animals at the end
of the cavalcade seemed to sway and keep step to the tune
that has stirred the hopes of many millions dead and living.

Then followed in the same fashion "Das zerbrochene
Ringlein":

"In einem kühlen Grunde, da geht ein Mühlenrad; mein'
  Liebste ist verschwunden, die dort gewohnet hat: mein'
  Liebste ist verschwunden, die dort gewohnet hat.
"Sie hat mir Treu versprochen, gab mir ein'n Ring dabei; sie
  hat die Treu gebrochen, mein Ringlein sprang entzwei; sie hat
  die Treu gebrochen, mein Ringlein sprang entzwei.
"Ich möcht als Spielmann reisen weit in die Welt hinaus, und
  singen meine Weisen, und gehn von Haus zu Haus; und
  singen meine Weisen, and gehn von Haus zu Haus."

The colony people did not confine their music and singing to the stirring religious hymns. They varied these
with folk songs familiar to all their members and the people everywhere who understand the German language.

There was struck up the old, old song, "Freut euch des

Lebens," sung the world around since 1793, followed by "O du lieber Augustin."

They often sang "Im Wald und auf der Heide," and "Lorelei," and "Kommt a Vogerl geflogen," and "Morgen musz ich fort von hier," and "Musz i denn, musz i denn," and they had in their memories and sang frequently, "O Tannenbaum, o Tannenbaum," and "Soviel Stern am Himmel stehen," "Steh ich in finstrer Mitternacht," "Stille Nacht! heilege nacht," "Wenn ich ein Vöglein wär," Mendelssohn's "Wer hat dich, du schöner Wald," "Du, du liegst mir in Herzen," and "Ein freies Leben führen wir"—

And many more, some of them composed and set to music by Dr. Keil and other members of the community.

Theirs was a singing covered wagon train. The very air was filled with music. Little wonder that the Indians were spell-bound by the strange caravan, different in so many things from any that had passed that way; so confident, so trusting, as though on a mission ordered by the Great Spirit, with which there was not so much as to be even imagined any thought of interference.

"Music oft hath such a charm to make bad good," wrote Shakespeare.

"Since nought so stockish, hard and full of rage, but music for the time doth change his nature," also penned the immortal bard.

"The man that hath no music in himself, nor is not moved with concord of sweet sounds, is fit for treasons, stratagems and spoils"; such words he put into the mouth of one of his characters.

"Music hath charms to soothe the savage breast," wrote Prior.

"The morning stars sang together" for Job as he scrolled the parchment of the oldest book in the world.

The planets, vibrantly swinging in their stellar spaces, seemed to sing for Pythagoras over five hundred years before the visit of the Wise Men of the East at the manger cradle of the Bethlehem Babe, teaching the ancient philosopher his doctrine of the harmony of the spheres in which he held that the celestial bodies are separated by intervals corresponding to the relative wave length of strings which produce harmonious tones. A multitude of the heavenly host of angels sang to the shepherds on the first Christmas morning. A strong bridge may be swayed to destruction by the power of rhythmic sound.

The colony train literally sang itself across the plains, on the march, at the noonday rest, and in the night bivouac —especially around the evening camp fires.

Who can doubt the saving grace of their music as they sang and played their way through the desert spaces, with savage tribes on all sides, able to utterly destroy them at any hour of the day or watch of the night?

There is a German proverb, incapable of being exactly translated into English words, but which has been expressed in this way:

"Where one sings, sit down in peace;
Bad people have no songs."

The colony train was organized with night watches, and with lookouts for day travel. Amos Cushman acting "instead of eyes" for them, had general charge of this part of the work. They were a careful people. They had not waited for a stampede of their cattle or a fright by Indians to force the observance of the ordinary precautions of travel in the plains country. Their tents were secure, their wagons stout, their clothing and blankets warm and their teams kept in good condition. At every camping place, they formed a circle with their wagons, leaving a space for an improvised portable gate for passing in and out, between the leading bier and the last wagon, with always a man on guard, garbed in black, on the driver's seat of the strange plains hearse.

Dr. Keil had learned from men who had made the plains journey the importance of precautions and good equipment, especially from the returned spies who had gone this way two years before.

The next camping place was ten miles on from the Big Blue halt, in the open country. The voyagers entered into the spirit of the music and songs of that evening with an abandon of cheerfulness. Their hearts were light.

Their course lay next over the ridges of the Big Sandy, then eighteen miles further to the Little Sandy, and on eight miles to the Little Blue River and up that stream for ten miles to a camping place on its bank.

The wind blew all that night, and the next day there was a dust storm that made it almost impossible for the drivers to see their teams. They were getting a taste of the disagreeable features of the long journey, but they were still cheerful. They had good road the following day, as they left the Little Blue and went over the hills to the Platte River. Here they saw their first buffalo and a few antelope.

The caravan passed Fort Kearney June 18th and camped beyond on the bank of the Platte, in cold rain, with no fuel but green willow brush. On they trekked up the Platte to where Plum Creek enters that stream. They began now to find buffalo chips for fuel where no other could be had.

On June 25th, the colony train camped opposite the main forks of the Platte, and some of the hunters saw a small herd of buffalo there and gave chase, wounding one animal, but it escaped. They had not learned the tricks of buffalo hunting.

The next day, the main bison herd was encountered. The wagon train was in danger of being overrun by the solid mass of moving animals in the hilly country back of the South Platte. By a desperate effort, the men succeeded in turning the course of the great dumb trek.

There was good traveling up the South Platte bottom, for eighteen miles, when camp was made for the night, and the next day the South Platte was crossed four miles further on, where the river was a half mile wide and only three to twelve inches deep; but the mud was much deeper, and the drivers dared not stop moving their wagons, on account of the quicksands. Safe across, the caravan headed over the divide between the North and South Platte; came to Ash Hollow, where a former year's immigrant train under Captain Gray had had trouble with the Sioux, and continued down the hollow. That night all the cattle were tied and guarded, fearing wolves.

Through heavy sand in the forenoon and over good roads in the afternoon, they traveled on, and saw at a distance an approaching band of Sioux Indians, the first considerable company of red men they had encountered since passing the Iowa mission. Their chief rode up at a furious pace, toward Amos, who met him cordially.

"Tell our people to sing," he had directed his companions in German, and the three outriders carried the word back, with prompt response, though seemingly a part of the regular routine.

Following their chief, these plains Indians showed curious interest in the leading bier; made signs to one another as the principal men of their motley cavalcade came close, and by the time the rest of the tribesmen had inspected at respectful range the strange sight, they were talking and gesticulating in a manner to show the colony people the deep impression made upon their superstitious natures.

In some way or other, the news of the charmed company had already traveled. The bier that led them, and the songs they sang, and the music, were big medicine to the Indian mind.

The next day the colony caravan crossed a stream that runs near the lone tower, called Chimney Rock, known as the "beacon of the plains," and camped on its bank. The following day's travel was with bluffs on the left having the appearance of an ancient city. The evening camp was opposite Chimney Rock—a huge mass that on a clear day was visible for over thirty miles to approaching travelers.

CHAPTER 12

IN THE INDIAN COUNTRY

THE colony caravan was now in the heart of the Indian country which then extended all the way from the Missouri to The Dalles of the Columbia River, across two thousand miles of prairies, plains and mountains. The Old Oregon Trail which they followed had in many places been worn down several feet by the tens of thousands of covered wagons that had passed over it in the twelve years beginning with 1843, and swelling annually in number, at least up to 1852, with no great falling off in 1853 and 1854.

Dr. Keil received another warning here, coming from the commandant of Fort Laramie, that grave danger loomed ahead. He was advised to turn back, or winter there. He would go on at his peril.

"The Sioux Indians threaten trouble, and they are in league with all the tribes. The Indians are in worse mood than they have been since the covered wagon movement westward with women and children began," said the commandant, adding that he was performing his simple duty, clothed with the authority of the United States government.

But Dr. Keil had come with his precious charge intending to go through regardless of all risks. Unafraid, under their leader, the colonists moved on. They made music and sang their familiar community songs as they measured off the dreary miles. With all their weariness they were buoyant, and they did not think of their tiresome marches as hardships. They were a compact com-

pany, all together, healthy, happy and of good cheer in
the hope of the great days at the end of the long, long trail
a-winding, often through axle deep dust and over in-
describably rough roads.

Twenty-five miles made the day's lap for July 2, reaching the Roubidoux trading post kept by the famous traders,
trappers and mountain men of that name, Antoine and
Joseph, brothers. The next camp was on Horse Creek, and
the morning of July 4, their country's natal day, the
travelers had a clear view of Laramie's Peak, a hundred
and fifty miles distant, appearing like a dark cloud rising
in the northwest.

Hard going thereafter for sixteen miles over low, sandy
hills brought them to a trading post right in a prairie dog
town, and after a four mile trek they found a third trading
post, where opportunity was offered by paying small boot
of exchanging some lame cattle for fresh ones. At the end
of fourteen miles of hilly road they camped on the bank of
the Laramie River, near the village of a large band of
Sioux Indians who were friendly but curious concerning
the music and songs of the colonists, and especially so about
the equipage that led their train.

"The news spreads ahead of us," remarked Dr. Keil.
"We could have no privacy in this wilderness, even if we
courted it. But it is well. The good God guides us. We will
halt here for a day in camp and shorten some of our wagon
beds, preparatory to crossing the Rocky Mountains, considered to commence here," he announced.

Twenty miles more brought them, July 8th, to the crossing of Bitter Cottonwood Creek and a second like stream,
and to the banks of a third. Having crossed Horseshoe
Creek, they made camp the next evening at The Dalles of
the Platte, near where the stream runs through a crevice
with banks a thousand feet high. The next day, seven miles

— BOB BOARDMAN.

The lone company of 1855 in the Indian Country; only covered wagon funeral train that crossed the plains; unique, in that it had no predecessor, could have had no contemporary, and can have no successor; weird, in that the strange leading bier piloted the devoted colonists in perfect safety as they sang and played their plodding way through the very jaws of death. (Conception of Bob Boardman, artist, Salem, Oregon.)

up, the road left the Platte and followed a ridge toward Laramie's Peak. Fifteen miles further on the pilgrims struck the Mormon trail and pitched their evening camp on beautiful LeBonte creek; thence the next morning six miles to Marble Creek, and fifteen miles further to Mike's Head Creek. Here Amos Cushman overtook and killed two buffaloes which gave the company a bounteous supply of fresh meat. Seventeen miles of travel brought them to the North Platte five miles below Deer Creek, and they drove to the stream and found it abounding in fish, of which they caught all they desired, with choice buffalo steaks—a great treat.

Arriving at the ferry, they crossed to the north side of the North Platte, traveled a couple of miles and halted where grass was abundant, and lay there until 5 o'clock in the evening, when they started across the thirty mile desert to Willow Springs, taking the whole night. They found grass there, negotiated a five mile lap from 4 o'clock in the afternoon, and on the 17th crossed Greasewood Creek and Alkali Ponds, and came to Independence Rock, 700 yards long, 200 wide, and fifty to eighty feet high. Many thousands of names of trappers, missionaries, explorers and immigrants who had passed that way were found written or engraved on the rock.

"Yonder monolithic mass, cloud crowned monumental pile of the pioneers, let us call God's great guest book, register of the plains." Thus spoke the leader with uncovered head as his followers reverently passed out of sight of the westward trail-marking Gibraltar and Rock of Ages.

The following day they came to the Devil's Gate on the Sweetwater, where that stream runs through a deep crevice worn by the swift running water in the rock, and traveled up the Sweetwater Valley thirteen miles. On up that lovely vale they went, near lofty peaks of gray granite as much as 1000 feet high, crossing Marble Creek where there was an abundance of beautiful white marble; up, up to an altitude of 7000 feet, and made their last camping place on the Sweetwater, within eight miles of the summit of the famous South Pass. Here attention was given to wagon repairs, especially the resetting of tires, as some of the wheels were rattling from usage and frequent drying and swelling.

Traveling over a beautiful road on a long dry ridge brought the company July 25th to the summit. They stopped and hailed Oregon, sunset land of their dreams. Near the crest of the Rockies, the backbone of the continent, they rested their cattle and partook of their noonday meal. Dr. Keil reminded them that not very far from here water runs in three directions; parting at a finger's breadth, a divided raindrop may seek the Gulf of Mexico, the Pacific and the waters of Hudson Bay—

> "From the same cradle side,
>   From the same mother's knee;
>   One to darkness and the frozen tide,
>   The other to the peaceful sea."

Eight miles further on brought the colonists to the far-famed Pacific Springs.

"Here we for the first time refresh ourselves and our tired animals with living, limpid water of the side of the mountains facing Balboa's restless ocean," announced their leader.

They were nearly half way to their new home in the Oregon Country. They had come nearly a thousand miles in sixty-three days. They were making good time, for the covered wagon train travel of their day. Ten miles the next day over a very sandy and dusty road brought them to the Little Sandy, and after following down that stream for six miles they camped. The next day, the 27th, after a sandy plain had been negotiated for eight miles they came to the Big Sandy, where they again pitched their camp. They followed down the course of that stream over a sage plain for seventeen miles the following day, with the Wind River Mountains on one side and the Bear River Mountains on the other, both ranges dotted with snowy peaks.

On the 29th, after ten miles, they came to the Green River ferry landing, where they crossed their wagons, swimming their oxen, and camped a mile and a half below. Seven miles further down, the next day, they left the main river, passed over the hills to Black Fork, that ran by famous Fort Bridger, and at sunset made camp on that beautiful stream. That was the 30th day of July. The next day they went up stream four miles to the trading post, where a stop was made for further wagon repairing by the men, and washing by the women.

They made eighteen miles the following day, up stream, and had good fishing in a creek putting into Black Fork, and on August 2nd they negotiated fifteen miles and camped on the river within three miles of Fort Bridger.

The next day's march was twenty miles, crossing a stream that empties into the Black Fork of the Green River, and reaching another that joins Ham's Fork, which flows into Black Fork, where the tents were pitched for the night. (Near the present town of Granger, Wyoming. The famous rendezvous for that year was held near here in 1834; where Jason Lee halted on his way to plant the first Christian mission in the Oregon Country, departing from the wild scenes twenty-one years plus a month and a day before.)

The weather was lovely. The health of the travelers was good. When the hour was up for the men on guard duty to sound the plains call, "Roll out," there came instead an announcement that they would lay by for the day, in respect to the sacred office of motherhood, for the population of the caravan had been increased during the night by the birth of twins, which on the suggestion of Dr. Keil were appropriately named Thomas and Didymus, for they were boys.

A little later in the morning, the alarm was given that five head of the loose cattle had been stolen. This was the work of Indians, of course. The thieves had driven the animals away almost from under the eyes of the guards, who perhaps had nodded in their seeming security, because they had come a long way since their last warning of danger without serious alarm.

A party of men in charge of Amos Cushman went out in search of the stolen cattle, with the blessing of Dr. Keil, and with the prayers for their safe return of the other members of the caravan, especially the women.

Soon the colony searchers scouring a canyon met a party of Indians driving the stock, and were on the point of making ready to take charge of their property by force. But eager peace signs were given by their red brothers. It transpired that they were driving the cattle into camp, as a friendly and grateful act. It was found that these tribesmen had been at the camp the evening before, where the men were given liberal presents of tobacco and the women among them had been furnished with articles of food and bright pieces of cloth and trinkets; and besides they had been moved by the music and awed by the leading bier.

They had taken the cattle away from the thieves and were returning them to their rightful owners.

Following a short distance behind the colony cavalcade for several days had been traveling another covered wagon train, under the lead of a man named Jackson, from Tennessee, acting as their guide and captain. In some way the members of the Jackson outfit had missed or had disregarded the warnings of the officers in charge of the frontier forces of the regular army, and had come thus far unscathed, though they had been engaged in a skirmish with the Indians and carried bitter hatred toward them.

"In my way o' thinkin' the only good Injun is a dead one," Jackson told Amos Cushman, with whom he had contacted daily.

"I've got a-plenty ammunition fer addin' a right smart sprinklin' o' extry nicks to this here gun butt, if any more stray bucks gets in our way," he boasted, as he displayed five freshly cut notches, "and there's space on the wooden part o' Old Sal, as I calls her, fer nicks for a hull tribe o' the red devils, perviden they gets handy to be nicked off. Whar we comes frum we don't think much more about pluggin' a roamin' or runaway nigger 'an we do a stray sheep killin' dawg, and I'm tellin' you a Injun's wurser nor a nigger any day er night, and cultuser, if any critter is," he confided.

The Jackson outfit passed the colony train at the Ham's Fork camp, without regret on the part of Amos or Dr. Keil, for they did not appreciate the near company of men holding that attitude toward a people to whose mercy (or lack of mercy) they were hourly entrusting the lives of their women and children, and their own.

The friendly Indians who had brought home the stolen cattle sent two of their number, of the Sioux tribe, to guide the colony train over the difficult way ahead. They found on breaking camp nineteen miles of rough road, but through grand scenery, with the Green River Valley in the east and the Bear River Mountains on the west. On the second day, the caravan met hundreds of Sioux, returning from a hunting expedition with plenty of game. With their guides in front, the colonists felt and were doubly safe.

The following three days of travel took the company up

a long ravine to the top of the divide between the Green River and Bear River valleys; then down the ridge to the right, to a ravine which followed five miles to the open valley, reaching Bear River at 10 o'clock at night. Thence their route ran past a huge spring, through a level stretch and over the spur of a mountain to a velvety valley carpeted with thousands of acres of wild flax, and on to the spring branch where Sublette's cutoff comes to the Bridger route; down Bear River to where Smith's Fork comes in, and on to Thomas' Fork, where they came to a bridge and trading post, and encountered many Indians.

A few miles after passing the trading post, they came across what was left of the Jackson train—and that was little, besides ashes and the iron parts of the wagons, which would not burn. There was nothing else to tell the story. Even the bodies had been burned or buried or otherwise taken out of sight. But behind a rock, where in some manner it had been cast or perhaps lost in his last desperate struggle, Amos Cushman found the gun of Jackson, plainly identified by the five telltale notches cut in the wood of the butt. Its owner had not been given time to make another notch, if he had it to his credit, or discredit.

The story of the tragedy of the Jackson train was never known. No one survived to tell it, excepting the Indians engaged in the fatal encounter, offending or offended in what led to it—sinning or sinned against—and the Indians wrote no history, nor told any for others to write. And, paraphrasing a German submarine commander's report during the World War, the gruesome incident was "spurlos versenkt" (sunk without a trace), other than the one that came to the notice of the devoted band of colonists through the accidental finding of the fateful gun with its identifying notches. How many like tragedies of the covered wagon days were enacted and never recorded no one will ever know; but their number was large.

The dreadful toll of them would certainly have been immensely increased in 1855, had not warnings held back the great tide that was ready for the coming of the grass on the prairies in the early spring of that year.

From the scene of the Jackson train tragedy the pilgrims resumed their march with thoughtful minds. Their guides were taciturn, true to the proverbial Indian trait; silent, then laconic.

"Mebbe so, big chief Jackson him got heap more as plenty fight nor what he could use; mebbe so, hees gros ventre (big belly) full, and, mebbe so, got hees scalp lifted for hees nicks," said one of them. They fully understood the significance of the notches on the gun butt.

August 11th the colony train had both rough and good going, climbing high ridges and passing through pleasant valleys. From a vantage point they saw Great Bear Lake to the south. After negotiating seventeen miles, they camped on a spring branch, all well and happy, and voicing their thankful spirits in song. Their new home seemed in sight. They followed the northward stream of the river all next day, over rough road to their camping place after twenty miles of going.

Seven miles the next morning found them at the far famed Lager Springs on Bear River. Grand scenery here; lovely swards of green grass adorned the valley; groves of fine timber studded the slopes; the summits were white with snow; bubbling streams coursed through the landscape; novelty and beauty on all sides. And a refreshing shower, the first drop for many dusty days.

August 14th they turned west with the river through a narrow gap, following down five miles where it opens into a wide valley, whence the stream turns south and the road swerves north, then over the hills to a spring where grass was plentiful. The rain had settled the dust. Then on north for sixteen miles the next day. The following day, when they encountered millions of crickets half an inch long and three-quarters of an inch in diameter, that fairly filled the air and crunched under the wagon wheels, they crossed the ridge between the Bear River Valley and the valley of the Snake. Their destination seemed nearer. They were to follow the waters of the Snake to the mouth of the Columbia, where they would mingle with the salt waves of the Pacific Ocean, together with those of the Willapa River on the banks of which their brothers were busy preparing for their coming. Down grade all the way, but up and over many a high hill, too. Their Sioux guides left them here, with liberal presents and profuse and sincere thanks, and God-speeds from a buoyant and grateful company.

The colonists were interested in the use made of the crickets by the Indians. They employed a peculiar device for catching them in a wholesale manner, by setting up sticks several of which they arranged to come together at the top, their lower ends far apart on the ground. The cricket armies on the march would crawl up the sticks, and thus the Indians caught them by scores and hundreds at a swoop. Their squaws boiled the crickets, the grease coming to the surface when the mess cooled, thus forming a protective covering, preserving them for winter food. Not an appetizing thought to the average reader of these lines, but substantial provision against the pangs of hunger for the tribesmen. And among the peoples who inhabit this globe, there are many quite as outlandish dietary requisites. But for hundreds of Indian dogs, many of them low in the scale of canine quality, the flesh of which came to be rather preferred as a delicacy, the Lewis and Clark exploring expedition would likely have ended in failure. In the sagas of the pioneers are many astounding tales of hunger appeasement the very thought of which by their descendants is apt to force a rising of the gorge.

CHAPTER 13

TREADING ON HISTORIC GROUND

W E ARE treading on historic ground," said Dr. Keil as the caravan stopped the next morning, August 18th, at Fort Hall to buy some needed supplies, explaining: "The first Christian sermon in all the Oregon Country was preached here, by Jason Lee, Sunday, July 27, 1834—twenty-one years, plus a month and nine days ago; and he held here the next day the first Christian funeral, over a man (a Hudson's Bay Company's trapper) killed the day before by accident, in a horse race. Captain Nathaniel Wyeth began building this fort while Lee was here. Enough history was made here to fill many interesting volumes.

"This seems the edge of civilization," continued the leader, "but we are still in the Indian country, with hundreds of weary miles yet ahead of us, and powerful tribes claiming every step of the way. We have been 'in perils of waters, in perils of robbers, . . . in perils by the heathen, . . . in perils of the wilderness,' even as Paul of Tarsus, but we have come through unscathed, the good God having guided us, and we need only still trust the kind Father of us all."

The strange leading bier at the head of the colony covered wagon column had undoubtedly been a safeguard, like the protecting cloud by day and the pillar of fire by night in that other wilderness journey, for, as all who are acquainted with their history know, the Indians of the plains were nothing if not superstitious. The like of this procession they had not before seen or even imagined. Nor had they been treated with such kindness coupled with genuine as well as seeming trustfulness. They were intrigued by the very strangeness of it all. The constant singing of the confiding company added to the awesomeness with which they were regarded by the tribesmen who but for it might have been easily incited to wipe out the company and take all their belongings.

The noon hour after leaving Fort Hall was spent on a clear creek thick with speckled trout. They also found here wild currants in great abundance. They prolonged the usual nooning time. Fried and planked trout and currant cobbler were added to the usual bill of fare, and they feasted like royal banqueters. The meal was prepared with the skill that was afterward to be famous throughout the Pacific Coast. The colony women were unsurpassed in the noble art of cooking. They were to become adepts at appealing to even jaded appetites. And the proverbial plains appetite was far from jaded. The toilers of the wagon train did not at any stage of their journey need the invocation of the host at Macbeth's famous board to his guests,

"Now, good digestion wait on appetite,
And health on both,"

And the plains meals these women did daily prepare! "With a Dutch oven and a spider, a long handled skillet, originally with legs for setting over coals, the colony cooks could prepare a feast to tickle the palate of an epicure," declared a member of the community long after the Keil wagon train crossed the plains.

That was true. And they could have made a meal to satisfy a plains appetite even without the use of a Dutch oven and a spider, after the fashion of the camp cookery of the modern Boy Scouts or Campfire Girls, with sticks and rocks and earth and leaves instead of those two standbys of the covered wagon days.

But these women had easier problems than most of their

sisters and brothers of that epoch in the preparation of meals, for in the shops at Bethel there had been prepared for them the handy utensils and devices of camp cookery known to their generation, down to the last detail, and all arranged for compact carrying and easy unpacking and packing. The food supplies, too, were varied and plentiful, so that, with the help of game and fish secured along the way, and the wild fruits and berries they gathered, little in the line of toothsome dietary essentials was lacking. The colonists had been busy for a whole year drying and storing fruits and vegetables, and curing meats, and milling grain.

Then, too, they were not in the class of an individual covered wagon complement, or a single family. They were as one family, with the task of each ordered and coordinated, making for economy of effort and rendering the task of no member of the company over burdensome. On the location of a camp site by the outriders, every member hurried to his or her appointed task, and in a jiffy tents were pitched, fires built, and the work in every particular proceeded in a manner to warm the cockles of the heart of a military leader or a circus manager. They had no matches. Safety matches were unknown in all the world up to 1855. In the community at Bethel, fires were never extinguished. In the plains journey, with flint and powder and lint and kindlings ready, lighting camp fires was the work of a moment. And the members knew all the other devices of the woodsman to start a fire, had occasion demanded. The list of recipes of the plains dishes would fill a page. As Dr. Keil had promised his people, there was "plenty to eat and plenty to do," and every member did justice to both requisites.

And careful provisions were made for the stock, so that the scarcity of grass at some camping places was not a serious hindrance, as it was with thousands who had passed this way in earlier years. Besides, they were not troubled, as so many who preceded them had been, with trains on ahead taking everything near the trail in the way of sustenance for their over burdened and emaciated teams. They had the broad prairies and plains and mountain places all to themselves in their long journey. There was plenty of feed for their cows, and there was milk for their cookery and cream for their coffee, and even butter for their bread, the whole way across. The Bethel shops had provided them with folding camp stools and collapsible tables, light and serviceable. All this was characteristic of the German thoroughness that marked the entire course of their colony life. The people were never over hurried; but they generally "arrived"; and on schedule time.

"Komm Herr Jesu sei unser Gast, und segne was Du uns und wir den Unseren bescheret haben."

That was the blessing at the breaking of bread repeated throughout many generations by German speaking people around the earth, slightly changed for community use: a free translation: "Come, dear Jesus, be our guest, and bless what You to us and we to ours have shared."

So spoke Dr. Keil as his people with bowed heads sat ready for the repast; thus was repeated the simple, beautiful prayer throughout colony life.

After their bounteous noonday feast, the colonists crossed the Portneuf River. They found the stream so high that they were obliged to block up their wagon beds to keep out the water. But they were prepared for this, too, and were soon safely over. They knew the trick before they started from Bethel, and the workmen there made proper provisions for the emergency. After covering twenty miles they camped on a small creek, and that night prowling Bannock Indians attempted to steal some of their horses, but the alert guards hailed them and they "ran like deer," as a member of the community long afterward expressed it.

The next day the wagon train climbed a hill, crossed a sage brush plain and made its camp at a large spring a mile above the American Falls of the Snake. The following day it pushed on fourteen miles over a rough and hilly road, and camped where the bluffs close in near to the river.

The 21st the road led down three miles to Beaver Dam Creek, followed the river bottom, led up a ravine to a sage plain; went over the sage plain to the head of another ravine, following it down to Raft River. Here they met plainsmen going east for their families who gave glowing reports of the country to the west but had startling news in regard to Indian troubles. Two guards at Marshy Springs, fifteen miles further west, had been shot while on duty. Raft River camp was where the California route turned off and followed up the stream. The colony train pushed on unafraid to Marshy Springs, one of the dustiest days of travel on the whole journey. They met Indians, but were not molested.

August 23d, they proceeded down the Marshy Springs branch and crossed; five miles further brought them to Goose Creek. The next day to Pool Creek, with dust filling the wagon tracks like water. Twin Falls, about two miles north, sounded like a continuous roar of distant thunder. The next day they reached Rock Creek, seeing many Indians. Their road the 26th led down that stream and to the crossing of it, descending long, steep hills, traversing dusty plains, and making camp at the Warm Springs branch.

After an early start on the 28th, Salmon Falls Creek was reached in three miles. There they rested the tired teams and fished the rest of the day. Following the creek a mile, the company reached the river the next morning, and a like distance brought them to where the water pours out of a

thousand springs and foams and tumbles into the Snake.
Four miles further brought them to the head of Salmon
Falls. Traveling down stream to where the road leaves the
river, the colonists encountered a large band of Snake Indians—thousands of them.

"They seemed countless in number," said a member of
the party in after years. "They reminded us of the buffalo
herds we saw in the Platte Valley. The sight made our
people 'drowsy' at first," he acknowledged.

But the Indians took note of the leading bier as they
passed by, Dr. Keil accosted the chiefs and gave them presents, the hands of their white sisters were liberal with the
Indian women in gifts of bright pieces of cloth and gay
trinkets, so the "drowsiness" of the encounter gave way to
friendly feelings and exchanges of various articles for salmon, with which the tribesmen were well supplied. The
Indian braves especially wanted shirts, many of them being devoid of covering from their waist up. Shirts were a
medium of exchange in pioneer days; were a thousand
times better than money, the value of which the Indians did
not understand.

(It should be recorded here that the river called Snake
had no generic name among the Indians. In its long course
from the mountains of Wyoming to Pasco and Kennewick
it bore many names, given it by tribes of restricted habitat.
The name Snake is a misnomer, whether applied to the
Indian tribe or the river. It came from a misinterpretation
of a gesture in the Indian sign language. When the first
white men met the Shoshone Indians in southern Idaho,
they inquired their names, and the answer was an undulat-
ing movement of the hand and the wrist, interpreted by the
white traders as signifying a snake. But the intent of the
Shoshones was to say that they were weavers of grass rugs.)

Dry Camp was reached at dark next day by the colony

train, and the upper crossing of the Snake the following day. The colonists commenced the work of getting over the stream on the last day of August, by calking two wagon beds and lashing them together, thus ferrying a wagon and its load at each trip. It was slow and dangerous business, but all were safely over on the first of September, the most difficult and hazardous task being the swimming of the stock.

Over ridges, bench lands and sage plains to a spring branch September 2nd, and the day following through dusty and stony country, passing Hot Springs branch and visiting the spring of boiling water; nooning on the 4th at Barrel Creek and making a dry camp at night, they found welcome water after three miles on the morning of the 5th and halted for a needed rest, going on a few miles to the first favorable camping place. They had hard going on the 6th, but reached the Boise Valley and two miles more brought them to the bank of that river for their night camp.

"We are still on historic ground here," announced Dr. Keil. "Near where we are camped the remnants of the Astor overland party, under Wilson Price Hunt, were the first white men to see this goodly land. With them was the Dorion Woman, who afterward went through some of her most tragic experiences near here.

"The Dog Rib Indians burned two Forts Boise, built by John Reed and his party in 1813, and left a trail of blood along this stream; murdered Reed and all his men; only the Dorion Woman and her two children escaping to spend their terrible winter in the Blue Mountains, furnishing a story of heroism that has gripped the imaginations of millions.

"Bonneville came in 1834 and changed the name of the river flowing by our camp from the Reed to the Boise," he added, "which should be changed back to the original."

Black-eared rabbits and prairie chickens, the latter in first plentiful supply there, furnished fresh meat to the colonists. Nine miles was the next day's stint, with quail added to the game that was in abundance; down stream the second day, crossing the river on the morning of the 9th and camping in the timber. The next day brought them to Fort Boise, of historic fame. They found many Indians fishing in the Snake and drying salmon for winter fare. They spent the 11th in ferrying the Snake and camped the following night on the Malheur, where they saw springs of hot water boiling up in the bottom, and the next day passed Sulphur Springs and went on to Birch Creek. Three miles over a rough road the next morning brought the cavalcade to the Snake River.

"We see this river for the last time on our long journey," announced Dr. Keil, "so take a farewell look at the Snake; its terrors have seared the memories of many who have gone before us; but it has not been unkind to our people, for which let us be thankful."

Over a ridge and down a stream to Burnt River the leading bier piloted the way with high mountains in sight. Up the river, through a gorge, the 15th, and over hills, through valleys and along streams for two days brought the company to the summit, whence they descended to the Powder River Valley.

The 19th the weary colonists made camp by a spring at the foot of the dividing ridge between the Powder River and Grand Ronde valleys. Over the Grand Ronde hill and down to the valley they plodded on the 20th, and found Cayuse Indians with peas and potatoes for sale. They began the climb of the Blue Mountains the following day and at its close camped in the long looked for pine woods of Oregon.

On the 22nd, the tired teams had extremely difficult

going; it was necessary for a man to guide each lead yoke of oxen and for a dozen men to support every wagon on the downhill side in many sidling places over spurs to keep it from upsetting. They were now in the Blue Mountains. The way led through rough country, much worse than they had found in the Rockies. The following day for five or six miles they had the hardest headway of the whole 2000 mile journey; but made thirteen miles, and fifteen the next day, turning down the mountain toward the Umatilla River and encountering on the western slope several bands of Cayuse Indians.

"We have done well," Dr. Keil told his nerve racked people here. "We have accomplished what up to twelve years ago was held to be impossible. In 1843 Sticcus, friendly Cayuse chief, piloted the first wagon train over the route we have just negotiated. That was the famous Applegate train.

"Men who were to become governors, senators, judges, statesmen, arbiters of peace between nations, empire builders, swung their axes and used their spades in preparing the way for the first thousand pioneers blazing the trail which we have even now found by no means an easy one, though following the tracks of wagons sufficient to transport a big army. I knew from our spies the difficulties we would find here. So let us thank the good God that we came safely through."

On the 25th the fagged out colonists remained in camp, to recuperate and recover their shattered nerves and allow their teams a much needed respite. Early next morning when ready to move on they found five of the loose horses gone. Some Indians agreed to find them at the equivalent of a dollar a head, which they did. This the colony leaders understood but kept smiling faces. They traveled down grade twelve miles the 26th, and sixteen miles the follow-

ing day, and on the 28th twelve miles, arriving at the Umatilla agency.

Here there was a rest. That evening, Dr. Keil spoke to
the assembled members of the train. It was a meeting of
rejoicing and thanksgiving. There was an abandon of music
and song. Even there was dancing in which the children
joined, and Dr. Keil with them. He was a lover of children, even as his Master loved the little ones, as will be
further disclosed in the pages that follow. Dr. Keil read
to his people from the eleventh chapter of Second Corin-
thians, from the 23d to the 33d verses, the letter in which
St. Paul told the church at Corinth of his "stripes above
measure," his "prisons more frequent," his "deaths oft,"
and of his shipwreck and wilderness wanderings and perils
of divers kinds; but declaring that in his necessities, in-
firmities, persecutions, distresses and weaknesses he was
strong—

Just as the colony caravan had proved in coming so far
through many dangers. They were all there, to the last
one, and in good health and spirits, and in high hopes, and
it was seemly that they show their gratitude. It was a true
thanksgiving service, there in the wilderness that is now
one of the great wheat belts of the United States.

The music and singing of that memorable thanksgiving
jubilee filled the clear evening air with concord of happy
melody—sounds as sweet as those of Narcissa Whitman,
who had served her generation so faithfully and gained the
martyr's crown not far away from this colony camp; Narcissa Whitman, to hear whose singing, it was related a
Flathead Indian woman walked a hundred and fifty miles
with her papoose strapped to her back, that she might have
the missionary woman with the pale face and golden hair
sing her baby to sleep; Narcissa Whitman, who had be-
guiled with song a chief trader of the Hudson's Bay Com-

pany, so movingly that this incident may have aided in leading to peace instead of war between the United States and Great Britain—

For the chiefs of that ancient monopoly were disturbed over the coming of the Christian teachers. They were more alarmed by the encroachments of the first covered wagon trains, pioneered by the missionaries, fearing for the security of their hold upon what they regarded as their country—the primeval and wild extension of Rupert's Land. Since the royal grant in 1769 of Charles the Second to his cousin, Prince Rupert, for nearly two hundred years they had held all but undisputed control of a vast empire the savage occupants of which they had governed and exploited, assuming for their purposes that it was fit only for the uses they made of it in contributing to the gigantic fur trade directed from the headquarters of their chartered company in London, which was for all practical purposes a long arm and a grasping hand of the British Empire, operating under the egis of Parliamentary law. The trail blazers of the covered wagon days, in cynical mood, were apt to say the initial letters of that concern's name stood for "Here Before Christ." It was and is yet, after a lapse of years approaching the three century mark, the largest fur trading company in the world.

CHAPTER 14

COUNTING THEIR BLESSINGS

THE PIONEERS

By E. O. LAUGHLIN

Over every modern luxury there lies
The shade of ancient hardship. He who flies
Across a continent on wings of gauze
Threads the thin paths of meteors because
His fathers, wingless, earthbound, as they groped
Through marsh and jungle, upward gazed and hoped.
The cars that roll so ceaselessly today
On velvet wheels along the concrete way
Would find no highways spanning hill and vale,
Had not the drudging oxcarts blazed the trial.

Though poverty awaited where the vast,
Stark prairie and horizon met at last,
Yet was their goal—how priceless still it seems!—
Unhampered freedom and untrammeled dreams.
Hovels are mansions, homesteads broad estates,
And settlements are cities now. The Fates
Caught up their severed flaxen threads and spun
With magic art the patterns they begun—
Caught up chimeric hopes, abandoned schemes,
And made a world more wondrous than their dreams.

The pioneers who broke the virgin soil
Ne'er garnered half the harvest of their toil.
To them the wearing days behind the plow!
To them the aching limb, the sweating brow!
To them the weary seedtime! Others reap
Today where'er they sowed. To them is—sleep.
Oh, aviator, conquering realms of blue,
A haunting specter flies along with you,
And vague-seen covered wagons bear strange loads
Of ghostly pilgrims down the long, paved roads!

THERE was no study hour in the school tent of Ruth Baker that evening. The children had been dismissed to take part in the general rejoicing and had joined in the singing and in disporting themselves in the ways of youth since the race was young. The school of the colony train, in the little red school house of the plains, had been planned at Bethel. A tent had been devised of stout home woven cloth dyed red, and folding seats had been fashioned with the same material and made very light, so that the whole equipment when gathered up for the day's travel took small space in one of the wagons and contributed only a few pounds of weight.

That beautiful evening, after a warm day, a cooling breeze wafted up the Columbia River gorge with the hint of approaching fall in its breath. All the way on the long journey it had been the self imposed and pleasant duty of Amos Cushman, at the end of each day's travel, to pitch the school tent and arrange the seats, with the help of Asa Cushman or some other member of the party, generally assisted by Ruth herself. It was the work of but a few minutes. This chore had been done as usual.

Amos and Ruth slipped away from the merry making crowd and repaired to the tented school room. They had time for a quiet talk; and opportunities for such leisure had been few in the more than four months since they fared forth from Bethel, for their duties were many and always pressing. There had been no time to waste and no duty that admitted of neglect, nor even the thought of such laxness had they allowed to enter their minds.

There had been many times when, as they rode through level stretches, they could exchange confidences, but they were usually short, and interrupted nearly always by some need arising in an unexpected place in the train. Their duties were in the nature of those of guardians and lookouts, together with their brother and sister. The Uncle Sam quartet, with their red, white and blue mounts were everywhere at once, it seemed. The young men had their turns at night guard duty added to the various details of the day's march. Amos and Asa had to be awake and watchful when others slept, and they were ready for any emergency every minute of their twenty-four hour day. Their companions came to wonder when they slept or how they could get along without sleeping, for they seemed always alert and on the spot where they were needed. Like Napoleon, they actually learned to sleep in the saddle.

They enjoyed the rest at the Umatilla agency.

Amos and Ruth talked long in the relaxed seclusion of that evening. They recounted the travail and the weariness of the long trail—the Old Oregon Trail. In the first part they had mushed it through mud hub deep. They had seen storms in which all the elements seemed to be in arms waging a war of unsurpassing vengeance. Hail had beaten against them until it became a hostile bombardment, the sleety force of which fairly cut their faces. Rain had come down in torrents, till it drenched them to the skin. In one such night, a member of the colony train on picket duty called to the next man on the thin sentinel line, "Two o'clock and all is wet!" The two brothers of the Uncle Sam quartet acted as guides in the mutual task of finding camping places and in fording the rivers, with Amos on his bay mount swimming many streams and Asa following on his proverbially patient Missouri mule. These alert guardians had learned to distinguish between the closely simulated howling of the thieving plains Indians and that of the wolves, which had allowed them in the experience of other covered wagon trains to deceive the men on picket duty, and creeping close stampede or drive off the stock. This had happened many times in the epochal westward movement in the forties and early fifties. But Amos and Asa had good ears that were far from tone deaf, and this delicate sense of hearing proved a protection against the wolf howl of the Indian counterfeiting that of his four footed brother thief of the wilderness.

Ruth and Amos recounted their experiences with the terrible torture of the dust after the mud had been left behind. They had been obliged to eat, drink and breathe dust, till breathing was difficult. For long stretches it was half leg deep to their animals. It was like a London fog, almost thick enough to cut with a knife. The high winds gathered it up and flung it into their faces with such impact as to sting them with pain, and to make it almost impossible for the oxen to go on. And the mosquitoes! These voracious insects, they reminded one another, had sung tenor at night, on long stretches, while the wolves accompanied them with a blood-curdling baritone.

"The mosquitoes went forty bushels to the acre in the vicinity of Fort Kearney," wrote an earlier covered wagon emigrant in his diary.

Lack of fuel had caused them to go to bed supperless except for cold lunches at a few camps. Dearth of grass and water had made the toilsome journey still more difficult over several barren stretches, sapping the strength of the oxen already pushed to the point of endurance. Water had sold at a dollar a gallon at one stage of the trail trek in 1850.

They had come upon many mute evidences of the death and disaster that had befallen the emigrants of former years. In June, 1849, Major Cross, in the lower part of the Platte Valley, said 20,000 people and 50,000 head of live stock had passed that point and were toiling westward beyond the forks of the Platte. Lines of wagons as far as the eye could see, lured by the California gold rush, urged

by the prospect of free land in the Oregon Country, fired
by the zeal of the spirit of Mormonism. It was the ever
westward march that had been going on since the dawn of
civilization. And this was the last major hegira, bound for
the ultimate West. Great as was the movement in 1849,
the wagon trains of 1850 were longer and more numerous.
They were to continue for years after the one in which the
Keil colony train crossed, when the Indian troubles of that
year and the years immediately following had subsided.

Ezra Meeker, the Old Oregon Trail blazer *[See note
at end of chapter], said in his Memoirs that the covered
wagon migrations of the early fifties (he crossed in 1852)
made up each season what would have amounted to "an
army 500 miles long, no inconsiderable part of it three
columns deep."

Another immigrant of 1852 said that for many days,
up the Platte Valley, he was seldom out of sight of some
party burying its dead, the losses being mostly from the
cholera especially prevalent and fatal that year. That dread
disease was at its worst in large crowds. It was estimated
that probably 6000 died from the cholera that year, nearly
all of them in the Platte Valley, most of them along the
lower reaches of that river. Many men, the mother of the
family having died, turned back.

Another immigrant says he never saw a woman turn
back. The women were braver and stronger for enduring
hardships than the men.

Amos and Ruth, outriders of the colony train, with their
brother and sister, had come across the remains of many
abandoned wagons of former years. Many had been burned
for fuel. Fine trunks, boxes, barrels, had been left behind,
to lighten loads or because the oxen dropped in their tracks
and could go no further. In 1850 there had been a hundred
carcasses to the mile in stretches east and west of Pacific

Springs. These outriders of the colony train had seen enough mute marks of awful death and sad loss to make their hearts sick. But they had steeled themselves to the tasks they had assumed, and they were not at any time in the least daunted or dismayed. They had strong wills, stout hearts, vigorous bodies and high hopes.

In the cool of the evening, in the seclusion of the colony school tent, they counted their blessings. They had prepared well. Their wagons were built for the service required, whether as caravels of the vast open spaces or boats of the river crossings, or to stand against the storms. They were colony honest and colony strong in their fashioning, and so with all their equipment, from their tents to their water bags. They were far better wains for the work for which they were intended than was the first one ever to cross the Rockies and the Blue mountains, the famous Conestoga wagon, called by the Indians the horse canoe, brought in 1836 by Dr. Marcus Whitman with the first Protestant missionaries to work in the Oregon Country east of the Cascades.

The colonists had been a compact company, well organized and disciplined, cooperating to the last man and woman and the least child. They had profited from the experiences of the people who had gone before. First there had been the buffalo and the Indian trails, then had come the trappers, then the missionaries, and after them the pack trains, followed by the covered wagon cavalcades of the Applegates and the many thousands that succeeded them. The trail was now well marked. The menace of Indian raids and massacres had been multiplied, but they were buoyed up by the spirit of the missionaries—and the strange leading "horse canoe" had protected them all the way, by virtue of the superstitious awe of the Indian tribes. Reports of the novel caravan had traveled in the many

astonishing methods of the spread of unusual news along
the trail. It was uncanny, like the grapevine telegraph of
the pioneer newspaper or the underground or undercover
information of prison cells, where the very walls have ears.
The vast waste spaces had been vibrant with tidings of the
charmed company in its lone march through what to an
ordinary covered wagon train would have been the hungry
and yawning jaws of death.

No one with retentive memory who has read pioneer
history will question the swift spread of reports through
Indian channels. Flashes on unusual events, by signal fires
and with fleet footed mouth-to-ear messengers, Mercury
winged carriers of tidings, frequently if not generally
reached out through such sources ahead of the swiftest
white couriers. It was the case with the 1843 drowning of
the missionary party at the falls of the Willamette, the
murder of Elijah at Fort Sutter in 1844, the Whitman
massacre of 1847. Indeed, that was the almost invariable
experience. Incredible to the novitiate mind as may seem
the general Indian knowledge of the presence on the plains
of the Keil funeral train, it was well within the regular
order of events.

As Ruth and Amos recounted mutual hardships and
dangers, they were both thankful and thoughtful, and each
divined the other's feelings. The love of the quiet Bethel
days had been tempered like steel in the fire of common
dangers. It had stood the acid test of the plains. That term,
it has been said, was coined in the covered wagon period.
It was at least a current expression that one who had come
to the end of that long journey unscathed by the lurid
flames of cynicism, and sweet tempered and loved by all
his or her companions, was an eligible candidate for the
circles of sainthood.

Amos spoke of the coming coveted time when with the

accrued muniment of an earned privilege he might claim Ruth as all his own. She answered in reciprocal words of loving kindness, but the feeling was alloyed with the former wish that they might remain with their blood relatives and their bond brothers and sisters of the community.

"The call of service brought you with us, Amos," pleaded Ruth. "You were needed and you came. You will still be needed in the new home."

"I am glad I came. I am proud to have been of help," answered Amos. "I would have hated myself for refusing the call of service. But when our people are settled in their new home there will be others in plenty to take over our duties. I want my place in the world, my chance to stand on my own feet as a man among men, and I want you for myself alone, to love and cherish and work for."

"But you will be your own man in the colony, and I will be yours and yours alone," said Ruth. "The only difference will be that we will have a partnership interest in a great undertaking instead of the individual ownership of a small one. And your natural industry and ability will make you a leader in the large undertaking," she went on. "You will be trusted with the oversight of big things for the good of many, instead of having the care of small affairs the result of which may miss the high hall mark of success however great your endeavors or skillful your management.

"Helena Giesy took greater risk for the sake of her conscience than I am called upon to make for mine. She pioneered in martyrdom of the heart, gave up assured happiness for a hope, a vision, a will-o-the-wisp. Now we know colony living is no freak experiment. I have the life of reality to guide me in the firm belief that it is the best way. 'The proof of the pudding is the eating thereof.' I have that proof. You have it. Helena, as you know, rejoices daily over the hard choice she made. In every kind of business there is a hazard. But no well managed community enterprise has ever failed or can fail, and you know the ability and prudence and honesty of Dr. Keil and the colony board of trustees."

"But I am willing to take the risk. I can try again or turn to something else if we meet misfortune or make mistakes. We are young and we have health and strength," urged Amos.

And so they talked and argued at length; but there was no decision, except an exchange of declarations of greater mutual love than they had before felt.

Amos made new resolves to win Ruth to his way, and Ruth hoped to prevail upon him to accept her own firm faith, that had been strengthened in the incidents of the trail journey by the many proofs of Dr. Keil's wise leadership. This feeling was shared by all the other members of the colony train. They had respected him at Bethel as a father and friend and safe leader. Now they loved him as a brother and sharer of dangers and difficulties. The change was like the refining of gold. His word had been law there; here his wish was a covenant and his glance a benediction.

As Amos and Ruth embraced and exchanged mutual good night salutations and sealed them with a loving kiss that was sweet to both as none before given or taken, and as Amos turned to go away to assume picket duty, Ruth detained him.

"I have a secret for you," she said. When she told him their brother and sister, Asa and Hannah, had decided to wed, as soon as they were settled and provided for in their new colony home, he was not surprised. He could have foretold this outcome back on the trail as far as the first few river fordings, when Asa was ready to risk his life for Hannah's safety, and guided and watched over her like a guardian angel.

But Ruth added that Asa and Hannah harbored no thought of leaving the colony people. He would study medicine and be a community doctor, for which his name marked him. Hannah would be a gracious and glorified nurse for her people, for did not the name given her at birth make her gracious? Asa and Hannah had formed their plans as the caravan moved. They hoped to aid in making their new community home a medical center, in order that they might not only give high service to their own people, but that they also might serve their neighbors and render help to all who came needing the facilities and skill of the institution they would establish for the good of humanity in the large.

"They are true community dreamers," Ruth reminded Amos. "Why should not we, too, dream dreams along some other line of community and general endeavor, and set ourselves to working them out in reality; in spirit and in truth?"

Amos went to his post of duty pondering these things in his heart. This way lay promise of security; Ruth's way. The other way offered hazards. But he did not fear to take chances. Was not the voyage of life one long series of risks?

* The Oregon Trail Memorial Association, founded by Ezra Meeker, who gave the last twenty years of his life almost to his ninety-eighth birthday to its objects, is still carrying on, with offices in New York City. Professor Howard Roscoe Driggs of New York University is president. A late circular of that association says: "Fully 350,000 Americans took these trails during the days of the covered wagon—from 1836 when Marcus Whitman and his wife first made their way to Oregon, to 1869 when the golden spike linking the Union Pacific and the Central Pacific was driven at Promontory Point at the north end of the Great Salt Lake in Utah."

"We are brought a little closer to the tragic cost of it all when we realize that fully 20,000 lost their lives in the effort to reach the Golden West," wrote President Driggs. (One writer says

30,000, another 32,000. Two-fifths of the "mountain men," the hunters and trappers who preceded the settlers, lost their lives.) "They had no means of marking the graves of the dead in those prairie stretches. Only one grave of all the 20,000, so far as we know, is surely marked. I refer here to the grave of the pioneer mother near Scott's Bluff, Nebraska. When Rebecca Winters passed away, one of the company had the forethought to pick up an old wagon tire that lay along the trail. Bending it into an oval he set the tire within the grave. On the top of the tire was chiseled the mother's name and age. A party of surveyors laying out a railroad along the old North Platte happened by mere chance to run their line over the mother's grave. Then the surveyors, with a touch of sympathy that is beautiful to think upon, went back for twenty miles and changed the line of survey that it might miss the mother's grave."

Part of the lettering on the monument erected over that known grave of a pioneer reads: "In memory of Rebecca Burdick, wife of Hiram Winters. She died a faithful Latter Day Saint, Aug. 15, 1852, aged 50 years, while making that memorable journey across the plains with her people to find a new home in the far distant Salt Lake Valley. She gave her life for her faith; her reward will be according to her works. This monument was erected in 1902, her centennial year, by her numerous descendants in Utah."

(However, another such known grave was thereafter marked, near the site of Laramie, Wyoming. Her widowed husband scratched deeply with his jackknife on a piece of sandstone the record: "Mary E. Homesley, died June 10, 1852, aged 29;" buried it with his wife's body and passed on to Oregon. Seventy-three years later the Wyoming Historical Society put a monument over the grave, and dedicated it with appropriate ceremonies, at which the mayor of Laramie presided.)

The Kiwanis Club of Bend has undertaken the task of erecting a monument to the unknown pioneer. A woman was buried under a gnarled juniper tree on the desert near Bend, Oregon, probably of the immigration of 1847. Her name was carved on the tree, with the dates of her birth and death. But the growth of the tree obliterated the name and date of death, and all else save the fact that a pioneer woman was buried there, almost within sight of the promised land, to which she was bound, with her people. All memory of her is lost. Such markers set up along the Old Oregon Trail, telling of all who perished, would extend the whole way across, and wayfarers of the present day would need no other guide posts.

CHAPTER 15

DOWN THE MIGHTY COLUMBIA

HERE at the Umatilla agency the road forked. The right hand way pointed down the left or south bank of the Columbia. The left hand trail led to Wells Springs (where, in 1848, General Cornelius Gilliam, commander of the citizen soldiers who went to punish the Indians for the massacre of the Whitmans, met his accidental death), toward the Barlow route, the first highway over the Cascades that admitted of the passage of wagons to the Willamette Valley, inadequately completed in 1846 only in time for part of the immigration of that year.

The colony caravan took the right hand road and reached the Columbia at the mouth of the Umatilla. They proceeded steadily on from this point, generally following the shore line of the great river. They crossed the John Day River near its mouth, the water being low at that season and the bed so rocky that one on foot could cross nearly dry shod. At this point they met rangers from the upper country hastening to The Dalles, with news of threatened outbreaks by the Cayuse Indians on the south side of the Columbia. They also feared that the Yakima Indians, on the north side, who had been defeating regular troops under Colonel Granville O. Haller, would cross the Columbia and attack The Dalles. The colonists put out double guards at night, but the alarm proved unfounded.

The wagon train crossed the Deschutes River at a dangerous ford near its entrance into the Columbia. A friendly Cayuse Indian guided the wagons over, and took his pay in a shirt and thanks and a good dinner, which he considered a fair exchange. Arriving at The Dalles, the colonists went into camp near the Methodist mission.

The building of the steamboat *Wasco* had but a month or two before been finished on the upper river and that vessel had commenced regular trips between The Dalles and the Cascades, and the portage on the Oregon side had for a few weeks been completed, connecting with the steamboat *Fashion* running on the Columbia below the Cascades. The portage consisted of a track on which cars drawn by mules were operated. Not long afterward, an engine built in San Francisco was substituted for the mule traction. And thus was operated the first railroad in Oregon.

The business of the portage road being new, a former member of the colony remembers that Dr. Keil was offered favorable terms for the transportation of his company and their equipment, as a sort of advertising stunt. So the colony people with all their belongings were with little delay transferred to the *Fashion* below the rapids and proceeded on down the Columbia past Fort Vancouver and thence to near the mouth of the river.

"We are passing highly historic places now," said Dr. Keil. "Captain Robert Gray in his good ship *Columbia* on May 11, 1792, discovered this long sought River of the West, on whose bosom we are now riding, and named it for his vessel; thus gaining for his government the next highest muniment of title to all the country drained by the great waterway and its tributaries.

"March 25, 1811, Astor's ship, the ill-fated *Tonquin*, came into these waters and on April 12 of that year work on Fort Astoria was commenced, founding the city we have just passed on our left, named for John Jacob Astor.

"On our right side a few days of 1805 were spent by the Lewis and Clark expedition, and on our left, at their Fort Clatsop, Christmas of that year was celebrated and the rest of the winter spent, until March 23, 1806—with Saca-jawea (Sacagewea has just been adopted by the U. S. Geographic Board as the proper spelling), the famous Bird Woman, a member of their party.

"After the arrival of the *Lausanne*, the Mayflower of the Pacific, in 1840, only fifteen years ago, the first Christian mission station was established on the coast of Oregon; a little below us, on our left—so you see, we are not far behind in the making of history with our contribution to the winning of the West."

From the north side of the Columbia, by way of the tide sloughs and over the densely timbered hills to Shoalwater Bay the Argonauts of the new dream proceeded. They were met there with boats by members of the colony who had been expecting them and so conducted over the bay to the Willapa River and up that stream to the place their spies had selected as the site of the new colony home. They were most warmly welcomed there by the members who had been preparing for their arrival, and by two small parties who had come by way of New York and across the Isthmus of Panama.

Among the latter were John Giesy, chairman of the board of trustees or head men, and his family, and Jacob Giesy, the latter to become known to many thousands of people up and down the Pacific coast as keeper of the Aurora hotel and restaurant, first in the overland stage days, then in the early railroad era, and for a number of years after the dissolution of the colony, a period covering two score years and more.

And John Giesy was to be head of the trustees of the colony at Aurora throughout its communal life, the first friend of Dr. Keil and administrator of his estate, and chief among those to effect the distribution of the common property of the colony, and wind up its affairs.

Before November 23, six months after the time of the departure of the covered wagon train from their Missouri home at Bethel, the members of the colony on the Pacific Coast were all together on the Willapa, and happy to be safe and well, though their accommodations were crowded and crude, the buildings being made from logs and other materials at hand. There had been born in the mean time to Christian Giesy and wife a son, who is now Dr. A. J. Giesy, long a leading physician and surgeon of Portland, Oregon. A second son was born to them, who is Christian Giesy of Aurora, Oregon.

The Keil wagon train arrived at the Willapa home Thursday, November 1, 1855. This date is verified by the fact that, the very next day, the population there was increased, over the "indirect immigration route," by one, who became a shining member and whose people extend loving felicitations each succeeding second day of the eleventh month, which was the ninth in the Roman calendar, signifying worthiness or completeness, like the present baseball aggregation.

Members of the community had taken up and taken over land for several miles up and down the Willapa River. They were all very busy getting roofs over their heads for several weeks after the arrival of the new comers in addition to those that had already been prepared by the advance guard.

The body of Willie Keil was not buried till the day after Christmas, on the afternoon of December 26, 1855. With reverent hands and with the singing by all the colony people of the song composed at Bethel for the occasion, "Das Grab ist tief und stille," they tenderly laid the body to rest on the Giesy farm near Crockett's Landing, and so dedicated a new cemetery. And thus was enacted the closing scene of the longest if not the only funeral march of

American history conducted by a cortege of covered wagons. Queen and Kate, the mule team, led the funeral procession that day, with the plains hearse, accompanied by the improvised band of the community, and the American flag carried in front of the musicians. That was a scene that lived through the remaining years in the memories of the colony people gathered there.

We will meet the historic mule team several times in succeeding pages.

Mother earth was to be opened slightly more than eighteen months later in the pioneer Willapa burying place for the grave of Christian Giesy, the devoted and tireless worker who had given such zestful and devoted enthusiasm to the gathering of the colony forces in Pennsylvania and at Bethel, and who was the chief of the spies sent to search for the new community home. He was drowned in crossing Willapa Bay in a boat in rough weather.

Dr. Keil, who was then with the colonists at Aurora, returned with a heavy heart to conduct the sad funeral rites of this strong protagonist of community ideals and his loyal supporter and friend. The ceremonies over and the return trip started, Dr. Keil was overtaken with dread news of the death in the same tragic manner of Henry Giesy, a younger member of the family and one of the four preachers of the ten Giesy brothers, and hurried back for the funeral and burial ceremonies. But the body was never recovered, though long and patient was the search.

Ground was opened for another notable member of the community in the third year thereafter—Andrew Giesy, father of the ten sons and four daughters, members of the community, at whose Pennsylvania home the movement began that led to its founding. His grave was third in the pioneer God's Acre, and next to that of his son, Christian. The inscriptions on the three grave stones read:

Grave of Willie Keil, son of the leader; died May 19, 1855, at Bethel, Missouri. Body buried December 26, 1855, at Willapa, Washington, over 2,000 miles away, after leading only covered wagon funeral train that crossed the plains.

View of Aurora town in overland stage days; first and temporary stage barn standing front.

Wm. Keil, born Jan. 12, 1836. Died May 19, 1855.

In memory of Christian Giesy, Sr., born in Switzerland, Sept. 20, 1813, died July 7, 1857.

In memory of Andrew Giesy, Sr., born Nov. 17th, 1791, died Oct., 1860.

(The reader will note that the date of Willie Keil's death corresponds with what has appeared in the foregoing pages—and that his grave is over two thousand miles from Bethel, where he died.)

That little cemetery is about half way between Raymond and Menlo, Washington, and near the village of Willapa, on the farm of Huldamay Giesy and Henry Giesy, cousins, Henry residing on the land. It is a beautiful spot, surrounded by rolling hills, reminding a recent visitor of those of his native Iowa, and in all the years the graves there have had careful and reverent attention from the hands of former members of the community and their descendants. Plain, neat headstones mark the resting places, erected in the long ago time when the bodies were laid there.

The stricken leader was bowed down with an especially heavy load of sorrow over the loss of two of his most enthusiastic preaching and teaching converts to his way of life. Henry Giesy, whose body was claimed and never given up by the waters of Willapa Bay, was one of the youngest members of the family. In especial honor to his memory, Dr. Keil wrote a song of eight verses and chorus, expressive of his profound grief, entitled and the first line reading:

"Ein Jüngling, der suchte sein himmliches Glück."

The song was set to music and used on occasions of deep emotional feeling in community singing throughout colony days. It still lingers in the memories of surviving members.

Something should be said here about published statements concerning the alleged illiteracy of Dr. Keil. He did not have the advantages of university training. But he was nevertheless a scholar in the true sense. Webster gives as one definition of a scholar, a student, and as a synonym, a learner. There is no record that Jesus of Nazareth attended a college, nor any but one that the Master ever made a motion to put into written form a word or a name, and then it was as if to write with his finger on the ground the name of a man without sin and thus worthy to cast the first stone at the woman taken in adultery. Yet Jesus was the prince of all teachers; the world's greatest student and learner. Abraham Lincoln never attended a college, but he was a profound student and a master learner, and the foremost teacher of democracy the world has produced.

In the same sense, Dr. Keil was a scholar. He was a student and a learner. He drew his knowledge from the vast library of nature, with its tongues in trees, its books in running brooks, its sermons in stones, and its good in everything. He understood the well springs of human nature and he found virtue in all men and women and in little children.

The writer has before him one of the several letters of Dr. Keil sent to the home people at Bethel describing the tragic ending of the lives of Christian and Henry Giesy, written in perfect German, in a hand and with the expressive language of a scholar and a man of deep human sympathy and clear understanding. In this letter, to one of the younger members of the community, he signed himself, after his name, "Your Teacher." He was a true teacher as well as a preacher and leader and brother and friend.

It was soon decided by Dr. Keil and the leading members of the community that the Willapa Valley location was not a suitable one for a successful settlement of the kind they had planned. The spies had given too literal heed to their instructions to select a timbered site, with supplies for their prospective saw mill and other wood working operations, and one removed from troublesome neighbors and with room for expansion. It was remote from markets. The cost of clearing the land for their orchards and general farm crops was too great.

The decision was shortly reached to seek a new location. A committee was selected to travel over the country looking for a better one. A number of men set out in a light wagon the team of which was driven by Amos Cushman—the mule team that drew the plains hearse. They searched as far east as The Dalles and as far south as Roseburg. They were proffered attractive inducements at several points, one of them more than a section of land at what is now the metropolitan city of Portland almost free of cost.

In the mean time Dr. Keil went to Portland and practiced medicine during the winter of 1855-56, where he was successful and built up a good clientele, the while receiving reports of the searching committee and keeping in touch by the slow mails of the period with the Bethel community, where Andrew Giesy, Jr., had been left in charge, and with the members of the community at Willapa.

It was finally decided that the beginnings of the far western home of the colonists should be made at what was to be called Aurora, in honor of a favorite daughter of Dr. Keil, where with $1000 down payment two quarter sections of land were contracted for, on one of which there was already a small saw mill and a grist mill. In the first years the place was known as Aurora Mills. There was a log house, and workmen occupied this and began in the spring of 1856 the construction of other residence buildings, and shops, and the improvement of the mills.

CHAPTER 16

D R. KEIL continued his practice in Portland, making frequent visits to Aurora, to help plan and direct the work of building and clearing and starting the farming and gardening operations and the setting out of orchards and vineyards. Good progress was made from the very first day. In the spring of 1857, the house that was to be the home of Dr. Keil and his family was finished and they moved in. This was "das grosze Haus," "the big house." During the first years, accommodations were afforded and meals served to overland stage passengers in this house, pending the completion of the Aurora hotel and restaurant. Part of the single men and women lived in "the big house," and a number of the detached men had rooms in "der Saal," "the hall," near by, in which, later, summer guests were accommodated. "The hall" was used for dancing and entertainments and public functions generally. There were to be from now on to the end of colony days twenty to forty people constantly at the hospitable board of the leader of the community; for visitors were usually entertained there, as well as some of the summer guests. So there was never much privacy for the head of the colony. He was preacher, counselor, confidant, friend. He was dictator and judge and jury. His word was law. He settled all disputes. No one questioned his authority. There was a board of "head men," trustees, and he took counsel with them, but on most questions his was the deciding voice. There were exceptions, some of which will be noted later on, but they only served to prove the rule.

"The Big House," Aurora colony home of Dr. Keil. Front view. First overland stage passengers were given meals and lodging in this house, before completion of famous Aurora colony hotel and restaurant.

Without money and without price: The building at Aurora in which were some of the shops, and the community store where every member was welcome, to supply his or her needs, and no charges were made, nor any books of account kept.

There was an "unter Haus," "house below," down the hill from "the big house," where some of the more detached members lived; and others were quartered in the various homes—as was the case with new comers, till houses for them could be built, and with the newly married couples, where no provision had been made for them.

By the time "the big house" was occupied, all the members of the colony who had come across the plains and by the isthmus route, and some others who had joined the colony forces, with the exception of a few who remained on the Willapa land till their holdings there could be disposed of, were settled at Aurora and on the farms that were being acquired and improved thereabouts.

There was much hard work, as there had been in the beginnings at Bethel; but the members of the colony were good farmers and craftsmen, and soon the community was prospering and extending its holdings and putting the land to good use. There had been school for the children from the first, and places for religious worship. There was contact with the neighboring farmers, and wayfarers were entertained and profitable trade established with the shops, and with the saw mill and grist mill.

Soon beginnings were made of a livery business and a restaurant, to accommodate the newly established overland stages that made Aurora a station. A colony store was opened for the needs of the members in supplying their wants—always without money and without price, and freely according to their needs, without even the scratch of a pen. And in a little while there was a general merchandise store to accommodate the trade of the surrounding country, at which goods and wares and implements were sold to people outside of the colony membership for the profits they brought to the common treasury, as was the case with all the shops and the surplus crops of every kind.

In the general merchandise store the postoffice was kept, by a member of the colony. So was the express office, which handled much money, there being no banks near at hand. The neighbors brought in their money, too, and the big safe in the general merchandise store constantly contained thousands of dollars, and this was true for years. Between the colony members there was perfect trust. This spirit was carried to the neighboring farmers. Locks and keys were scarcely necessary, in fact, they were not common in the colony homes. There were no tramps in those days. Everybody trusted everybody else, and the latchstring of every door hung hospitably loose on the outside.

"Our diligence and activity must be an open fountain in order to do good to the poor," said their fundamental law, adopted in the beginnings of Bethel. No one was turned away hungry. No one was refused shelter. A traveling photographer came to the community. He was thriftless and left his wife and small daughter on the hands of the kindly colonists. They were willingly kept, and the daughter was cared for during several years, without ever being members. There were other cases of this kind throughout the life of the colony.

A saw mill and grist mill were on the land at Aurora when the colonists bought it, as before related. These were enlarged and improved. A tannery was built, a brick yard established, and a drug store opened. Some of the colony members were master craftsmen. They made good furniture. They built their houses well and substantially; were painstaking and thorough in all they did.

They saved. They were thrifty. In 1872 Dr. Keil told Nordhoff, the historian, that when they first settled at Aurora, having no fruit of their own, he "used to buy summer apples for his people from the nearest farmers for a dollar a bushel. These were eaten in the families; but he taught them to save the parings, and make them into vinegar, which they then sold," at good prices, adding a neat net revenue for the common treasury.

There was never any skimping or niggardliness in the colony life; but nothing was wasted. They did not need to skimp. They all worked, and there was plenty for every one. And, by conserving, good management and saving, there was something over, for their own young people coming on, and for the needy who applied to them for help or came to them by accident or through misfortune.

Each shop had its foreman, and general supervision over all the farm work was arranged, so that there might be no lack of seasonal help on the land, nor any poorly planned, slack or misdirected methods. But the foremen and overseers had their tasks by the law of natural selection. The fittest man came to his place. Nor was any one confined or regimented to a single routine or task. And there was no forced labor, nor long hours save under unavoidable conditions incidental to the planting and harvest seasons and the like.

There was much leisure, and many celebrations. Saturday afternoon was observed as a half holiday—and this was long before that custom was anything like a common one in America or elsewhere. There was a great deal of music. Funerals were attended by all, and the bands played appropriately solemn music. The processions started from the big house of the leader.

There was usually a lay-off at the end of a heavy or laborious task. Then the men generally went hunting. They made up big parties, prepared to camp, and took what at that time seemed long journeys. But the limit of them was usually small, compared to present practices. Some of them ended about where Tonquin on the Oregon Electric railroad is now, approximately half way to Portland. That section was then a timbered wilderness, filled with deer and other game, extending up and down both sides of the Willamette River. The hunting parties always brought plentiful supplies from the chase. The deer meat was consumed or preserved in various ways; but the venison hams were smoked, as only the colony experts knew how. Henry T. Finck told, sixty years later, after he had written eighteen books, that the taste of those venison hams lingered still.

The early lack of fruit at Aurora was not to last long. They were soon to have the "most extensive orchards in the state," which Nordhoff found in 1872, with apples, pears, plums, prunes "and all the commoner large and small fruits." And Nordhoff found their orchards "in fine order." They were thorough in all undertakings, and neglected nothing. They employed outside laborers when there was a rush of work, as Nordhoff found. He related a conversation with a member concerning this:

" 'We will employ and pay you as long as we need your labor,' " a foreman would say to an outsider. " 'If after a while you are thoroughly satisfied that this is the best life, and if we approve of you, we will take you in.' "

It was not necessary that the new comer should bring money with him, Nordhoff found; "but if he had means he was required to put them into the common treasury;" for he MUST believe that "all selfish accumulation is wrong, contrary to God's law and to natural laws."

There was no drunkeness in colony life. The idle or dissolute person had no favor with the colony people; he had no connection with the industries; as he did not work he could not be so brazen as to ask for supplies. So he presently disappeared of his own volition. No force was ever necessary.

Nordhoff asked about disagreements from envy or jealousy.

"We have them very seldom now," answered Dr. Keil. "The people . . . are too well satisfied of the wisdom of our plan of life; they are practiced in self-sacrifice, and know that selfishness is evil and the source of unhappiness. In the early days we used sometimes to have trouble.

"Thus a man would say, 'I brought money into the society, and this other man brought none; why should he have as much as I?' but my reply was, 'Here is your money —take it; it is not necessary; but while you remain, remember that you are no better than he.'

"Again, another might say, 'My labor brings a thousand dollars a year to the society, *his* only two hundred and fifty;' but my answer was, 'Thank God that He made you so much abler, stronger, to help your brother; but take care lest your poorer brother do not some day have to help you, when you are crippled, or ill, or disabled.'"

Nordhoff found that the children in all the time of the colony life at Bethel and Aurora, up to his visits in 1872, had generally remained. He said he spoke to a number of men who had thus passed all but their earliest years in the society, and who were content.

"Men sometimes return, repenting, after leaving the society," he said.

"The boys and girls know that they can leave at any time; there is no compulsion upon any one; hence no one cares to go," he wrote.

"'They generally see that this is the best place. We are prosperous and as happy as any one; we have here all we need.'" Thus he quoted one of the members.

"As to the people—there can be no doubt that they are happy and contented," said Nordhoff, adding: "In a country where labor is scarce, and highly paid, and where the rewards of patient industry in any calling are sure and large, it is not to be supposed that such a society as Aurora would have held together . . . if its members were not in every way satisfied with their plan of life, and with the results they have attained under it."

CHAPTER 17

AURORA as before mentioned, was named for a daughter of Dr. Keil, one of his nine children. Aurora was the Roman goddess of the morning. The word means the dawn of day, the rising light of the morning.

During the beginning days there, Dr. Keil composed and set to music a song, entitled Aurora, consisting of ten verses and chorus. It had a beautiful tune, and it was much used throughout the life of the colony and for a long time thereafter, by the bands and orchestras and in community singing. It has survived there throughout the years and is still employed in orchestral playing and in community singing. It is the favorite and the true community song. The first verse and chorus follow:

> Alles lebt in einem Lichte,
> Yedes Auge der Natur—
> Und die ganze Weltgeschichte
> Predigt von Aurora nur.

> *Chorus:*
> Aurora, Aurora, du bist mein holdes Licht,
> Wann kehrst du wieder,
> Wann kehrst du wieder?—
> Vergistmeinnicht.

If all the songs composed in the Bethel and Aurora communities, by Dr. Keil and Prof. Finck, and others, and set to music and used by their bands and orchestras and in community singing, could be gathered together, the collection would yield some beautiful words and harmonies the outside world has not seen or heard. Here is the lead to a veritable mine for some one, though many of the precious gems may now be beyond the possibility of unearthing.

There was steady progress at Aurora. More land was acquired, additional acres cleared. Shops were added and enlarged; new houses built, in the town and on the farms. Where log cabins had been at first, comfortable frame dwellings were erected, with lumber from the saw mill and materials from the output of the shops.

They were preparing for further accessions. A second large wagon train was being outfitted in Bethel. This came in 1863, captained by Prof. Wolff. It arrived in the early fall over nearly the same route as that followed by the Dr. Keil train, excepting that the Lander cutoff, then new, was taken near the summit of the Rockies, leading by a shorter route to near Fort Hall—and at Umatilla the left hand trail was chosen and the covered wagons came clear through, over the Barlow road. A paragraph in Bancroft's Oregon reads: "The immigration of 1863 was escorted . . . by a volunteer company under Captain Medorem Crawford, who went east to organize it, Congress having appropriated $30,000 to meet the expense. . . . Among them was a large train bound for the town of Aurora, founded by Dr. Keil . . . several years ago, upon the community system." This was the covered wagon train led by Prof. Wolff. With the protection afforded by Captain Crawford's dragoons, it was immune from hostile Indian attack. Crawford had come west in 1842, with the first considerable immigration of settlers that reached the Pacific Coast, by pack train from Fort Hall, where wagons were abandoned. The Lander cutoff was named for the famous surveyor seeking a route for the first transcontinental railroad, afterward Union general, whose gripping life story makes up a heroic chapter of American history. The Wolff train added over two hundred to the community population at Aurora.

Another wagon train came from Bethel in 1865, captained by John Vogt, bringing some eighty people. Still another arrived in 1868, led by George Link, captain, with about sixty, including the Becke family from Nineveh. This train, even at that late date, encountered hostile Indian interference, at one point giving Good Samaritan aid to dying and wounded victims of arrows shot from ambush into a covered wagon company overtaken by them. Their own escape was regarded as a miracle, some members thankfully believing it divinely ordered.

In addition to the covered wagon train passengers, approximately a hundred colonists came from time to time by way of the Isthmus of Panama from Missouri to Aurora, together with a considerable number who were added from the Willapa section of the colony.

All in all, at one time more than a thousand people belonged to the community, about three-fourths of them at Aurora, and they owned a total of more than 23,500 acres of good land. Nordhoff reported that they had some 18,000 acres in the Aurora community in 1872, in Marion and Clackamas counties. Their final holdings at Aurora were estimated to be worth a million dollars. At Bethel and Nineveh they were in the flourishing days worth more than two hundred thousand dollars. At present day or at least recent day prices, all this property represented a total value of three million dollars.

All this accumulation grew through labor and management from the original investment of $30,802.75, most of it in horses and mules and oxen and cows, and implements, tools and equipment—every dollar of which was paid back in money, to the original contributors or their representatives or heirs. In view of this fact, it may be truly said their constantly swelling possessions came from scratch, for what was accumulated represented solely their labor and its usufruct. And they had expended large sums on their wagon trains and other means of travel, and had helped all needy persons who applied to them. In Civil War times, at Bethel, they had been at large expense in supplying the soldiers who came there—both those wearing the blue and the men who wore the gray—for Missouri was a border state.

The colonists at Bethel tried to be neutral. But their sympathies were against slavery, and in Aurora they were all Republicans, with a single exception, and voted the ticket straight during the whole time they had their property in common, and generally for a long while afterward, even up to this day. The single Democrat was a physician and druggist, and he was by no means radical, merely liking a little variety.

This party loyalty made the colony people a power to be reckoned with, or at least worked with, and they contributed from their number two Marion county commissioners, a county treasurer, members of the legislature, a mayor of Oregon's capital city, a county clerk and other men to public office. John Giesy, chairman of the board of trustees, was county commissioner when the present Marion County court house was erected. That was in the first years of the seventies, and the building stands now one of the most beautiful of its kind in the United States. This is notable, as indicating thoroughness, for so early a time in the development of Oregon. Its cost was less than $100,000, though now it could not be duplicated for less than $200,000. The colony people paid taxes along with their neighbors, but they added no burden during all the community life to nation, state, county or district, in the way of court costs. No man at either Bethel or Aurora was ever charged with crime or arrested. No law suit was ever started. Their settlement in the United States court when they decided upon a division to wind up their community business was through a bill in equity, in the nature of the administration of an estate. There was never a divorce suit or separation. No one was sent to an insane asylum. There were few if any cripples. No children went to reform schools or institutions for the deaf or blind or feeble minded. They arranged their own differences by methods of friendly arbitration. Of course, there were no paupers, no money from the poor funds. They provided for their own. No one was poor; all had plenty. The aged and sick were cared for tenderly. The law they lived by was the law of love, the fundamental statute of their community life.

In all the colony days at Aurora, no dwelling or barn or outbuilding was burned or seriously injured by fire, though that was before the time of electric illumination. At first, they had only lights from the ancient lamps such as were used by the wise virgins of the parable, or tallow candles, which they themselves made. The virgin lamps and the candle molds are precious heirlooms in the families of colony descendants to this day. The first coal oil lamps in that part of the state came to the Aurora colony. Likewise the first cooking stove or range. Also the first sewing machine. These were all great curiosities, which people came far to see.

Busy days followed the coming of the big wagon train of 1863, and throughout the sixties, after the arrival of the third and fourth trains, and the accessions by way of Panama. John Giesy, chairman of the board of trustees, had come with his family from Willapa in 1862. Prof. Finck, the music master, had arrived by way of the Panama route in the fall of the same year. Still more land was acquired

Colony church at Aurora. Note balconies for bands and orchestras around steeple.

Colony church at Bethel. Note steeple balcony for band.

and cleared; more fences built, additional orchards set out, more homes and outbuildings constructed. Shops and stores were enlarged and new equipment provided for the workers on the land and in the town. But complete cooperation prevailed and every stroke counted. Nor even then were tasks over hard, or much over time required. It was not like former Governor Isaac Lee Patterson of Oregon said of his boyhood in that state on a farm: "Work as soon as you can see and as long as you can see."

The colony church had been planned before the arrival of the prairie schooner train of 1863. Work on the building was begun the following year, but it was not fully completed and ready for dedication till the latter part of 1867. It was one of the outstanding church edifices of the Oregon of that day. The steeple pierced the sky 114 feet from the ground. Musical chimes were installed, made in Germany, the first of the kind, it is believed, brought to the Pacific Coast of America. Rose windows were features of beautification. Two balconies around the steeple were provided for observation, and to accommodate the two bands, with sixty members; brass bands—plus, having some novel instruments brought from Germany. They frequently played antiphonal music from the balconies, and in concert on great occasions. Aurora had the best band on the Pacific Coast. It was never defeated in a contest. Urgent call and ready response brought the sweet or sad strains of the organization to enliven or solemnize many high events of Oregon's pioneer period. Prof. Finck was a music master who magnified his worthy calling and lived up to his splendid reputation. He composed music. So did Dr. Keil, and, as heretofore related, the head of the colony wrote many community songs. Every member played or was expected to learn to play with proficiency some tuneful instrument, and several of them were no less than wonderful performers. The colony was indeed outstanding in the field of melody.

Materials and fixtures of various kinds that adorned the church were made in the colony shops. Numerous pillars of turned woodwork weighing several tons each beautified the interior. The men entered one doorway and the women another, and they sat on opposite sides. The church was large, and it was always filled at services, which were regular. No one had to go to church. All in the colony came, and neighbors and visitors frequently attended.

With the chimes and the bands and orchestras, and community singing, much was made of holidays. Everybody sang. The observance of Christmas extended through the holiday week and included the New Year; and memories of the good times linger yet with the old colony survivors, tender recollections of events never to transpire again this side of the fields of asphodel beyond the stars.

The celebration of Dr. Keil's birthday, March 6, was annually made a high tide event. There was music, and community singing, and feasting and dancing. On this day all the children danced, and Dr. Keil danced with them, in "the hall," with a dancing floor large enough for a considerable proportion of the members of the colony. When he had danced with the children the leader retired, and so did the children, leaving the rest of the evening for the enjoyment of their elders. Dr. Keil regarded the children with a love akin to that of the Master, who said, "Forbid them not." His affection for all the little ones was like that of a fond father, and this was returned with interest. Every colony child seemed a favorite of the leader. His heart was big enough for them all.* [See note ending chapter.]

The leader was a regular physician. He used the ordinary remedies and the colony maintained drug stores and other practitioners at both Bethel and Aurora. But, before

Interior, Aurora colony church, front view with pulpit.

Interior Aurora colony church, back view with stairway and balcony.

Mrs. Eddy had proclaimed Christian Science or her doctrines began, in 1866, to be spread abroad, and when psychiatry was little known, Dr. Keil employed mental healing. The sick came. He talked with them, and they went away well. Or he sent them home, telling them they would be well on the morrow, or the day after, or within a week or other fixed time—and they recovered according to his promises. The average reader will have and is entitled to his own explanation. The fact remains.

Dr. Keil was a convincing speaker. He had the power of eloquence, and there are tales and traditions in plenty, some of them almost beyond belief, of how his hearers were deeply moved and led to show their feelings in ways out of the ordinary, at times to the point of requiring quieting admonitions on the part of the speaker.

The leader had a piercing look that Nordhoff described as an evidence of fanaticism. But not one of the colonists or their neighbors ever thought of him as a fanatic, though none denied the power of his earnestness, nor questioned his sincerity. His sermons were much given to exhortations against the sin of selfishness. "Thou shalt not covet" were words repeated often. "And all that believed were together, and had all things common," was a text the changes of which he rang on many occasions, and "As every man hath received the gift, even so minister the same one to another," were words that rolled often from the tongue of the leader. "If ye fulfill the royal law, Thou shalt love thy neighbor as thyself, ye do well; but if ye have respect to persons, ye commit sin." This was a golden message sounded down the ages to the community members, literally construed, its obedience invoked in letter and spirit. "This commandment have we from Him, That he who loveth God, love his brother also," repeated oft, was a fundamental of the Keil teaching. The community was built on love of brothers and sisters, a foundation that made it strong.

A near neighbor was J. W. Grim, a pioneer and patriarchal character of those days, well known in that section of Oregon, a man of parts and probity, very much resembling Dr. Keil in appearance. Judge Grim had come in the 1847 immigration of about 5000 people, doubling the population of the Oregon Country of that day; was a member of the first territorial legislature of 1849; was elected as county commissioner acting as probate judge in 1850, and reelected in 1852; was in the state senate from 1858 to 1866 and from 1878 to 1882. His wife was a Geer of the pioneer stock which produced a governor and various other high officials, and they had a numerous family. Judge Grim was always present in the colony on festive and great days, as an urgently invited and welcome guest. The leader and the patriarch were great friends and good neighbors; so were their families. Judge Grim had aided the searching party of 1856 from Willapa in locating their first holdings at Aurora. One of the Grim sons was the first director of the Oregon State Agricultural College experiment station and afterward in the federal customs service, and for thirty years city judge and recorder of Nome, Alaska, living now in Salem, Oregon.

F. X. Matthieu and his family were also near neighbors and fast friends of the colonists. Matthieu was one of the settlers of French descent whose votes were required at the famous Champoeg meeting of May 2, 1843, to turn the scale that put the Stars and Stripes over the Oregon Country, from Mexican California to Russian Alaska. It was his voice and vote that influenced the decision of others, especially that of Etienne Lucier. If Matthieu as a boy in Canada, near Montreal, had not joined the Sons of Liberty and been obliged to flee the country to keep from being hanged in the public square at Terra Bonne, and had not in 1842 found his way with the early trappers and the first large party of settlers to the Oregon Country, the British flag might now float over much more of the territory fronting Balboa's restless sea; might indeed kiss all the breezes that blow from the snows of the Rockies to the sands of the Pacific—all this but for the influences that brought the covered wagon immigration of which that company was the forerunner, the influences attending the response of the forces of Christianity and American civilization to the Macedonian call, in the early thirties of the last century, of the Indians of the ultimate West. Matthieu was born in 1818 and lived nearly 100 years.

There were other prominent pioneers among the neighbors of the colony people at Aurora. They were all good neighbors, neighborly to the full extent of sincerity the term implies. It was the case there as it was with all the American communistic communities, each one of which was visited by Nordhoff, that they improved the condition of their neighborhoods; enhanced the values of adjacent property; imparted a law abiding and progressive life and were helpful in bringing improved live stock and setting examples of good farming and gardening, and marketing, besides furnishing frequent employment to labor, and at all times having the facilities for making and repairing machinery and implements needed in the work of the surrounding country; besides affording the necessary equipment and methods for curing, processing and otherwise rendering fit for market products of the soil.

That steadying, stabilizing influence lasts to this day in firm farm land and other property values and exceptionally good credit, over a wide territory of which the old colony district is the center.

In its closing years, at least, the colony at Aurora had a

surplus of cash assets. Besides extending liberal credit in
the mills, shops and stores to neighbors, it loaned money
to good borrowers, including some of the leading merchants of Portland, taking their notes, generally in the
name of Dr. Keil. The final settlement papers revealed
that state of affairs, showing also that no loss of colony
funds was thus suffered, in either principal or interest.

There was another notable feature of community life at
Aurora, as in the other American colonies. Their labor was
ordered. Their hours were regular. There was system.
There was always water for the kitchens. There were ample labor saving devices. At Aurora there were many bake
ovens. There were cellars for storing vegetables and fruits.
The women worked, but their labor was made as light and
pleasant as possible. They had no worries about the wood
piles, and the wood was always split. Men did the heavy
tasks. This made a pleasing contrast to the homes of many
neighboring farm women.

And there was cleanliness in all such communities. Dirt
was tabu. New comers with uncleanly traits reformed. A
new family with outlandish habits came to Aurora from
the "old country." They kept their chickens under their
beds. The pigs had free range of the kitchen. This did not
last. Everybody in colony life knows everybody else and
his habits. The "old country" new comers reformed. They
were amenable to the discipline of public opinion.

Another thing, there were flowers and trees and vines.
All homes had flowers, and all had vines. There were flowers in the gardens, floral beauty everywhere, beauty of
bloom for all occasions, the whole year through. Aurora
was a community of beauty and music.

* [Singularly coincident, Dr. Keil and his wife were born on the
same day, so the high event observance of his birthday was a double
celebration.]

CHAPTER 18

A DOUBLE WEDDING

THE Cushman and Baker families were among the first to go to Aurora when the site had been selected for the colony there, after spending the winter of 1855 at Willapa. The skill of Levi Cushman was needed in the furniture factory, which was among the first of the shops to be opened. The services of Amos Cushman were of high value to the colonists, because he was strong and industrious and made a full hand in the operation of the saw mill, besides being useful in all dealings with the neighbors, since he spoke better English than the majority of his brother colonists.

Hiram and Mary Baker soon had their harness and saddlery and glovemaking shops going, for the good of the colony work, and presently a trade was opened with the ranchers of the surrounding country, bringing needed revenues to the common treasury. Ruth kept on with her work as teacher of the colony school.

Among the first two dwellings to be built at the new colony home were those for the Cushman and Baker families. Shortly an extra dwelling was planned, for Asa Cushman and Hannah Baker were to be married and to establish their home. Already Asa had taken up his medical studies and was busy in the drug store of the colony, which was also drawing trade from outside the community. There was little need for the ministrations of Hannah in her chosen calling as nurse, because there was little sickness among the members of the community. They all worked hard at first, for there was much to do, and it was the gen-

eral expression that there was no time to be sick. An occasional smashed finger or hurt hand was about the extent of
the need of a nurse or doctor. In Hawthorne's "Scarlet
Letter" these words are used: "The founders of a new
colony, whatever Utopia of human virtue and happiness
they might originally project, have invariably recognized
it among their earliest practical necessities to allot a portion of the virgin soil as a cemetery, and another as a site
of a prison." As to the site of a prison, this was not true of
the Aurora colony. No jail was ever provided or needed
there. And it was a long time before a cemetery was required.

"Somebody will have to get killed by accident before we
can start a graveyard," it was often remarked in those beginning days. And that was almost what happened. Some
of the survivors still believe the first grave was opened for
Henry Roser, a young man fatally injured by a falling
tree. It was actually the second one. The first in the plat
which became the community cemetery was for a woman
afflicted with smallpox, Lucinda Wolfer, aged 67; the date
she died November 3, 1862. Roser's death was February
1, 1864; their green sodded graves are side by side. The
woman contracted the malady from germs carried by her
husband, John Wolfer, a faithful member who responded
to an urgent call on behalf of a stricken neighbor, when no
one outside of the colony would go, because of the ancient
terror over the scourge. He, too, faced death, Jenner's then
rather young discovery of vaccination not having been
availed of to immunize him. But his fear of the dread mes-
senger was not as acute, by the third fraction of a feather's
weight to ten times that of the Washington Monument, as
the lively colony conscience awe of penalty pangs from a
neglected known call of duty. Instantly, with Dr. Keil's
counseled advice and blessing, Wolfer hurried to the suf-

fering neighbor's bedside—and a precious son and three loved and lovely daughters of the devoted leader contracted and died of the lethal disease—from the identical original source, through the same clarion call and quick response to duty. Their names: Elias, 19; Louisa, 18; Gloriunda, 15; and Aurora, 13. Dates of their passing: November 22, December 11, December 11, and December 14, 1862, respectively, resting together in the private burial place of the Keil family and intimates, as heretofore recorded. The occasion for first opening the ground in that hallowed God's Acre, in the receding morning shadows of towering, majestic Mount Hood, was the death of Elias Keil, and his grave is between that of Louisa and the one of Gloriunda, next to go, on the self same day; and to the left of the first three rests Aurora, for whom the town was named.

The spot was in the colony orchard. Often Elias sat there, with his book, and drank in the wonder scene of nature's profligate bounty and superb beauty. Once he remarked casually that he could not imagine another spot as fit for his grave, not sensing in buoyant love of life the near need. His father was told it, and the son's wish decided his last resting place.

Further along, the reader will note a reverential reference of Dr. Keil himself to the sad loss of his cherished children, setting him apart in resignation with Job, that exemplar of the boldest and grandest effort of the ancient world to "justify the will of God to men," according to earth's reputedly oldest scroll, found bound under the covers of the Book of Books.

"Though He slay me, yet will I trust in Him," cried Job. "He gave them, and I thanked Him; He took them, and now I can thank Him too," echoed Keil across the centuries.

John Wolfer contracted the smallpox from the sick neighbor, but recovered. His intimates of the colony were wont to tell him in after and less tragic days that his flaming red hair was the talismanic charm that saved and brought him through to a ripe old age.

Young Roser had approached Dr. Keil saying he had decided to try his fortune "in der Welt" (in the world; or outside world), and inquiring if he might come back in case he found things unsatisfactory.

"You may go, as a matter of course," the leader assured him. "Every one is free to go at any time. And you may come back when you please."

The young man returned to the Rudolph Giesy place where he had been working and had gone to where the men were clearing a piece of land, intending to bid them good-bye. A falling tree struck him. They gave Henry Roser all the honors of the regular colony funeral, nor even referred to the fact that he had been about to depart from them.

The members of the Aurora colony had long lives. This was true at Bethel and it was common in all such communities. Freedom from worry was one cause, regular habits another, abundant and healthful food a contributing factor. Constantly available medical attention was another. Comfortable surroundings helped. The fact that the women were not overworked or weighted with tasks too heavy for them, and had competent and loving care in the trying times of motherhood, were important aids to longevity. Social activities made for health. There was never any sense of loneliness in colony life, nor of neglect, helplessness or lack of sympathy. Premature old age was rare. The resiliency of youth lasted longer than was the average in the life of their neighbors surrounded even with the best conditions of individual living. The colonists as a rule lived long, and they enjoyed life in their old age.

The infant death rate in the Keil colony was very low. And there were no undernourished children. The youngsters in the community were utter strangers to rickets. This is reported to be true in like communities now with some improvements in dietary rules that have come about with the rapid advance of medical science.

The rumor was whispered among the colonists that the Cushman-Baker nuptials might mark a double wedding, and it was generally hoped that this might prove true. Every one had long known of the attachment of the teacher and Amos Cushman, and they were favorites among all their people. Of course Ruth and Amos knew of the reports. They realized, too, that in each case the rumor or wish was father to the thought. But their bond and blood brother and sisters did not realize the one and only obstacle. The time for the wedding of Asa and Hannah was approaching, work on the dwelling intended for their home under way. Amos and Ruth in their daily companionship in the colony had retained the freshness and fervor of their long attachment. They were true lovers. But he could not agree to give up his dream of an independent life in a home of their own, and she was unable to bring herself to a decision that their true place was not among their own people.

"Ruth, I have found a rich farm in Yamhill County, that can be ours for the asking," Amos announced after a trip in that direction looking for milk cows to complement the colony possessions of live stock.

"The land, a whole mile square section of it, is in a beautiful spot in what is known as one of the best sections of a district famous for its good crops. The owner must return to Indiana, where his father has died and left the family needing his help to carry on. We can have the land, with the home he has built and his start of live stock, cows and teams and tools and outbuildings, for two thousand dollars, and all on credit. For a two thousand dollar mortgage securing our notes payable in annual installments for ten years, and at a low interest rate, we can move in when he moves out. At first in Oregon no taxes were assessed against land, and they are next to nothing now. We can pay off the notes before the last one comes due, and have a home of our own and be independent."

"But we now have an undivided interest in thousands of acres of land as good as that," Ruth argued, "and we have the help of all our people in making it fruitful and life pleasant and worth while. We have no worries here over interest payments or meeting annual installments. You are in high favor here, where your ability is known and your services valued. Here our future is secure, and we have neighbors. Everybody is a brother or sister here. Every one places his neighbor's good and happiness on a full equality with or above his own. This is the true working out of the Golden Rule," added Ruth, "and you know our people practice the Golden Rule, and that they go even further than that. They observe what Dr. Keil is pleased to call the Diamond Rule of community life.

"Each one here does as he would be done by, and more. He follows the course that invokes the duty embraced in the words of the Diamond Rule, 'in honor preferring one another.' As you know, it is the idea of Dr. Keil that we should not merely wish for ourselves the treatment from others that we would like for ourselves; we must go a step further and wish for our brother or sister even better treatment and greater preferment than we crave for ourselves.

"This means service above self; it is the absolute negation of selfishness, which is the cardinal sin of community life. Dear Amos, we both recall how Dr. Keil often cites

Abraham, father of the three great religions, as first among the heroes of faith to practice the Diamond Rule, at the parting of the ways between community living and individual life—and God prospered him exceedingly—and Lot, who made the wordly and selfish choice, suffered many grievous afflictions, after he 'pitched his tent toward Sodom.'" (See Genesis 13:5-12.)

"I know all this, and I appreciate your loyalty," Amos replied, "but independence is in my blood, coming down through my ancestry, and I cannot shake it off or thin the flow of it through my veins."

Amos had been obliged to tell her that the place in Yamhill County was in a newly settled district, with no near neighbors.

"But there will soon be neighbors," he urged, "and no doubt a near town before long, for immigrants are constantly coming, and all the unoccupied land of such excellence will soon be taken, and prices will increase. We are fortunate in being on hand at the right time. Such chances will not last. It is better than free land, for what has already been done on the place, with the stock and implements, is worth more than the price we will have to pay. We will not be obliged to wait for an income, like we would on a tract of free land from the government. The initial capital is provided."

"Admitting all this, which I do freely," countered Ruth, "we still have the risks of ill luck and misfortune, which every one in individual life must face. In case of sickness, or when there are diseases among the stock, or pests and unfavorable weather to ruin our crops, we would be far from help. And in harvest time there will be none to assist, for the neighbors will have the problem of their own ripened crops. There will not be available abundant help called from all other occupations, and with quick and willing response as with us, for here the good of every one is the interest of all."

But Amos was adamant in his obstinacy. He believed they would throw away the chance of a lifetime if they did not take the offer that had come to them; it seemed to him an act of divine guiding.

It was a long debate, not easy for either, and it was not decided then; but ended in a love-armed truce. Ruth hoped to finally prevail. She had no idea of surrender, nor any thought of giving up hope of winning Amos to her way. Nor did Amos believe he would be forced to abandon his plans for an independent home—now heightened by the dream that had appeared to him as it seemed like a rainbow of hope in a mistless sky.

The wedding day of Asa and Hannah had been set. Their new home would be ready. There would be a house warming in celebration of the two events—their marriage and the completion of their home. Amos came to Ruth with a last plea.

"Let us make it a double wedding," he pleaded, following this with the brightest word picture he knew how to paint of the setting in the Yamhill home, which seemed a real paradise to him, lacking only Ruth's angelic presence.

"I freely consent," responded Ruth; "let us make it a double wedding, and let us remain with our people. What would become of the school if I deserted it?" she asked.

"There are others who can carry on with the school," answered Amos, "till the arrival from Bethel of good Prof. Ruge, who is anxious to be in Aurora and is scheduled to come."

"But no home is planned for us here, and one is ready for us there," urged Amos.

Ruth answered that there was ample room and welcome

for them at either the Baker or the Cushman home, or dozens of others. She said every home was the home of every member of the colony. It was all a matter of convenience or pleasure, or adaptation. Often newly married couples went to established homes until their own dwellings were provided. The big house in which Dr. Keil and family and a number of single men and women lived was available.

"You well know, Amos," added Ruth, "that we can have a separate home here if we want it; that work will be commenced on the plans for it tomorrow, if we announce our engagement today. And you know, too, that it will be our own for our use as completely as if we owned it in fee simple or by the entirety, for ourselves and our children if we have any, and for our children's children."

"Yes, I know that full well," said Amos. "But all that does not mean perfect freedom of action, in which we may ourselves sell or give or bestow and work out our own futures as we deem best, without being subject to any whim or notion of a paternal overlord or board of trustees, and if we do not take up the offer in Yamhill County now we will lose it, and another as attractive may never come, and certainly there will not be another one so exactly in the nick of time. But I am willing to give up that hope and have the double wedding without going to Yamhill, only asking your promise that we are finally to try our fortunes in the outside world."

"If we are not wed now or in the future, I will not marry at all," said Ruth. "I have room in my heart and my life for only one such love. If I am not married to you, Amos," she added with all the feeling of finality in her being, "I will never marry at all. I will live for my people. I will give my blood and bond brothers and sisters and their children all the love I have left, and I will serve like Helena Giesy has served and is serving, to the end of my allotted time, wholly and joyfully."

"I do not deserve this loyalty," said Amos. "What you have said makes me humble, gives me the feelings of an ingrate, cuts to the quick. But I am what I am and what I have heard and seen and experienced, and I want my chance to prove my mettle. But I will not go alone. You must go or I stay. Or you must promise to go with me when another opportunity offers, which we can together agree is a worthy one, though I feel it will not be a better one, or as good."

"You make it hard for me to refuse," said Ruth. "Let us put it this way: We will have the double wedding. We will accept the offer. I will go with you, and we will plan together and work hard together. We will mutually promise that if the results prove you are right, we will not come back. We two will be the judges. If the years show life is better here than there or elsewhere for us, we will come back. And you alone shall be the judge of this."

"That is more than fair," said Amos. "I am willing to have a joint vote decide the latter event as well as the former."

"No," insisted Ruth, "that decision must be with you alone, and I will at no time be a special pleader to sway it, and I will promise to work and pray for the other result, nor at any time will I utter a word or give a sign against your hope of success."

So it was agreed, and they put into their kiss that sealed the covenant all the fondness and love that had grown in their hearts since they were children together in the school at Bethel teaching each other the better use of the words of the two languages they now used indiscriminately. And their embraces were a witness of the covenant which showed that the language of love is universal and needs no mother tongue or dialect or alphabet.

And so there was a double wedding and a joyful house-warming, and Asa and Hannah devoted themselves to their chosen work, and Amos and Ruth went to the big house of the colony's leader and made plans for their departure for their new home on the west side of the Willamette River. Dr. Keil was told of their pre-nuptial compact, just as he had received many intimate confidences from his people, as a sort of father confessor. He kept the secret and passed the word to the trustees to be generous with their outfitting, in liberal fulfillment of the colony's rule, "You shall not let your brother go away from you empty."

Without intimating a thought that they might need the assurance, he told the bride and groom they would be welcome home at any time, and that they were not to hesitate in making known their needs if ever they were hard pressed or visited with any misfortune. He wanted them to feel that they were never to consider themselves as strangers, for they were more; they were blood brother and sister and children of some of their people, and they were bond brother and sister to all.

"We are bound by our rules to help the needy stranger to the extent of our surplus means; but such as you," he said, "are assured of help to the uttermost. You must never think of yourselves as outsiders or suppliants."

CHAPTER 19

THE year 1863 was the beginning time of high tide in communal life, in the communities of Bethel and Aurora and the seventy others scattered throughout the United States; and that means in the whole communal life of the world, in small societies holding their property in common, for in no other country did this movement have anything approaching such a sweep as it attained in America. At Aurora the hotel was being finished, work on the church was proceeding, the colony school had been completed, and the town enlarged with mills and shops and stores and homes. Much farm land had been cleared and stocked, barns and granaries built and the facilities of prosperous agriculture provided.

A correction should be made here concerning a statement in the book of Nordhoff, "The Communistic Societies of the United States," in which he said the Aurora homes were "of uncommon size," and "three stories high, sometimes nearly a hundred feet deep, and look like factories." There was no home in the Aurora community three stories high, nor any nearly a hundred feet deep. The only building there that could be so described with near truth was the hotel, which had (and has) two stories and a basement. The homes were of various sizes, most of the larger ones of two stories, some of them with lower porches and also upper ones, verandahs or loggias, extending along the entire fronts, in the style of many pioneer dwellings in the West, like the first home in Salem, Oregon, still standing, built by Jason Lee, the pioneer

Christian missionary of the old Oregon Country. But there was no uniform style or size of dwellings in the community, excepting that they were all substantially built and comfortable.

(Nordhoff also said: "There is not even a hall for public meetings in the village." That was a whopper, a stretching of the long bow beyond the breaking point. It did rank injustice to a small community which had the finest park in Oregon, with an auditorium seating 1500 people, as shown elsewhere in these pages; that had the largest and finest church building in the state outside of the cities and larger towns, and where two halls "for public meetings" were well maintained, each of them unusually large and convenient for a community of that size.)

The children were in school, the bands were organized, the classes in higher learning were being carried on under the able teaching of Prof. Wolff. There was no breath of dissension, outside of friendly differences among the leaders. Dr. Keil was undisputed autocrat, executive, legislature, judge and jury. His word was fundamental law. His wish was the unwritten law. He was called in jest "King Keil." But he was an honest, wise and just ruler—and some one said long ago that the best government would be one with a wise, honest and just king, if such there could be found and given perpetual life; or if having been found he could be endowed with such prepotency as to transmit those attributes to his descendants indefinitely—which never has happened for even two generations, much less for several or many, or perpetually. However, in the period being described a family that had contributed nothing in money or goods to the community, a family the members of which came in empty handed, demanded a thousand dollars in order to leave Aurora and secure a footing in individual life. Demanded this sum for services rendered, and threatened suit. There was no action at law. The sum asked for was paid, in more than ample fulfillment of the community rule taken from the Word of God: "You shall not let your brother go away from you empty."

It may interest some reader to know that this thousand dollar payment was invested in real property outside the community the title of which proved defective, and the money was lost.

"This case taught the colonists at Aurora the futility of violating the spirit of the compact under which they lived; it was considered a 'horrible example,' " remembers one of the survivors. "It was made comparable to the experience of Ananias and Sapphira, who 'lied to God' in holding back part of the purchase price of their land from the first Christian church, where 'the multitude of them that believed were of one heart and of one soul; neither said any of them that ought of the things which he possessed was his own; but they had all things common,' and, hearing the condemning words of Peter, 'fell down, and gave up the ghost: and great fear came on all of them that heard these things,' as told by Luke in The Acts.

"This was the only Ananias and Sapphira case in the history of the colony."

But this incident led to an agreement of Dr. Keil under which he covenanted with the board of trustees that he would convey to them all the property in his name, save "his two dwelling houses, garden and A MULE TEAM." The exact words of the exception are quoted. And the trustees covenanted with Dr. Keil that they would assume the trust and carry on the affairs of the community as they had thus far been administered by their "beloved" leader. This agreement was duly signed, sealed and witnessed on April 5th, 1866.

Queen and Kate were the mule team meant in this historic agreement, the team that had drawn the plains hearse leading the covered wagon train eleven years before. Dr. Keil could not overlook those faithful animals as he thought of the terms of the solemn instrument. The same day there was drawn up an agreement to be signed by all the members of the community then and to come in later, by which each one was bound to abide by the rules set out in the contract between Dr. Keil and the trustees and accepted by them, embodying the same principles in effect as were in the original constitution made and adopted at the beginning of the colony enterprise at Bethel.

Dr. Keil himself and his wife were among the first to sign this agreement, merely as members of the community. It served to establish the legal status, so that there could not thereafter be any claims like the one of the family that demanded and received a thousand dollars. But the signing and witnessing of this general agreement by all the members of the colony at Aurora was not a simple matter. It went on day after day, by groups, families and individuals. Some refused to sign. It became a matter of discussion, was for months the principal topic.

Finally an expedient was thought of and carried out, to bring in a considerable group. They were allowed to sign with an extra stipulation that they were still to be under the leadership of Dr. Keil, and this stipulation was carefully written in long hand after the names of those special groups or individuals. There were no typewriters in those days. This now all but universal convenience had not been invented.

An amusing incident attended the signing of the agreement. Nearly all the members had signed. But one Peter Ziegelmeier was obdurate. He would not sign. He was as chilled steel against all approaches. His wife wanted to sign. She appealed to and argued with him to the limit of her powers of wifely entreaty. She was unable to move him. He feared for their future with the supreme authority of Dr. Keil, their beloved leader, taken away and placed in the hands of a board of trustees.

A committee was appointed to go and wrestle with Peter. He heard about this and learned of the time of their coming to present their arguments—and he bolted. He ran away. He kept going till he reached East Portland. At that time the old Stark Street ferry carried all the traffic to the west side of the Willamette, where most of the city was located. There were then two cities, Portland and East Portland. But there was not much of East Portland, excepting sloughs and mud flats. When stages arrived, the hotels sent their runners with their 'buses to the east side of the river, and at the ferry landing on that side they made a great hullabaloo, calling the names of their hotels. It was a new experience for Peter. He was alarmed. He did not understand. He conceived the idea that the news of his running away had reached Portland, and everybody was after him with hue and cry and a demand for his capture—so he bolted again.

He ran back toward Aurora and made the return trip in less time than it had taken him to reach East Portland. He landed at his home a badly scared and a very tired man, in nautical lingo a blue Peter. He was ready to sign and to have his wife sign with him. And he never heard the last of the friendly jibes after the whole truth of his marathon leaked out.

When all the signatures had been duly made, and the document filed for the addition of new names as other members were admitted or the children attained legal age, nothing was done. The power was vested in the trustees, but it was never exercised so that any member of the colony felt that Dr. Keil had lost any part of his authority, though it must not be understood that the leader himself did not often consult with the members of the board of trustees, and frequently there were meetings to decide upon important matters. And all the members were consulted in arriving at weighty decisions affecting the interests of the whole community. Dr. Keil never claimed autocratic powers. He was accorded such powers as a matter of course, by common understanding because his people looked to him for authority and guidance.

He never conveyed the property, or any part of it, to the board of trustees, according to the mutual agreement with them of April 5th, 1866. However, in 1872 he deeded and distributed to various members of the community most of the real and personal property, taking their receipts. But few if any of the deeds were recorded, and the life of the community went on the same as it had proceeded before the agreements were signed and the distributions made, to the last day of Dr. Keil's life.

Though legally held in severalty, the property was considered as common, as well as the usufruct of it, and the labor of the members—and in the end, in the final division, under the decrees of the court, it was all pronounced common, to the last part of it, and every deed made as one of trust, and Dr. Keil as having held all in trust for the whole community, even including "his two dwelling houses, garden and A MULE TEAM."

In the general division, however, the heirs of Dr. Keil were treated well and were satisfied with the property allotted to them, though they took merely as members, like all the rest, and not as heirs. That this was as Dr. Keil himself would have wished it was shown by his trusted friends in whom he confided while he lived.

CHAPTER 20

HISTORIC DREAMS

IN THE time of high tide in the communal life at Aurora there was what may be termed an adjourned meeting of the three leaders of thought of the colony— adjourned from the meetings they had at Bethel while they were preparing the first covered wagon train for the journey to the Oregon Country. The three were Dr. Keil, Prof. Wolff and Prof. Ruge.

Prof. Ruge said their excursions into the land of historic dreams reminded him of the quotation about "Moses' inspiration, Aaron's tongue," applied to the leader and Prof. Wolff, though their white hair did not alone qualify them in point of age for their comparative parts. He said Moses complained to God that he was not eloquent; that he was slow of tongue, whereupon the leader of the Israelites was directed to take along his brother Aaron, and "he shall be to thee instead of a mouth, and thou shalt be to him instead of God;" and at that time of the great undertaking of leading a nation out of bondage Moses was eighty, and Aaron was three years older—and that was a case of old men for both counsel and eloquence and young men for war.

Prof. Wolff reviewed again the historic dreams of the thinkers of the past ages, and he gave this outline of the key words or slogans expressing in small space what was in the mind of each, in chronological order, beginning over five centuries before the Christian era:

"Friends should have all things in common."—Pythagoras.

"The perfect society would be that in which each class and each unit would be doing the work to which its nature and aptitude best adapted it."—Plato's idea in his "Republic."

"And all that believed were together and had all things common."—Acts, 2:44.

"Though no man has anything, every man is rich."—More's "Utopia."

"Wherever there is any want it is immediately supplied by unanimous consent and distribution."—Jonathan Swift's Houyhnhnms in "Gulliver's Travels."

"Labor according to capacity, reward according to services."—Saint-Simon.

"The earth must belong to all, and its fruits must be common property."—Baboeuf.

"Labor according to capacity and reward according to exertion, talent and capital."—Fourier.

"For the equality of all and the brotherhood of man."—Cabet of Icaria.

Prof. Wolff recounted additional high light excerpts from the writings of Fourier and Saint-Simon and their followers, and others. For instance, Fourier said in one of his books: "Labor is divided into three classes—necessary, useful, and agreeable; the highest reward accruing to the first and the smallest to the last division, according to the principles of equity."

This division, Prof. Wolff explained, was for the Fourieristic societies, with their phalansteries, which Fourier proposed in his ambitious scheme of reorganizing the entire world, for a better and happier state of society for the whole of humanity.

"There was another formula of Saint-Simon, himself," said Prof. Wolff, "which was contained in four words, thus: 'Recompense according to works,' and another in five words, 'Recompense in proportion to merit.'"

"And the Saint-Simonians, organized on the basis of their master's teaching, had another: 'To each one accord-

ing to his capacity; to each capacity according to its works.'
And still another: 'Each one should labor according to his
capacity and be rewarded according to service rendered.' "

(The three men at Aurora could not have known it at
that time, for his book, "The Coming Race," had not been
published, but the Right Hon. Lord Lytton was soon, in
that book, to make his contribution, in these words: "The
poor man's need is the rich man's shame," and these: "No
happiness without order, no order without authority, no
authority without unity.")

Prof. Wolff, in his capacity as a teacher, was pleased to
revert to Plato, the greatest teacher of his time, as main-
taining that democracy means perfect equality of opportunity, especially in education. And Prof. Wolff held that
there could not be a perfect equality of opportunity outside of a society in which there was a community of property. He maintained that any other plan would defeat itself.

"You might divide all the property of the State of Oregon equally," he said, "giving every man, woman and
child his or her just share of the total wealth of whatever
kind, today, and tomorrow a proportion of the people
would have nothing, and large numbers would possess
unequal shares, and in ten years there would be many
rich and many poor in their possessions, and a great many
would have nothing."

"In the Proverbs of the Old Testament," he added,
"we find the words in the 30th chapter and 8th and 9th
verses: 'Give me neither poverty nor riches; feed me with
food convenient for me; lest I be full and deny thee, and
say Who is the Lord? or lest I be poor and steal.' Those
were words of wisdom. In our colony life we have neither
poverty nor riches, or rather we are all rich, and there is
no occasion to steal, for everything we all own belongs

to each one alike. In such a society there can be no thieves."

"The Master on a certain occasion," he went on, "uttered these words: 'Ye have the poor always with you.' But He did not mean this statement to apply to other conditions than he found in the land where He labored. They do not apply in our colony life. We have no poor. Every member owns an equal share in all our wealth. It would be the same if all humanity were organized as we are here bound together—poverty would be banished from the earth—there would in all the world be no poor."

The three colony leaders resumed their discussion around the evening lamp in "the big house." They came to the head of neighbors.

Dr. Keil liked Luke, as Prof. Wolff knew. The inspired writer was also a physician.

"When the Master was approaching the end of his earthly labors in the flesh, according to Luke," said Wolff, "a certain lawyer stood up and tempted him, saying, 'Master, what shall I do to inherit eternal life?' And the Prince of Peace, answering the conspiring quibbler's question, Yankee fashion, by asking another, said, 'What is written in the law? How readest thou? And the lawyer quoted: 'Thou shalt love the Lord thy God with all thy heart, and with all thy soul, and with all thy strength, and with all thy mind; and thy neighbor as thyself.'

"Jesus told him, 'Thou hast answered right: this do, and thou shalt live.'

"Then came from the lawyer the question of the ages," said Wolff—

" 'And who is my neighbor?'

"Followed the parable of the Good Samaritan," continued Wolff. "That is the supreme test; it is the Rosetta Stone, the rule of interpretation for the language of love for human society. Our neighbor is any one of God's crea-

tures who needs our help. The hated Samaritan becomes
the lover of the race; the helper; the sympathizer.

"Here in Aurora we act the part of neighbors. We let
no known need go unhelped. We ask no questions about
race or religion. The need is the touchstone, the open
sesame of sympathy. It was and is so in Bethel. Bond and
free were and are the same. Our rules recognize neither
slave nor master. Each is the other's equal to us. There
is no servant and no master, rather all are servants and
all masters.

"We have the Aaron Greenbaum family, Jews. In the
next town a Jew cannot belong to a club or society; the
children of Jews do not mingle on full equality with the
children of the so-called Christians. Here in Aurora all
are equal, brothers and sisters. All are our neighbors."

"Here, too," added Prof. Ruge, "we know neither
Catholic nor Protestant, and our neighbors live in all lands.
We are Americans but not chauvinists. The Chinese are
our neighbors, whether here or in their own country. So
are the Japanese and the people of India, and all the rest.
Our neighbor may live next door or his home may be a
hollow log under the equator or an igloo within the Arctic
Circle."

Prof. Wolff quoted again from the inspired physician
who wrote that God "hath made of one blood all nations
of men."

"Blood heat," he went on to say, "meaning the tempera-
ture of human blood, is the same in Africa and the Arctic,
in torrid summer or winter cold, at sea level and on the
highest mountain peak, whether the skin under which it
courses be white or brown, red or black, or mixed. And
there is no counterfeit for human blood; not even in that
of other animals, as all the world has known since chemi-
cal science learned to make comparative tests and criminal
courts have had expert witnesses.

"Children draw no color line, as any high class Southern man who suckled at the breast of a black 'mammy' will testify. They see no social line, as every nurse maid knows. Children mark no difference between prince and pauper, rich or poor—until the barbaric cleavage of cruel custom creates barriers. These ancient attitudes of thought have no rightful place in civilized society—and they are not tolerated here, where all are neighbors under the egis of the rule given in the parable of the Good Samaritan.

"The delusion of superior races was hatched in hell. It falls flat under the acid test of fact. A Sioux Indian baby found orphaned on the field of carnage was given the rearing and cultural advantages of a good Christian home. He became a great physician. A like quip of fortune took the infant child of a slain Australian bush mother to an environment of culture. Parented, on both sides, in the world's supposedly most backward tribe, he grew into an ornament of high English society. History abounds with such incidents. Henry George was fond of saying a normal American girl baby, taken in infancy and reared in the center of China, would grow up with mincing steps from bound feet, and with the olive complexion and slanting eyes of the women of that country. No race, nation, color or continent has valid right to a spirit of chauvinism or assumed superiority. All mankind, subjected for one generation to the conditions we here enjoy, might emerge from the deadly sins of selfishness, ripe for orderly security, ready for realization of the dreams of a world without the wail of want or the dread of war."

Prof. Wolff had read widely and thought profoundly. He had come to believe with the full conclusion of finality that there was no way of complete social justice outside of a society with all property held in common, the usufruct of it kept in a common treasury, and the work of all for the benefit of each.

"The true rule," he said, "is the rule we have adopted and by which we live, FROM EVERY MAN ACCORDING TO HIS CAPACITY, TO EVERY MAN ACCORDING TO HIS NEEDS. That is the whole of the law and the prophets. It is the Golden Rule of the perfect society. And the Diamond Rule to supplement and complement it, and give it full sanction, must be also strictly observed, purging community life of the least eidolon of selfishness; laying the last eerie and ancient shade or effluvium of self seeking that might hamper the working efficiency of the whole order; in short, obeying the final and all inclusive one, the tenth of the Ten Commandments, 'Thou shalt not covet.' I have reference in my figure, showing the need, in such a society as ours, of driving out, as it were with a whip of scorpions, the cardinal sins of selfishness and self seeking, to the speculations of the ancient Greek sages, Empedocles and Epicurus, and of Democritus, 'the laughing philosopher.' "

To this the three agreed. They had built their colony life on these foundations. They had made much from small beginnings, felt they had so far builded wisely and well, and in looking backward were content with their progress.

Prof. Ruge said the colony life as they had developed it was comparable to the family systems in some European and other countries. No account was kept as between the members of the families; their property was held as in common, and the use and earnings of it were regarded as belonging to each; his or her needs supplied in sickness or health, weakness or strength, youth or age. Some of these families had maintained such relations through many generations, amassing great fortunes, like that of the Rothschilds.

Prof. Wolff was more of an idealist than Dr. Keil. The

beloved leader, practical in most matters, was apt to stress
the words of the original colony constitution, "Having
therefore food and raiment, let us be content." He had
told the members who came in originally that he would
give them "plenty to wear and plenty to eat, and plenty
to do." The colonists as they set out from Bethel for the
Oregon Country were promised "plenty to eat and plenty
to do." Dr. Keil, strong on the essentials, was apt to think
the pioneers of such a community might well wait for
larger prosperity in material things before faring forth
into the realms of luxurious living and soaring to the
heights of culture.

"Let them walk safely first; then they may learn to
run," he was wont to say. "They will enjoy luxuries more
for being obliged to do without them till they are sure
we can afford them."

But Prof. Wolff having himself explored the empyrean
realms was anxious to have all the members of the community enjoy their fiery spaces. He wanted the Aurora
community to be a seat of learning as well as a center of
music and a patron of the arts. He believed there was
nothing too good for those people, and nothing desirable in life beyond their power to secure and enjoy. He
was not for waiting; believed the foundations were already laid. At one time, there was more or less of an es-
trangement between the leader and the teacher on account
of Dr. Keil's conservative attitude and Prof. Wolff's im-
petuosity to be on the way and marching to the heights.

Prof. Ruge was by nature less aggressive than Prof.
Wolff, but he was also ambitious to have his people enjoy the fine things of life, especially in matters of the
proper training of their minds. But he was a gentle soul
and did not chafe at slow progress.

Prof. Wolff acted as the keeper of the colony's store,

the one that kept no books as between the members. He was in sympathy with the women and girls who asked for the beautiful things they delighted to wear. There were no more substantially clothed people in Oregon, and the men were always well dressed when they went abroad or appeared on public occasions at home. There was a colony tailor, who was a master at his trade and did well at it, after the colony was dissolved, in his Portland establishment. There were plenty of assistants. And there were competent dressmakers. Shoemaking was done by skilled tradesmen in the colony shops. They themselves tanned the skins and hides and had the best. They made good gloves. Finished products of the Bethel glove factory won a first premium at the World's Fair in New York in 1853, the second of its kind ever held, and the first in the United States. The Bethel plow became famous throughout the Middle West. The same workmen or those of equal ability were in the shops at Aurora.

The keystone of the arch of Dr. Keil's planning was that the colony should be self contained, and that all its products should be honest and of the best quality. In the light of after events, who shall say the lofty dreams of Wolff and Ruge might not have been realized, had the community life kept on to this day?

The three colony leaders were not far apart in point of age. The physical appearance of Dr. Keil has been described elsewhere in these pages by one who knew him well. Nordhoff described Prof. Ruge as strongly resembling Horace Greeley. All three at this time had white hair. Prof. Wolff was about five feet seven, and well proportioned, rather above the average weight for his height. He wore a full beard, carefully trimmed. A survivor describes him as usually carrying a cane, and says he was a great worker; that he took a cross-cut saw on his back to the woods in after years and made his work count, whistling the while, and that he was of a lively disposition; that he taught music and had his house full of books, and no one knows what became of them. He was never married, nor was Prof. Ruge. It was known at Aurora that Ruge in early life had been engaged to a young woman in Germany, and that she died. There were rumors of a youthful love affair of Prof. Wolff, about which he himself was uncommunicative. The members of the community had deep sentiments with regard to affairs of the heart. They were likely to remain true to their first loves. They "staid put" when married, and few widowers took second wives. The "triangle" was unknown, and a scandal monger would have been without occupation for lack of materials.

Henry T. Finck, as mentioned elsewhere, said that in the earlier days of Aurora Prof. Wolff took a cold plunge every morning, even if he had to cut a hole in the ice, that this among other odd practices marked him among the younger members as queer and freakish. The neat marble headstone over his grave in the community cemetery reads: "Christopher W. Wolff, born 27 Aug., 1810, died 25 May, 1894."

Prof. Ruge spent his declining years at Aurora and died there. He was the notary public and did most of the legal work of all kinds for the community, and for the people thereabouts, after the colony had been dissolved, including the performance of marriage ceremonies. Both Wolff and Ruge had rooms during colony days in "the hall" and generally took their meals at the well filled tables in the big house of the leader, and were therefore in constant contact with him.

CHAPTER 21

A MUSICAL OASIS

AS MENTIONED before, Henry T. Finck, author of eighteen books and countless magazine articles, musical critic of the *New York Evening Post* for forty-three years, up to the last week in May, 1924, was born at Bethel and spent his ten years before entering Harvard University at Aurora. In his autobiography, "My Adventures in the Golden Age of Music," finished and the final revision of the proofs completed within a few days of his death, Mr. Finck told many interesting things about his boyhood at Aurora. He was eight when he came to Aurora. He was eighteen when he went to Harvard from there, and he was the first Oregon student to enter that university. He received his entire preparation at Aurora, and was upon examination in Latin and Greek promoted at once to the sophomore classics!

He was born September 22, 1854. He graduated at 22 with the famous Harvard Centennial class of 1876. His father was Henry Conrad Finck, born near Stuttgart, Germany, who had come to America in his youth and had met at St. Louis, Christian Giesy, who had induced him to go to Bethel, where he was professional apothecary and amateur musician, and physician in case of need. His chief delight was the training of the Bethel band and orchestras and choir. He was a born musician, and old time Oregonians will tell you he became one of the best on the Pacific Coast. He played many instruments, the violin being among his favorites. His distinguished son said in his last book that he was "the best guitar player I ever heard."

The younger Finck was certainly a competent judge. He heard the world's best. In this book he relates that his father was the alter ego of Dr. Keil, who had gone to Oregon, and whenever a letter for his Bethel congregation came from him it was sent to Prof. Finck, as he was known both in Missouri and Oregon, and he read it aloud. Prof. Finck was postmaster at Bethel. After the colony people were well settled and organized at Aurora, inducements were offered him to move hither. Plans were made as early as 1859. Christian Giesy, who had induced the music master to go to Bethel, pleaded with him to move to Oregon, though he did not live to see his friend in the new colony home.

In 1862, with his five motherless children, six, eight, ten, twelve and fourteen years old, Henry T. being the eight-year-old one, Prof. Finck moved to Oregon, going by way of New York, the Panama railroad across the isthmus, thence to San Francisco and Portland, and by stage to Aurora. His wife, native of the same district in Germany where he himself was born, had died at Bethel. Oregon at that time had no railroad. Prof. Finck had considered the covered wagon trip across the plains, but it was out of the question, with five half orphan children. Let Henry T. Finck, in "My Adventures in the Golden Age of Music," tell in his own words of his early life in Oregon:

It has always been a matter of special satisfaction and pride to me that my early life, from my eighth year to my eighteenth, was associated inseparably with Oregon apples. If there is anything in all the wide world better to eat than an Oregon apple I have not found it though I have been an indefatigable traveler on four out of five continents of this globe of ours.

The term "Oregon apples" includes, of course, those grown in the State of Washington which formerly was a part of Oregon

Territory, the grandest corner of the United States, because of its glorious snow peaks and forests. When once a foolish notion is spread abroad it is almost impossible to annihilate it. All my life I have been fighting the outrageous lie that the highbred Oregon apples, while large and beautiful to look at, are inferior in flavor to the underbred, puny eastern apples. During every one of the forty-three years I spent in New York City, the greatest apple market in the world, I compared the Oregon fruit with the Eastern, and almost invariably found the Western better.

My testimony is of exceptional weight because I have always been an ultra epicure, almost like a dog in the keenness of my olfactory sense, upon which our discriminating enjoyment of fruit and all foods depend chiefly. [Mr. Finck had explained this in two of his former books, "Food and Flavor" and "Girth Control."] Nor is this superiority of Oregon fruit due chiefly to the greater and more scientific care bestowed on orchard culture on the Pacific Coast. It is largely due to soil and climate, just as the quality and aroma of choice wines like Chambertin, Chateau Yquem, Barolo or Budai are dependent on climatic and soil peculiarities in France, Italy, and Hungary. Oregon apples can be grown only in Oregon. Hence my aforesaid pride. My youth was spent in the midst of a large orchard which supported our family and, later on, paid for my education at Harvard. It came about in this way:

When we came from Missouri via New York and Panama to Portland, situated some hundred miles up the Columbia and Willamette rivers, we did not stop at this metropolis of Oregon, which, with its view of five giant snow peaks, is undoubtedly the most picturesquely situated city in the United States, but took the stage for a village named Aurora Mills, twenty-nine miles south of Portland. Here Dr. Keil had made his home—apparently because he could buy there a flour mill and a saw mill—and was gradually importing his colony from Missouri. We did not exactly belong to this colony, but we shared some of its socialistic advantages, while the colony benefited by my father's musical endeavors to help make life worth living.

By rare good luck, which I shall never cease to chuckle over, he was able to buy a house with a fine apple orchard on a hill only half a mile from the village. [The house still stands, though unoc-

Henry T. Finck, first Oregon student at Harvard; author of eighteen books; product of colony train-ing; leading dramatic critic and judge of good music of his time.

ɛupied and in poor repair.] It was, as I have since discovered, one of the very first and best of the many commercial orchards for which Oregon soon became famous. I find from my diary that we harvested up to 2000 bushels in one year.

What did we do with them? My first impression is that we ate most of them: but there were plenty left to ship to San Francisco. There they were sold at auction, and the proceeds paid our living expenses, with a margin for other things. (In 1853 four bushels of Oregon apples were sold in San Francisco for $500. The following year forty bushels brought $2500 in the same market. In 1861 the shipment of apples from Oregon amounted to over 75,000 bushels.) . . .

Of course we had the luscious Gravensteins, . . . winesaps, excellent Newton pippins; with other favorites of our time, like Baldwins and greenings. . . . We doted on white winter pearmains and on the russets, both golden and Roxbury which, alas, have become so scarce. We had green Newtons which were even more juicy than the yellow. What has become of them and what of the mealy bellflowers, and the unique western seek-no-further and others worth perpetuating? . . . There were rambos, too; you can never get them now. . . .

You may not believe it, but it is a positive fact that we never needed to spray against pernicious insects and we never had it plowed. No need of these things . . . Surely, Oregon is the natural home of the apple.

Henry T. Finck quotes from his Oregon diary kept at Aurora, under date of June 4, 1870: "The Oregon and California Railroad is coming right through the middle of town; today they commenced to move an old shop. The store and a stable must likewise be removed." On July 14: "R. R. men leave town now and it will be quiet again till the tracklayers come."

On August 24, 1870, the diary read: "How this man has changed the whole country! Our town looks unlike what it was last year." Reference was made to Ben Holladay, pioneer Oregon railroad magnate.

Mr. Finck related that, "Holladay's most important achievement was that he opened up the Puget Sound region. Having unlimited means he hired a large steamer in San Francisco and took a number of prominent persons from that city and Portland into those amazingly interesting waters which have since enabled Washington to forge ahead of her placid twin sister, Oregon. For this occasion Holladay engaged the Aurora band."

The historic steamship *Oriflamme* was the vessel employed for the excursion. The start was made from Portland, Oregon, April 21, 1869, as was reported in the *Oregonian* of that city. It was double leaded front page stuff. The big news articles were written by the world famous editor, Harvey W. Scott, who was a member of the party. He wrote that it departed "with flying colors, the Aurora band on board playing lively airs, and the whole excursion party in a state of happy expectation regarding the pleasures of the trip." The party visited all the chief points of the Puget Sound section, consuming the time with receptions and visits by the high officials and principal business men and other citizens anxious to interest the then leading transportation magnate of the Pacific Northwest, and with lavish entertainment of his distinguished guests, till May third, when Portland was reached on the return trip. Says a note in Harvey W. Scott's six volume book on the history of the Oregon Country: "The Aurora brass band was composed of players from the German colony at Aurora, Oregon. It was considered the best musical organization of its time." There were two Aurora bands, and several orchestras, all trained by Prof. Finck.

Henry T. Finck tells of the wonderful Oregon salmon, the trout, crawfish, strawberries, blackberries, thimble berries, and so on, and of the pigeons that used to thicken the air; and the grouse, and the venison. "Oregon was indeed a great state for epicures," he declares. Of the Aurora colonists he says: "If the whole world were made up of such, there would be no need of locks and keys and safes. I would have trusted my bottom dollar to any one of them." He added: "They wore their best clothes on Sundays and the flowers in their gardens showed that they loved beautiful things."

In his last book, under the heading, "What a Wolf Did for Me," Henry T. Finck tells of his training for college in the Aurora colony. Christopher W. Wolff was his teacher:

"When he heard," wrote Finck, "that I got up at 5 o'clock in the morning to prepare myself for college by learning Latin and Greek all by my lonely self, he took pity on me and kindly offered to teach me—free, of course. He felt that such ambition ought to be encouraged. I gladly accepted his offer. It was the most fortunate thing that ever happened to me in all my long life. For Wolff not only taught me the old languages, but he helped to open my eyes to the countless beauties of nature about us.

"As a born gardener I naturally loved flowers, wild as well as cultivated, but it was he who revealed to me the lure of botany, the scientific side of plant-life. I soon found it great fun to be able to discover the name of any strange plant I came across by comparing its leaves and roots and stems and corollas and stamens and pistils with the classified descriptions given in my botanical text-book.

"By the time I was fourteen I had already gathered over four hundred different kinds of plants growing in our neighborhood, all of them carefully dried and put away, with their names, in old almanacs and magazines. This herbarium was afterwards enlarged to over five hundred. How fragrant it was when I came across it many years later!"

Mr. Finck goes on to say that Prof. Wolff also made him familiar with the enchantments of mineralogy, and astronomy being one of his hobbies he found his pupil a most willing companion in the study of it. He relates that this longing for knowledge of the stars—("we know now there are at least three billions of them")—at seventy haunted him and almost tormented him all his life.

Prof. Wolff had as one of his maxims *festina lente;* he believed in losing no time. He taught his pupil French, *beginning* by having the boy read to him Voltaire's "History of Charles XII"! But it was Greek grammar and literature with which his studies with Wolff were chiefly concerned. The pupil was soon disputing with his teacher the proper translation of certain sentences—and nothing could have pleased the teacher more than that. Prof. Wolff was proud of his pupil, and one day when another teacher was visiting in the colony he asked him to choose any page in Heroditus for the boy to translate—and he read it off as easily as if it had been English or German.

Teacher and pupil climbed Mount Hood together, a great feat for that early day. They met Prof. Thomas Condon at The Dalles—the grand old man of Oregon scholarship in her early days. Learning that young Finck was soon to depart for Harvard, Prof. Condon taught him from his collection in a half hour about the geology of Oregon, which he said might be useful when he was questioned at Harvard about this subject.

July 31, 1872, arrived, and Henry T. Finck, prepared in the Aurora colony for college, and the first Oregon boy to enter that institution, was off for Harvard.

He astonished the sage examiners in Latin and Greek there by offering to translate at sight from those languages, and from English into those classics. He asked no quarter, saying any writer would suit him, "Plato, Xenophon,

Heroditus, Thucydides, Homer, Cicero, Horace, Ovid, Vergil, Tacitus," or any other they liked. The professors at Harvard had never had an experience like that before. One of them told him afterwards that they put their heads together and decided that if he was bluffing they would give him a chance to regret it. So they selected some of the most difficult pages they could find. Some of these young Finck had not seen before, but he translated them all swimmingly, and the delighted examiners promptly promoted him to the sophomore classes.

Henry T. Finck at Harvard sat at the feet of the great teachers of that day there—President Eliot, Professor Norton, Professor Paine and the rest. His skill in playing the violoncello became a bridge by means of which he entered the best society in Cambridge, including the home of Longfellow, the poet, at which he spent many happy evenings playing with one of his daughters. His violoncello also opened to him the door to the home of William Dean Howells.

After graduation at Harvard he spent a year at Bayreuth and Munich, then was awarded the Harris fellowship by the Harvard faculty, which meant three years more of study in Europe. He steered straight for Berlin, where he studied two winters; the summers he spent in Heidelberg, and the third winter saw him in Vienna. Strauss was then adding regularly to his list of masterworks: "The Bat," "The Merry War," "The Queen's Lace Handkerchief," "The Gypsy Baron," and so on, and Suppe and Milloecker were shaking from their sleeves their tuneful "Fatinitzas," "Beggar Students," and so on. It was the golden age of the operetta, and Mr. Finck was on the spot when these musical gold coins came fresh from the mint by wholesale.

A surprise awaited him when he was preparing to return to his native country. He was offered the place of musical editor of the *New York Evening Post*, which he assumed in August, 1881, and held for forty-three years— one of the outstanding dramatic and musical critics of his generation, in some respects the greatest of them all, the friend and intimate of the world renowned artists in the higher ranges of musical and dramatic creation and interpretation in a time that will be looked upon as the veritable golden age of music.

Prominent in colony life

1. Professor Charles Ruge, colony teacher at Bethel and Aurora. 2. Professor Henry Conrad Finck, "The Music Master." 3. Helena Giesy, good mother by proxy of colony children, good angel of plains journey. Was to be bride of John A. Roebling, builder of Brooklyn Bridge. Picture shows her in old age. 4. George Groher, colony cabinet maker, carpenter, and finished worker in wood. 5. John D. Ehlen, first music teacher of the colony; basket maker at Bethel and Aurora.

CHAPTER 22

HENRY CONRAD FINCK

HENRY CONRAD FINCK was the man who made the Aurora colony the "musical oasis" of that part of Oregon in the sixties and seventies. He led the colony band and orchestras and choir at Bethel.

At Aurora he organized and trained two bands and several orchestras. The bands and the orchestras and the community singing made the colony famous throughout the West. The bands were in demand for celebrations and political and other meetings all over the coast. They furnished the music for the Oregon State Fair at Salem. As before said, every Aurora funeral had band music, and they played antiphonal pieces from the two balconies of the Aurora church on festival occasions and holidays. Railroad excursions from Portland and elsewhere were welcomed by the bands.

Such excursions were frequent at Aurora in colony days. As told elsewhere in these pages, Prof. Finck had given twelve acres for a park some rods east of the church. This park was improved. A mound was built and planted with flowers and kept fresh and beautiful with green grass, topped by a band stand from which music was played on many occasions. The school house was near by. A cook house was built for the use of the colony people and for excursionists. The Fourth of July speakers orated at the park. A company was organized and gave military drills. There was even an Aurora flag, though it was always displayed along with the Stars and Stripes. Close by the cook house were two large bake ovens. Nothing was left undone that would add to the many pleasures of colony life.

This musical atmosphere aided in making Aurora a summer resort town. Rich families came from Portland and other cities. They were provided with rooms in "the hall," the house close to the residence of Dr. Keil, and meals were served to them at the Keil tables and at the Aurora hotel. As stated elsewhere, the house by the Keil home contained a hall for dancing and other entertainments. Some of the teaching in the higher branches was carried on there. Prof. Wolff taught Henry T. Finck in that house. Families came and remained for weeks.

Prof. Finck was a true music master. He composed much music. Chamber music was common in the Finck home. Everybody present played and sang. All of the Finck children played and sang well. The members of the colony, mostly of German extraction, were natural musicians. They loved music and responded to the fine training of Prof. Finck in a way to delight his soul. The atmosphere of music permeated the whole community. No wonder that it produced the world's greatest musical critic and personal friend and companion of the chief musical celebrities of his time.

Prof. Finck could not abide poor music. His distinguished and ultra musical son, even in his early 'teens, wrote in his diary: "Brass band music has this peculiarity that it always reminds me of a threshing machine through which live cats are being chased." The boy belonged to one of the Aurora bands at the time, or soon after, and the snare-drum was his chosen instrument. "But it wasn't a brass band, but had wood wind-instruments too, and it played civilized music. At the Salem State Fair it always got the first prize in contests with bands from Portland and elsewhere," wrote the son in his memoirs.

A fine Portland lady, supposed to be a talented musician, was one of the frequent sojourners at Aurora, and she insisted on playing the piano when she visited the Finck home. When Prof. Finck could stand it no longer, which was each time the lady visited the home, he would retreat to a vantage point behind the smoke house and stop up his ears! Discord drove him out of his home.

After the dissolution of the colony, when Prof. Finck had moved to Portland, where his son Edward was a leading music teacher, he visited one of his married daughters at Anaheim, California, and while he was there he trained a boys' band. There followed a visit to Germany to see his old home people after long absence, and to feast his soul with high class German music, which he longed to hear in its native land once more, before his gentle spirit was translated to the fields of asphodel beyond the stars, where, let us assume, there are no discords to trouble it.

After some months in the fatherland, Prof. Finck returned to Anaheim, on his way home to Oregon. The juvenile band had in his absence kept up its practice, without any teacher. The aggregation met him on the arrival of his train and gave him a cordial welcome by essaying the pieces he had taught them. So out of time and tune had they fared in his absence that they so shocked their beloved teacher that he actually cried. The boys were pleased that their warm welcome had brought tears to the dear music master—and they never knew the exhibition of his feelings came from the agony of his soul over the discordance they made!

To weep over the beauties of music is a common experience of emotional people, even of great musicians; but the emotions of Prof. Finck at Anaheim were of a far different kind.

Prof. John B. Horner, one of the oldest members in point of service of the Oregon State Agricultural College, and leading writer of books on Oregon history, contributes the following words for these pages:

"The orchestra of Aurora, the peculiar community on Pudding River, was noted throughout Oregon in early days. The eighteen members, bearded men of modest mien, were artists, each man upon his favorite instrument. They belonged to that class of early musicians who lived close to nature and drew music from the skies, but were likewise earnest students of the great composers.

"There was considerable rejoicing, therefore, in college circles at Philomath in 1877, when it was learned that this orchestra had been engaged for the following commencement exercises; and it may be stated also that the sight of the musicians arriving with their instruments on one of Ben Holladay's stage coaches was somewhat striking.

"Although there was as yet no railway communication with Philomath, the important event of commencement brought visitors from Washington, Idaho, Montana, California and various parts of Oregon; and so great was the gathering that no building in that vicinity was large enough to accommodate the audience on that occasion. But as usual in the event of necessity in the West, the unexpected occurred. Samuel McLain—a man unlearned in books, though a college builder—donated a beautiful maple grove to serve as an academy for this and subsequent commencement exercises.

"Although it was the first year of President Walker's brilliant administration in that institution, there were six graduates in the class—a goodly number representing 200 students who daily touched the raiment of the great educator.

"At the appointed hour the academic grove was dedicated with noble music by the orchestra and prayer by Bishop Castle. Senator John H. Mitchell, who made a special journey from Washington, D.C., to be present, delivered the address to the graduates; and the scholarly charge was given by President Walker. Then followed the final selections by the orchestra, to which a chorus of birds above in the trees responded; and the grove, the programme and the orchestra were as classic as if the Grove of Academus had been really transferred from Athens to Oregon."

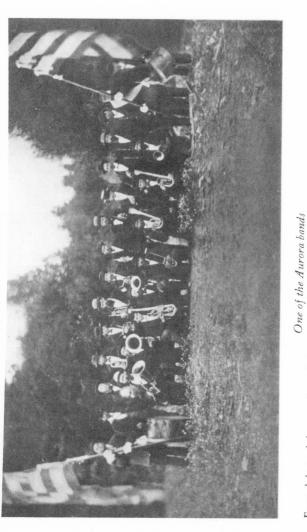

One of the Aurora bands

From left to right, standing: John Giesy (with flag), John Link, Henry Myer, Henry Ehlen, Jr., Wm. Kraus, Geo. Kraus, Wm. Schwader, Chas. Snyder, Fred'k Keil, Dr. A. J. Giesy, Fred Giesy, Wm. Miley, Lawrence Ehlen, Emanuel Keil, Adolph Pflug (with flag). Sitting: Henry Ehlen, Sr., Urban Will, Henry Giesy, Samuel Giesy, Geo. Will, Henry Vogt, Chas. Becke, Jr., Nicholas Giesy. The photo from which this picture was made was taken in 1876, the summer when this band spent a month in Portland, Oregon, helping in the observances attending the centennial celebration of American liberty. This was by the colonists usually called the big band, the other the little band—indicating the higher average age of its members, not superior number.

At that time, Philomath College, Philomath, and Willamette University, Salem, were the leading and largest institutions of higher learning in Oregon. Prof. Horner graduated from both of them, from Philomath in 1877 and Willamette in 1885. Philomath College was established by the United Brethren denomination in 1867, just ten years after Rev. Milton Wright, later bishop of that denomination, father of the world famous aeronauts, Orville and Wilbur Wright, opened the Institute at Sublimity, near Salem. The Sublimity school long since ceased functioning; that is now a Catholic community. Willamette University, Salem, the beginnings of which were made in 1842, in the first log cabin of the Jason Lee mission, was the first degree granting institution west of the Missouri River, and is now growing great in endowments, efficiency and size. The Sublimity Institute and Philomath College represented in their early days the only institutions of their stamp on the Pacific Coast under the sponsorship of the United Brethren church. Philomath was up to a short time ago still going, though not by any means of as relatively great importance as when the Aurora orchestra furnished the music for the commencement exercises of 1877.

AFTER Prof. Finck had been at Aurora a year or more and had organized two bands and the orchestras, and whipped them into shape by giving them diligent practice, he saw the need of a suitable place where all the members of the colony might meet and have the benefit of the music and be trained in community singing. The tract of land Prof. Finck had acquired, mostly west of and above what became the site of the church, contained besides the apple orchard a natural grove of beautiful fir trees. He gave this tract, containing twelve acres, for a park.

The colony people as heretofore mentioned, improved and beautified it, built a grand stand, provided seats for large crowds and erected a commodious kitchen and constructed a big bakery for the preparation of meals on public occasions. They hauled dirt and formed a great mound in a place convenient to the grand stand and to the amphitheater for the seats, and the spacious refectory. They covered the mound with a beautiful growth of grass bordered with flowers—made a lawn of it—and provided a most unique and ornamental place on the top for the bands.

They planted flower beds along the walks leading to the park, gave the whole tract and the ways leading to it such attention as only patient and thorough workers and competent gardeners can do—in short, they made the gift of Prof. Finck the finest park in Oregon at the time; and the most attractive and convenient for large gatherings. They omitted no detail, nor failed to keep neat and orderly the whole of it and its surroundings.

"I often think, when working over my plants," said John Fiske, "of what Linnaeus once said of the unfolding of a blossom: 'I saw God in His glory passing over me, and bowed my head in worship.' "

A survivor of colony days, who was a small boy then, remembers that Adolph Findling spent what seemed to his youthful fancy his whole time in hauling fertilizer from the barns to the park and the flower beds leading to it. This survivor, long since grown to manhood's estate, did not then appreciate the love of Adolph Findling for the beautiful flowers and shrubs and plants he tended in a seeming dreary round. But Adolph Findling, now for two generations gathered to his fathers, "saw God in His glory passing over" him in the creations of bloom he was aiding in their unfolding. And Adolph Findling was not the only worker in and around the park. He had ample help and superintendence, for all the colony people were by instinct and teaching lovers of the beautiful.

The fame of the Aurora park spread. Excursions came from long distances. Many state-wide meetings were held there in the sixties and seventies. The Portland Turnverein came annually in a great excursion, by boats and carriages the first years and by railroad trains in the seventies.

The Fourth of July celebrations of those days for that section were all held in the Aurora park, and the flights of oratory of the period, when political feelings ran high, were memorable. They "made the American eagle scream" in the approved manner of the "Oregon style" of the pioneer epoch, in plain, blunt words, not devoid of invective nor always of personal allusion and abuse. The "Oregon style" is proverbial throughout the United States.

These uses of the park lasted on after the dissolution of the colony, notably for Fourth of July celebrations and large political meetings for which sufficient room was not available elsewhere. But gradually the mound was neglected and grew up to weeds, the flower beds went back to nature for want of attention, the buildings fell into desuetude and decay, and the whole beautiful tract reverted to the underbrush entangled wild state in which the colonists found it. The park was one of the finest examples of the colony spirit of cooperation and care, and of attention to the amenities and pleasures of life.

The children, now scattered to the four winds, of some of the leading families of Portland and other Oregon cities—those of them yet in the land of the living, though on the sundown side of life—must think with regret of the neglect and the reversion to primitive solitude of that wonderful park, for they spent many happy hours there in the far off days when their parents brought them thither as summer visitors.

Everything that was popular in that time in the way of facilities for the recreation and amusement of both the elders and the children was provided in the park. There were sand piles and swings and teeter boards and coasting chutes and all the rest; there was even a merry-go-round for the youngsters. Dr. Keil never forgot the children.

The merry-go-round was stout in its construction and gay in its appearance—and the motive power was Queen and Kate, the "mule team" of historic significance in the memorials of community life at Bethel and Aurora, the span that drew the plains hearse over two thousand miles in the covered wagon journey of 1855. The long eared hybrids, patient above the average of their tribe of Missouri mules of quip and story and song, were the prized pets of all the youngsters, who regarded them as special creations set apart for the one purpose in life of giving them pleasure.

Albeit the new arrivals among the tots were under the necessity of being reassured after their initial terror over the raucous and unmusical sounds when the animals raised their voices to bray, in the manner of their kind.

A then "broth of a boy," scion of a prominent pioneer family, recalls that many summer visitors were at Aurora when, August 2, 1873, the great fire that burned over twenty-three downtown Portland blocks raged—and a big crowd of them, some of the number owners of properties in the path of the flames, had their first news of the holocaust when they watched the whole fire fighting force of Salem speed by on a special train of engine and flat cars, hurrying to give aid to their hard pressed brothers waging battle in the sister city on the lower Willamette River. This boy, now a man of patriarchal years, will not forget that sight while life lasts. The special train made the speed record to date in Oregon railroading, then in its swaddling clothes period.

Ben Holladay and his wife and their guests were frequent summer visitors, and Dr. Keil and this pioneer railroad builder of Oregon and former magnate of the overland stage lines were fast friends and mutual admirers. They were kindred spirits in the attributes that make the true pioneer, though vastly different in their moral and spiritual ideals.

In the high tide days of Aurora community life few weeks of the summer passed without some kind of excursion to or convention in the Aurora park. At the big events the Aurora bands played and the colony orchestras furnished music, and the Aurora militia company paraded in full uniform, with guns and sabers and all the furnishings and furbelows Dr. Keil and some of the older members of the colony had seen in Germany; and with the flag, too. No copy of that flag is known to exist now. There were two members of the colony at Aurora who had served at Waterloo, one with Napoleon and the other with Wellington, under Blucher. Their reminiscences, in which they recalled the great days and fought over that fateful battle, were always interesting. These doughty veterans lived in the community away past their ninetieth birthdays, and they measured up to the ideals of colony life, as did the members of their families.* [See note, end of chapter.]

The Aurora militia company was not organized for protection. It was merely for show. The members of the community had no quarrel with their neighbors, nor was there a neighbor who had a grudge of any kind against them.

The second annual reunion of the Oregon Pioneer Association, on June 16, 1874, was held in the Aurora park. "After the procession, numbering some 1500, had been comfortably seated in the Aurora park," according to the written record of the secretary, the program proceeded. The principal speakers were Governor L. F. Grover and Secretary of State S. F. Chadwick. The famous Joe Meek was one of the speakers. So was Dr. Keil who the previous year had assisted in organizing the association. Two halls were filled with dancers in the evening, and the terpsichorean music was furnished by the Aurora orchestras.

Along with an excursion in the middle sixties, Amos Cushman and his wife who had been Ruth Baker came for one of their few visits since their marriage to spend the day with their people. They brought with them their four children, living witnesses of what may be termed Exhibit Number One of the toilsome days they had spent on their Yamhill County farm since their wedding week in the colony. They brought other witnesses, in their careworn faces and work-begrimed hands and more or less shabby and scant wearing apparel in striking contrast to the natty appearance of the colony members in their Sunday best, showing the careful workmanship of the tailoring, dressmaking and shoemaking shops of the colony, all under the eyes of masters of their trades. Their old neigh-bors asked the Cushmans many questions about their life on the farm. Some of them directed at Ruth by the women were more sympathetic than polite, but she gave no least sign of disillusionment, nor let any word of self pity or reproach pass her lips.

"We have worked hard and deprived ourselves of so-cial contacts, by necessity and on account of being so far away from neighbors," Ruth admitted, "but we have come through in one way and another. We have met our pay-ments and made some improvements, and we are hop-ing for the best. We have our children to love and work for, and we have not lost either our youthful attachment or our mutual love."

"But how can you enjoy such a lonely life?" asked one of her old pupils who had been growing up while Ruth was away, adding, "How we would like to have you back as a teacher; we have missed you so much, all of us."

Amos was as free from signs of repining as Ruth, but he admitted to one of his old colony confidants that he had been almost ready to give up, on several occasions, the struggle was so hard.

"Especially is it hard on Ruth," he added, "and the worst part is the loneliness. She has the children to tie her at home and take up her time, together with all the house-hold duties, but she misses the loving companionship and the sympathetic touch of her blood and bond sisters of colony life, which she had from childhood up to the time of our marriage. I am a man and can endure it, but she is a woman with all the cares and worries of motherhood, and if she would urge it, or even mention it, I would throw off the load and come back. But Ruth will not even breathe a complaint," he added. "She is a good sport and a brave soldier, and it makes me love her the more; but it compels me to almost pray for a disaster of some kind that would drive us back to Aurora.

"There are times," Amos confessed, "when I would welcome an earthquake or a flood or a hurricane or a fire, to make us move out, for her sake; but nothing happens in the dreariness and drabness of our daily round of duties on the farm, and how long I can endure it, and pocket my pride, I do not know. We are thankful for some things, however; we have health and we have our mutual love, and we have work that keeps us so busy that we scarcely have time for worrying, and that is perhaps all for the best.

"But what we are going to do when the children grow older and must have schooling, I cannot say. For the present, Ruth employs her teaching knowledge part of the time in giving the two older children their first rudiments of learning. She has established a sort of home kindergarten. That is fine, and they could not have a better teacher. But the time will come when we will have to find other ways, and there is only a district school seven miles distant, where a three months term is kept each year, by a green girl who, although she does her best, is woefully incompetent."

"But we have our colony school the whole year through," said the confidant of Amos, "and I can never see why that is not the best for the children."

Amos knew this well, and the thought of it did not make him comfortable in the part circumstances had maneuvered him to the necessity of playing. As Amos and Ruth returned home to their farm after their visit to the colony people, with the wonderful band and orchestral music and the community songs ringing in their ears, and the thoughts of their welcome among their old friends singing in their hearts, they were thoughtful and their excursion was the talk of their home for weeks and months.

But never a word of reproach or self pity escaped Ruth's lips. All of which added to the admiration of Amos, however poignantly it gave him concern for the problems of the future.

There should be added here an explanation of the individual property held in the Aurora colony by Prof. Finck. This was not the only case. There were several. Even some relatives of prominent members who had come to Aurora acquired farm lands in their individual names, but participated in all or most respects in the colony life, using and giving the use of their holdings absolutely or nearly as if they had been held in common. Some of the mechanics and tradesmen operated in much the same way —or under special agreements made with Dr. Keil and approved or participated in by the trustees. Prof. Finck left the colony and took up his residence in Portland, shortly before the death of Dr. Keil and the beginning of the dissolution of the colony.

* The Aurora bands and orchestras played no poor music; never descended to anything resembling jazz. Frequently, for dancing, at the park, where great crowds gathered, or in the halls, they used Mozart's Quadrille. It was the only piece of the kind the master magician ever composed, a brain and heart child of necessity. He was in a company the members of which wished to dance in that style. Presto! Wolfgang Mozart dashed off the necessary music. A living member of the Aurora bands and orchestras declares that when the strains of Mozart's Quadrille issued forth the feet of the most staid moved as it were by electrical urge to rhythmic time and step. To hear this now grayed grandfather call up the fond story is enough to hark the memories of his oldest hearer to the ecstacies of youthful days when "on with the dance, let joy be unconfined," was the frequent order.

CHAPTER 24

THE AURORA HOTEL

THE best known building in the colony was the Aurora hotel, in which was the famous Aurora restaurant, where meals were served to the general and traveling public, to overland stage passengers before the coming of the railroad and to train passengers long before the time of dining cars in Oregon—throughout the life of the colony and for years thereafter. Thousands of people traveling in or through Oregon had cause to anticipate with pleasure the stop there for meals, or to remember with satisfaction the dishes set before them.

Not only were the travelers on the passenger trains accommodated with meals at the Aurora restaurant tables, but lunches were put up there for freight train engineers, firemen and brakemen, and they were carried to like workers at division points all up and down the line for two hundred miles. The excellence of the Aurora community cooks was shown beyond peradventure at their colony restaurant. They would have become famous for the high quality of their handiwork even with indifferent equipment and ordinary supplies, as witness the wonderful meals they served to their people of the covered wagon trains; but their equipment was out of the ordinary and their supplies, furnished from the colony gardens, orchards and fields, including frequent wild game from the nearby forests and fish and crustaceans from the streams, were fresher, better and more appetizing than could be afforded even at the best hotels of the cities of that time, before cold storage facilities were known or ice plants were built,

Famous colony hotel and restaurant at Auror in its palmy days.

excepting the occasional ice house to preserve a lake or stream supply, held over from the winter—and in the mild Oregon climate there was not every year sufficient below freezing weather for even this.

The tables in the homes of Aurora were not less sumptuous in their delectable viands to tempt the jaded appetite than were those found at the famous Aurora restaurant. Edward M. Miller, a staff writer of the *Portland Oregonian*, recalling memories of the old days, recently said in that newspaper:

A narrative of the Aurora colony would not be complete without a brief discourse upon the glories of the Aurora table viands. Even as Henry Theophlius Finck, metropolitan music critic, praised Aurora pig sausage, so have countless hundreds of Aurora guests marveled at the substantial delicacies of the Aurora boards. Aurora fried potatoes surpass all other fried potatoes. Aurora home-baked bread is without a peer in this broad land. Aurora pig sausage has a secret, if captured, that would make a fortune for an enterprising packer. Then there were the other dishes. It is doubtful if even the colony descendants can spell their names, so we make no apologies for our attempts in that line. There is stearum, a cross between a pancake and an omelette, fried in a smoking iron pan, difficult to fry, but delightful to partake; there is smear-case, the granddaddy of all cottage cheese; animal cookies, with candy eyes and draped with a sugar that glistens with a luster peculiar to Aurora; Christmas candies, German jellies, cakes drowned in chocolate frosting, and pies too deep to be true. Crullers, home-smoked hams, green onions and a heavenly chicken dressing savored with garlic water prepared the night before. A chicken was honored to find a place in an Aurora frying pan.

The writer knows. A picture of his paternal great-grandparents hangs on the walls of Aunt Annie Fry's colony home at Aurora; and when a visit is made to Aurora, nourishments are never lacking, and supplies are usually carried away. Aunt Annie, 86, would fain speak German on these visits, but of this the fourth generation knows nothing, save "No sprecken dee Dutch," and therein Aunt

Annie is greatly disappointed. In the old days the Pioneer Hotel, now gaunt beside the Southern Pacific tracks, was the stopping place for train meals. The trainmen and the passengers knew that Portland was not far away, but they knew that the best meals on the coast were to be had at Jacob Giesy's Pioneer Hotel.

The keeping of a hotel and restaurant for the accommodation of the traveling public, and to entertain visitors, was the rule with almost every one of the numerous American communal settlements of the latter part of the last century. It is (or at least up to a recent date was) continued by the Community of True Inspiration at Amana, Iowa, as thousands of visitors to that colony each year could attest with pleasant memories. But in no other such community was this feature more efficiently carried on, if as well. At the Aurora restaurant there was a woman in charge of each department, and she had efficient and ample help, so that the work was not over hard for any one. It was organized in a manner that would do credit to the high class hotels and restaurants of the present day. There was no lack in either quality or quantity of food, and the service was peculiarly efficient.

Henry T. Finck without doubt secured the background for several of his famous books at Aurora. "Gardening With Brains" is one of these books, used in schools and technical institutions and quoted by experts, commended by the great Luther Burbank, wizard of the plant world. "Girth Control" is another and "Food and Flavor" a third —the last named a book that advanced a new idea concerning the dependence of the appetite on the sense of smell.

And Mr. Finck absorbed the background of others of his books and magazine articles at Aurora, like "Primitive Love and Love Stories," "The Evolution of Girlhood," and "Romantic Love and Personal Beauty." He showed in "The Evolution of Girlhood" that there was no such thing in any country in the world up to a few years before the time he wrote; that is, girlhood as we see it today in the high schools and elsewhere, from the ages of fifteen to thirty or older—because all were married and began rearing families when they were in their tender years, in past times. In "Romantic Love and Personal Beauty" he traced the standards throughout history in all countries, making an original contribution to literature.

Mr. Finck in his last book, "My Adventures in the Golden Age of Music," as heretofore mentioned, designated Oregon as "a great state for epicures," and of course he had reference to the Aurora community.

The taste of the good things lingered with this epicure of the epicures who had fared forth throughout the whole world, and he reverted to the viands on the Aurora boards as the best this wide earth afforded.

The Aurora restaurant could not be duplicated in this day, because there is no other place just like that, in soil and sunshine and showers, and the famous cooks of the colony days cannot be called back from the present place of their gentle spirits along the streets of gold in the eternal city of which it is written: "And there shall be no night there: and they need no candle, neither light of the sun; for the Lord God giveth them light: and they shall reign forever and ever."

And if a restaurant is needed there, they surely went prepared to make it the best in all the diamond bedecked length and breadth of the continuing city not made with hands.

CHAPTER 25

THE BREAKING POINT

LIFE on their Yamhill Country farm went on as usual with Amos and Ruth Cushman and their little brood after the return from the hurried visit to their Aurora brothers and sisters. Silas Hobson and his young wife, homesteaders five miles distant, had attended to their stock while they were away and were on hand to share in their reminiscences when they returned.

These good neighbors, the nearest in point of distance of the human kind, were often willing helpers at the Cushman home, for Amos was constantly clearing more land and adding to his cultivated fields, and increasing his live stock. He would have been called a prosperous farmer. The knowledge of a number of trades, gained at Bethel and Aurora, stood him in good stead in a district far removed from the services of trained mechanics with their tools and machines. He added many touches to the comforts of the cabin home of the Hobsons, and Drusilla was always a most welcome visitor and guest under the Cushman roof. A cordial attachment grew up between these neighbors and their children, for there were three tots in the Hobson cabin, two boys and a girl, corresponding in age to the Cushman children.

The year following their visit at Aurora was what Silas Hobson called an unlucky one in the life of the Cushmans. The children were all sick at once. Physicians were scarce and not of the best on the average in the days when any one with a little reading or what he regarded as a knack in prescribing pills, poultices and potions might hang out his shingle and with a saddle pony and a medicine case go on his way with all the seeming confidence of a true disciple of Aesculapius or Luke. The pioneer doctor of medicine in Oregon was akin to the circuit rider of religion, often uncouth and of scant schooling, to which rule, however, there were notable exceptions to the tyros in both callings. There were learned and able circuit riders. They were in fact in the majority. There were physicians who held high university honors and were graduates of great schools of medicine.

Old Saddlebags was the name by which one of the circuit riders of the cloth was known to the settlers of the backwoods districts of Yamhill County. He was unlettered and largely unlearned. "Edication is the ruination of the world!" he was wont to thunder in stentorian tones when he had developed his theme to the high pitch of his oracular diatribes. That was one of the favorite subjects of his sermonizing talks in the remote homes.

"Edication" of the young, he had convinced himself and come to sincerely believe, was carrying the growing youth to the danger point of disrespect for their elders, and to the brink and frequently to the depths of hopeless damnation. This hardshell harbinger of the old fashioned gospel of hell fire and brimstone would have regarded himself as sinfully recreant to his duty had he omitted the least of his philippics against the curse of "edication," for he had worked himself to the point of believing that even a little learning is a dangerous thing, though he had never heard of the ancient sage admonition, "Drink deep, or taste not the Pierian spring." He would not have known a Pierian spring from a hawk or a handsaw, or a wheelbarrow, no matter what the quarter of the wind. The jibes of the young people in the homes he visited at the peculiar beliefs of Old Saddlebags did not help in turning him to favor school facilities for the growing generation, but rather made him more "sot" in his ideas. It is not necessary with the vanishing race of Oregon pioneers to say in defense of veracity that Old Saddlebags was no mythical character, though it is admitted that he was a rare specimen even in his class.

Ruth Cushman and Drusilla Hobson had worn themselves out with anxious days and sleepless nights in the care of the four Cushman children, following the directions of a "Doctor" Johnson of the class of pioneer practitioners who got their learning from a casual book or came by it through what they thought was a knack. Rhoda, the eldest of the Cushman children, had died. Her little body had been laid in a homemade coffin, fashioned by Amos and Silas from materials at hand. The distracted women had dressed the cold form in what had been her poor Sunday best. There was no time for a formal funeral, nor was a minister available. But they improvised a brief burial service at the side of the grave that had been opened and prepared by Silas on a nearby knoll, in which the four elders sang as best they could with their hearts in their throats—

And there was a prayer by Amos that had the benediction of a mother's tears, uttered in accents broken with sobs, commending the spirit of little Rhoda to God who gave it and her body to the dust from which it came. And Ruth and Amos and Drusilla essayed the colony funeral song, "Das Grab ist tief und stille," and the father and mother broke down in the attempt and Drusilla went on alone, but could not get to the third verse with the words and tune. It was all their pitiful best; and never were the royal ceremonials for a king's daughter more beautiful in sincerity of feeling.

"We must find a way to save the lives of the other children," said Ruth after the grave had been filled and the little mound rounded and covered with wild flowers wet with tears.

"But what way?" in agonized accents asked Amos, his frame shaking with the fears that bespoke his thoughts of the futility of their situation.

"I have heard of a Doctor Dagon, at Lafayette, and they say he makes wonderful cures, and I will ride fast and bring him if possible," spoke up Silas.

There were anxious hearts in the Cushman home when Silas was gone. The three remaining children showed no signs of improvement.

"Can you save my children?" inquired the distracted mother, when Silas had returned and the doctor, after a few curt questions, had proceeded to work.

"I will do my part and hope for the best," was the reply, "and the rest will depend on careful nursing and the mercy of the good God."

Dr. Dagon was a recluse, living alone. He was a graduate of one of the German universities and medical colleges. There were stories of what seemed to the early settlers his marvelous cures. Strange reports leaked out about his past. After Dr. Dagon's death, years later, there were rumors of buried treasure, for he had practiced long and was not known to have spent any unnecessary money in his living expenses.

"I will stay till the worst is over," he told Ruth, to her great relief, expressed in thankful words, for the kindly doctor of the old school had come a long way and his services were in demand and needed elsewhere.

"My three patients are out of danger," he told the mother after a few days, "but I fear little Dan may get up from his bed a cripple; perhaps for life," he added, showing his sympathy in his words and face. Dan, next in age to the child resting in the new made grave, was the life of the home, the restless spirit of his father mingled with the calm and sweet disposition of the mother.

When the doctor was ready to depart, announcing that the children were on the way to recovery and needed only attentive and efficient nursing, which he assured the two women they were giving, as well as could be expected from any one trained in the profession, Ruth demanded:

"Could you have saved Rhoda? Could you have saved Dan from the danger of becoming a cripple?"

"That is not for me to say," said the doctor. "It might have been. I am sorry I was not called earlier. Of course I would have done my best, as with the other little ones. But we must not think of things that cannot be helped. Too late are two of the saddest words in any language. Perhaps I could not have been of service. Let us leave it at that."

Promising to return soon to observe the condition of little Dan, and giving directions, Dr. Dagon rode away.

Ruth had some needed rest now, and so did her kind neighbor from the homestead. By the time of the return of Dr. Dagon the two younger children were recovered; but the affliction of Dan was the same. The good doctor could do no more, for he declared the cure of Dan's lameness was beyond his power; possibly no one could help. It was a case for a specialist.

"Then, doctor, what is there for us to do; what can we do?" inquired Ruth, with her whole anxious soul in the words.

"I cannot give you advice," Dr. Dagon said, "but if Dan were my boy, and it were possible, I would get him to a specialist; that is the only hope. It may be merely a dim candle light of hope. But even so, there are places in the world for cripples. Many men in worse bodily condition than Dan is likely to be, even though his lameness may be incurable, have made high marks in the world and accomplished great things. History is full of them. This seeming handicap has been in innumerable cases a turning point from mediocrity to greatness, which in my theory of the world's work is usefulness. Dan's handicap may be his help. It may be the tide in his life which taken at the flood will lead on to fortune."

The men and Drusilla were listening. They were thoughtful after the good doctor had ridden away, with an "auf wiedersehen" and a wave of the hand and a "God bless you all."

Every one familiar with western history knows of the Whitman massacre on November 29th, 1847. In one of the companies of the 1844 covered wagon train immigration, hailing from Missouri, traveled Henry Sager and wife and their seven children. The parents died of camp fever on the Old Oregon Trail, the father at Green River and the mother a few weeks later. The family of William Shaw and wife, the latter a sister of Colonel Cornelius Gilliam, a heroic figure in early Oregon history and afterward patriarch of a famous and numerous pioneer family, took the orphaned children on to Waiilatpu, mission station of Dr. Marcus Whitman and his wife Narcissa, who adopted them. The two boys of the Sager family, John, 17, and Francis, 15, were killed in the massacre, and the younger children, all girls, taken captive by the Indians, and finally rescued, four of them to become maternal heads of leading pioneer families. Dr. Theophilus Dagon was a member of that covered wagon train, and ministered to the stricken members of the Sager family, as he was to perform like offices of mercy and healing on the Yamhill County farm. He went to Southern Oregon and in the early fifties kept a drug store in the then booming pioneer and now ghost city of

Scottsburg for about a year; acquired real property and after disposing of his drug store built a log house about eleven miles east of that city, on the highway leading to Wilbur and Roseburg and on to Yreka, California—the highway built under the direction of Col. Joseph Hooker, who became "Fighting Joe" Hooker, Brigadier and Major General leading Union forces in the Civil War. Dr. Dagon made his place a road house, which he kept until 1855, when he enlisted to fight Indians in the Rogue River war. The old muster rolls of Company 1, Second Regiment of Oregon Mounted Volunteers, show him as No. 21, and A. C. Gibbs as No. 38; both privates. Gibbs became the second Governor of the State of Oregon. They served from November 8, 1855, to February 14, 1856; and three years after the latter date Oregon became the Valentine State, adding the 33d star to the flag. Dr. Dagon later went back to Southern Oregon. He filed for a homestead entry in Douglas County in 1875, and received property by deed there in 1883. He died in or near that year—"was found dead in his cabin and was buried by neighbors, on the old Smith hill and Price lane road on his little place near the summit of Smith hill and about one mile south of the old Smith place." Part of this information comes from a grandson of Jesse Applegate, most prominent early Oregon pioneer, of the epoch making 1843 covered wagon immigration. He was called Theo., but more generally Dr. Dagon was known as "the old Dutch doctor." The writer retains grateful and loving memories of him, dating from days when that kind and sapient oldtime practitioner and philosopher administered to patients in the parental household of which he was a youthful member, not far from the historic Yoncalla (Indian for Eagle Bird) of the famed Applegate settlement, where were inspired and set in motion so many movements relating its hills and vales with the destiny of states and of nations in all the ends of the earth for time and eternity.

A few days after Dr. Dagon had ridden away from the Yamhill County home, Silas Hobson returned with interesting news. A Mr. Spencer from the East was searching for land on which to establish a large stock ranch. Silas had met him and they had talked of the chances of getting what was wanted in that section. The newcomer had asked Silas to make inquiries while he went further up the valley in his quest. Silas suggested that both families might dispose of their equities to advantage, and he advanced the thought that they might all be better off with the men working for good wages or engaged in some small business.

The following Sunday the two families were together at the Cushman home, Mr. Spencer having returned with an offer, and they talked over the idea of making a move.

"Our equities are small," said Amos. "We have worked hard and made headway. We have so far kept up our annual payments and interest, but we have not much to show for all this. We have had unexpected expenses. Four babies, welcome as they have been, have taken their toll from our scanty income. It is an uphill pull."

He suggested the idea of returning to Aurora, which was a delightful note to Ruth. He said the Hobsons might go with them to the colony, where they would be welcome, and where they would all find their places and be safe from worries and every one would be a neighbor.

"It is like this," said Amos: "A congressman told a story of the burros in the forests of Brazil, where there is a vast back country little explored by people from the outside world. There are large bands of the burros, for they have been able to hold their own against their savage enemies, the wild beasts subsisting on the flesh of weaker animals, on account of a peculiar habit the burros have. When they are attacked they bunch together with their heads near

the center of a circle and their feet out; so they protect
their heads and their lives with their heels. But the average
community of human beings, though able to protect themselves against their enemies and all adverse circumstances,
when they are in danger or distress, proceed the other way
around. They bunch together with their heads out and
their heels in, and so kick themselves to death. I have tried
both ways and I am about ready to follow the example
of the Brazilian burros."

But Silas, admitting the force of the illustration, advanced another idea. He was for leaving the homestead.
He had been a well paid mechanic in one of the big iron
foundries and machine shops of Portland, but the lure of
free government land had drawn him and Drusilla to their
present life. They had been disillusioned and were ready to
go back. Amos and Ruth and their children would fare
better there than here, and Silas was sure Amos could get
employment along with him in the shops.

Drusilla understood the German language. She had
learned it with English as a child, for her mother was a
German of American birth and they had lived in a settlement of German people. But Silas knew only English, and
the Hobsons feared he might be slow in acquiring another
tongue. Their people were in Portland, and they would be
oriented there immediately on their return.

"I am for going back to my job in the machine shops,
but I will abide the decision of the rest of you," agreed
Silas, after much discussion.

"I want to make a suggestion," said Drusilla. "Let's
draw straws. Let fate decide it. Then no one will be to
blame if we find we have made a poor choice; we can blame
it on the deciding straw. What say you? Isn't that fair?"

They drew straws. Portland won.

The new owner of the land furnished a driver for the

Cushman team, that now belonged to him, and the two families with their scant furniture and other personal belongings moved to Portland. Amos and Silas were taken on at the factory.

"The sooner the quicker," said the old foreman of his department, after expressing his pleasure over the chance of getting Silas back, answering the query as to when he should report for duty, along with Amos. Work was brisk; they could come as soon as they were settled and ready.

Houses for rent were scarce, but there was much building. A bargain was struck quickly for two dwellings not yet completed but which gave them roofs over their heads, and they could themselves add the finishing touches at odd times out of working hours at the plant. They bought on the monthly installment plan, making small down payments. All went well with the families who had been far neighbors. They now lived next door.

"Two things led me to be resigned to coming to Portland instead of going to Aurora," Ruth said to Amos after they had made themselves as comfortable as conditions would permit. "One thing was my promise to leave the decision to you. The other you know. I am praying to God that we may find a specialist who can cure Dan's lameness. It may turn out that the angels of mercy made the choice of the long straw."

"Your first reason makes me ashamed of my selfishness," answered Amos. "I have been selfish from the beginning, and you have been wonderful. You have observed the Diamond Rule of colony life, while I have fallen short of measuring up to the demands of even the Golden Rule. But I have had the same thoughts about Dan, I feel less of shame when I think of him. We will look for a specialist now. We will take the risk of finding ways to meet the attendant expense."

"Yes, we will save all we can, and I will work, too, if I can find a way," said Ruth. "There may be a place for me in the public schools, or perhaps I can get a chance to teach German children. There are many Germans here. The Turnverein shows a large membership, and from what sister Hannah told me at Aurora of the annual picnics at the park there, I might be led to the conclusion that half the people of Portland are German. I will welcome any kind of honorable service that I can perform. It is 'service above self' for poor Dan, and I would scrub floors or wash dishes the rest of my days if by that way I could aid in ending his handicap."

Ruth found no chance for a teaching position, nor other steady employment, but the Cushmans through the inquiries of Amos at the shops made a contact with one of the leading physicians of the city. After several examinations, the anxious mother was told that a cure of her boy's lameness was beyond his power.

"And I think it is not in the power of medical science," he honestly confided to her. "My advice is to make the best of the situation and be thankful that it is no worse, and to fit the boy for an occupation in which his handicap will interfere the least."

"It is the hardest blow of my life," Ruth between heartbroken sobs told Amos when he returned from work that evening, "for me to come to the point of feeling that I am in a blind alley of fate, with no clew; no way out, and no ray of light, when the very flesh of my flesh and bone of my bone appeal to me for help and there is no help. And I am sure I voice only the feelings of any true mother in my position," she added.

"I have run true to the name given me at birth; I have been a burden to you," sobbed Amos so shaken with grief and black despair that Ruth was spurred to reason with him in a vein of hopefulness, following the cue they had been given by the good old Dr. Dagon on the Yamhill farm. They would do their best and still hope for new medical discoveries.

Time wore on. Each day was like its yesterday, with the round of duties at the factory for Amos and the grind of household tasks at home for Ruth. The installment payments on their home came due with the regularity of the routine of the shops where Amos toiled, and there were other installment payments on houshold furniture; and the children were in school with books to buy and shoes to provide for their feet and presentable clothing to make them companionable with the other children. They were existing, the Cushmans were, but they were not living, and it was the same drab story with their neighbors, the Hobsons.

Gathered under the Cushman roof one evening, after a year of the treadmill grind, the two families resumed under the head of unfinished business the talk of the future they had discussed on the Yamhill County farm.

"We are mere cogs in a big wheel at the factory," admitted Amos. "We are not individuals; we are numbers. We file in as the whistle blows in the morning; we perform our tasks like automatons. At the noon hour we mix with the other numbers and eat our lunches and listen to nasty stories and ribald jokes, and we fit into our places again when the siren calls us to resume the round for the afternoon shift, and in the evening we file out. Morning, noon and night it is all the same, and day after day the endless course proceeds. Why? This is the industrial age we hear so much about, a fine figure of speech; but what is the outcome?"

"Oh well, it all comes to the same thing, whatever we do, six feet of earth and a funeral notice in the paper, whether we are cogs in the wheel or own the factory or the bank," was the answer of Silas Hobson.

"Who knows us here, outside of the other cogs in the

big wheel?" asked Amos. "If we have sickness or if we are injured and cannot work, what will become of us? Who will pay the installments and buy the groceries and keep the children in school? Who cares whether we live or die, excepting the foreman in the shops? And we would be missed for only a day, for there are other cogs ready to be substituted."

Ruth confided to Drusilla the next day that what Amos had said was like balm of Gilead to her soul. She revealed to her good neighbor their understanding before their marriage, and how she had kept the faith. She proposed to stand steadfast in holding to her promise, but she had not ceased to hope for the coming of the turning point in their lives that would lead them back to Aurora.

"I am hoping we can all go together," she told Drusilla. Her neighbor was anxious to learn more of the life in the colony, and Ruth painted a word picture for her of the spirit of brotherly and sisterly kindness there.

"I recall a sermon I heard Dr. Keil preach," Ruth said, "taking his text from the Sermon on the Mount, in which the Master during the early days of his short public career taught his disciples." As her mind went back to the setting of the sermon, she outlined it as best she could, something like this:

" 'Blessed are the poor in spirit, for theirs is the kingdom of heaven. Blessed are those that mourn, for they shall be comforted. Blessed are the meek, for they shall inherit the earth. Blessed are they which do hunger and thirst after righteousness, for they shall be filled. Blessed are the merciful, for they shall obtain mercy. Blessed are the pure in heart, for they shall see God. Blessed are the peacemakers, for they shall be called the children of God. Blessed are ye when men shall revile you and say evil things about you falsely.

" 'The old law was against murder; but Christ's new law was against even anger with a brother. The old law was against adultery, the new one against thoughts of adultery. The old law was vindictive, an eye for an eye and a tooth for a tooth, but the new law admonished against returning evil with evil, against all forms of retributive vengeance.

" 'The new law is THE LAW OF LOVE, love for both friends and enemies, charity even for one who steals from you, pity even for one who does you injury, the turning of the other cheek if one strikes you.

" 'Judge not that ye be not judged is the new law.

" 'The Golden Rule is the heart of that law which the Master that day in old Judea taught his disciples when they had withdrawn apart from the crowds that followed: 'All things whatsoever ye would that men should do to you, do ye even so to them.' "

"These things I remember of the lesson of that sermon, and I recall also another and concluding appeal, when, quoting the words of St. Paul to the church at Rome, 'Be kindly affectioned one to another with brotherly love; in honor preferring one another,' the leader called that the Diamond Rule of colony life; said it is not enough to do as you would be done by; you must go further, following the later rule, and prefer your brother's or your sister's welfare to your own. Yes, even you must be willing to die for others, as Christ suffered disgraceful death of the body on the cross," concluded Ruth.

"And then," she went on, "Dr. Keil said the text showed that 'when Jesus ended these sayings, the people were astonished at his doctrine, for he taught them as one having authority and not as the scribes.' And no wonder! It was a new doctrine in the world. No one had heard it before. The people of the world are still 'astonished at his doctrine.' They have for over eighteen hundred years, in increasing numbers, been pretending to believe in and follow these doctrines.

"But no one has yet lived up to the Sermon on the Mount. No one has truly loved his enemies and lived literally the Golden Rule, much less the Diamond Rule. We in Aurora attempt it. We go as far as our selfish natures will permit us to go. We are making progress in banishing selfishness from our hearts.

"It is like a perfect sphere or square or point of a needle or a perfect clock or watch. There is no such thing. The clock must be regulated. The perfect needle point is approximated in the bee's sting. Perfect time is kept under God's laws in the revolutions of the earth. We can only initiate and hope in time to reach perfection.

"But we have here in the Aurora community the rules of perfection. We try to follow them. We hope to banish selfishness entirely, to live the law of love, which tells us to place our brother's or our sister's good on an equality with and even above our own. 'Our great task,' said Dr. Keil, 'is to Christianize Christianity. Let us each day devoutly pray for more light to see and greater strength to do the tasks set by the Master Teacher sent by God that men might have the perfect rules.' "

There was such earnestness and sincerity in the manner of Ruth, and her words carried such conviction, that Drusilla was moved to tears.

"My poor recital was so weak compared with the original in the words, voice and gestures of Dr. Keil that I only wish you might have heard the original, and might have lived with the people who are attempting to measure up to the high ideals of their leader," concluded Ruth.

"I am willing to cast my lot with them and to make a trial with your people of living up to those words," was the expressed reaction of Drusilla. "I may make a dismal failure, but I want to have a chance to try. It seems to me that in such an atmosphere the almost impossible attempt to live such a life any where else would be made possible and even easy there. I crave the chance to make the attempt. There is no other thing I want as much as that chance."

CHAPTER 26

OPPORTUNITY KNOCKS

WHEN Silas Hobson returned home from the shops that evening, he found Drusilla in a frame of mind that was new to him. She was in the state of one who has made a great discovery. She was anxious to tell about the life of the Aurora colony. She relayed to him in detail her talk with Ruth. She was for joining the colony forthwith, and getting the Cushmans to go with them.

Ruth said nothing to Amos about her talk with Drusilla. She was playing the part of a good sport, as she intended to do. She had learned by word and example from Dr. Keil that a promise was a promise, something to be kept and fulfilled to the letter. She would keep her promise. Amos must make his own decision. But she was hopeful. She knew Drusilla's mind, and she realized the dissatisfaction of Amos with the present situation.

A short time after this a brother of Silas Hobson who with a partner had a small general store in Portland was seized with a desire to go to the mines of eastern Oregon and Idaho, where there was great excitement over the discovery of gold. Benton W. Hobson, the brother, and his partner had been searching for a buyer of their business. They had not found one. They were determined to try their fortunes in the mines.

Finally they offered to sell the business, doing a flourishing trade in a growing section of Portland, for less than the invoice price, and take the notes of Amos and Silas for the amount, on long time.

"Opportunity is surely knocking at our doors in this offer," Silas urged. "We have a chance of being more than cogs in a wheel, to be our own men. We may become leaders in business. It is like a rainbow in a clear sky. In justice to ourselves and our families, we must grasp it; we must not pass it up; we would be recreant to our duties and trusts as husbands and fathers to refuse it."

This was an important matter under the head of unfinished business in the two families. Against the forcibly urged objections of Drusilla, and contrary to the secret hopes of Ruth, the store won over the colony. The two men convinced themselves that this was a case of a "time in the affairs of men which, taken at the flood, leads on to fortune."

Due to his experience in the trade of the colony in Bethel and Aurora, and what he had learned when he was employed in the store at Quincy, Amos was the better qualified of the two to give expert help in carrying on in the new line they took over as equal partners. The firm prospered. Hard work and youthful enthusiasm carried them fast. They were meeting their obligations and were able to maintain a better standard of living in their homes.

Another daughter came to the Cushmans to fill the place of little Rhoda. A son arrived at the home of the Hobsons. The hope of greater independence induced the partners to take on larger stocks, make more extended engagements, and employ additional clerks.

Portland was growing. Amos and Silas considered themselves justified in joining clubs and lodges, and they were soon supporting horses and buggies and taking their families and friends on trips. They were enjoying life.

Their prosperity attracted others. There was opposition. Stores were opened carrying the lines they majored in. Some of the new merchants had larger capital than Amos and Silas commanded, or greater credit, or were more reckless. The first department stores, in which an expanding list of articles might be had under one roof, were cutting into the trade of smaller concerns with fewer lines. Chain stores came, backed by greater purchasing power and more experienced buying methods. They were obliged to meet the competition of cut rates and bargain days of opposition stores.

That was time of "dog eat dog" in business.

"It will never be different," Amos admitted in a family council, "for it is the natural thing. Business is a game of 'every fellow for himself and the devil take the hindmost.' Our lodges and service clubs have high-flown words to sickly over the bluntness and brutality of it all, but the fact remains. The rule is, 'get yours while the getting is good,' or 'do the other fellow who would do you if he could, and do him first.' We may as well admit it, and accept the rules of the game and fight with our backs to the wall."

Silas admitted that they had "taken on too much steam," as he expressed it, and they must trim sail and cut corners, and work harder and put in longer hours. They agreed that they must "deal their cards close to the belly," as the numerous professional gamblers of those days were wont to say, and they might pull through. Thus far they had met all their installments.

So there was taking of stock all around, in their homes and in their store, but some of their creditors noticed this and became less liberal in their offerings, and more insistent upon prompt and frequent settlements. Amos and Silas walked the floor and spent sleepless nights. They had been proud of their prompt payments. They had discounted their bills. Now they must ask for extensions. They had not been obliged to explain. Now they spent a good deal of time in explaining.

"If we would work more and worry less," said Silas one morning, "we would get along better."

"I wish I could learn to do so," answered Amos, "but I fear I cannot get the habit of it. This is worse than farming in Yamhill, and it is worse than being a cog in a big wheel at the shops. I would be willing to go back to the farm or the job, but there is no way. We have got to fight it out or admit defeat and let the tail go with the hide, and I will never be ready for that, unless they hang up the sheriff's red flag in front of the store."

Amos and Silas admitted to one another that anything might happen. Suits were threatened, but they allowed their installments to lapse and paid the jobbers and wholesalers. They robbed Peter to pay Paul.

Something did happen. A fire in an adjoining store spread to their own in the night, and they woke up to see their property in ashes. Insurance rates had been high and they had cut down on this charge. They found themselves, after adjustment of their losses and payment of their bills, about where they were before becoming merchants. They had not enough left to meet the back installments on their homes.

CHAPTER 27

AT THE STATE FAIR

HENRY T. FINCK says in his last book, "My Adventures in the Golden Age of Music," which was his autobiography: "At the Salem State Fair the meals used to be wretched till an Aurora restaurant was started. It was a huge success from the start. It needed a regular circus tent to accommodate all who crowded in at mealtime; and nearly the whole Aurora colony, men, women and children, were in Salem for a week, cooking and serving meals."

The circus tent was used at first; but the Oregon State Fair management granted a continuous concession, the Aurora establishment was so well favored; and the colony people erected a large building on the grounds, with facilities for baking and for doing all the work of a first class restaurant. The main building still stands, removed a few hundred feet from its original location. In the final settlement of the colony's affairs, the dishes and other equipment were listed among the colony's assets.

It is remembered by a survivor that in the late sixties and the seventies about two hundred of the Aurora people went each fall to the fair. The members of the band were included, but they assisted in the restaurant work. There were twenty to twenty-five waiters, two meat cutters, and four to ten dishwashers. Sleeping places were provided for the women and girls in the main building, and the men slept in tents near by. The provisions were nearly all from the colony mills, gardens, farms, ranges and stores, so the revenues brought a neat net income annually to the com-

Colony restaurant building at Oregon State Fair as it appears now.

Refectory and speakers' stand at beautiful Aurora Park. Speakers
addressed 1,500 hearers seated in front. View taken several years
after dissolution of colony, showing neglect.

munity treasury, besides the money paid to the band and the prizes won on exhibits.

And State Fair week was one of the big things in the high tide of colony life. Attendance was a privilege that was passed around. One of the surviving members prizes his ticket which he has kept since 1873. The opening date was Monday, October 6th, and at that time the fair grounds property was owned by the Oregon State Agricultural Society. It did not come into possession of the state with the exhibitions under state control till nearly twenty years later, November 6, 1891.

The turn in the affairs of the Cushman and Hobson families that was forced by the fire came shortly before the fair of that year. Hannah had written to Ruth that she and Asa would be there in the capacity of helpers and ready to give first aid and nursing attention in case they were needed. She had suggested that their brother and sister and the Hobsons and their children attend. They would all be welcome guests of the colony people.

"In a body, and with bells," as Silas expressed it, the two families were on hand the day previous to the opening. Upon their arrival, Amos was eagerly urged to assist in the management of the restaurant, getting the supplies delivered and the public accommodated—at good wages— and Silas was prevailed upon to take charge of the supply wagons between Aurora and the city of Salem and the grounds. The crowds were unusually large; it was a rush week, and there was work for all the colony people who could be spared and for a number of outsiders whom they employed.

It was a glorious week for the two families. The Hobsons had not experienced anything like it. With all their work, the members of the colony and their visitors took time between meals and in the evenings to see the exhibits, including the side-shows. They had an open sesame to everything; were a favored and privileged crowd, on account of the large part they took in providing good food, and giving high class music for the major and minor activities. They took time, too, for visiting and dancing, and for singing their community songs.

The Cushman and Hobson children never forgot the gala days they enjoyed that week. They were made much over by the Aurora people and formed friendships, especially with the colony children, that were lifelong. The Cushman and Hobson families were taken home by the colony people after fair week was over and the restaurant closed and locked up for the season. Silas summed it all up like this:

"It was the treat of my life; to see everything at the fair, and enjoy the visit with the colony folks, and have all of us fed and lodged in a style we never dreamed of— and then to be paid good wages for merely having such a wonderful time—it is too much!"

But that was not all. The reader has been told of the colony custom, after a heavy piece of work had been finished, to celebrate the completion of it by some special relaxation. Often it was a hunting and fishing trip, or a picnic in the park, with music and singing and general jollification. The end of the annual State Fair was classed with such events. Among the forms of relaxation was a dance at "the hall" near Dr. Keil's house. Everybody danced. Especially the children. Dr. Keil danced with the little ones, as always on such occasions. He took all the tots under his protection and held high revel with them in ways that made them love him, as he loved them.

Ruth and Amos knew this custom, but it was a pleasing revelation to Drusilla and Silas. Drusilla exclaimed to Ruth the next day: "How can any one help feeling the love bordering on worship which all these people have for

Dr. Keil? My youngsters can talk of nothing else—they dreamed of Dr. Keil last night, and they were talking of the great time they had with him as soon as they were awake this morning."

Drusilla was for joining the colony that very day.

"Count my vote with the ayes," spoke up Silas.

"I am ready now and glad to make the decision. I say yes, with all my mind and all my soul and all my strength," Amos told Ruth, as his tears mingled with hers, tears of joy.

"In the words of the historic Ruth of 'the days when the judges ruled,' whose name meant friend, I say to the Ruth of my heart, my wife, my friend, and sweetheart of my youth, 'Whither thou goest I will go! and where thou lodgest I will lodge; thy people shall be my people, and thy God my God; where thou diest will I die, and there will I be buried.' I will change my name to Amoz, and be strong. I move to make it unanimous," Amos concluded.

"You have been strong always, and a burden bearer rather than a burden," Ruth protested, as they sealed their covenant with mutual signs of love.

Four names were that day added to the roll of members of the colony, the date and first signing of which was April 5th, 1866, and the original of which, with all the names signed, some in German and some in English, is in the big vault of the United States Court for the District of Oregon in the federal building in Portland.

One of the most marked of all the things noted in the life of the colony by the new members, Silas and Drusilla, was the gentleness and politeness of the members of the community, in every relation with one another, as well as with outsiders and strangers. During the first week of their membership, there was an illustration of this the memory of which remained with them.

The only head of a Jewish family in the colony was

Aaron Greenbaum. He was a loyal member, a believer in the principles of the community. Aaron frequently drove the team of Dr. Keil, "a mule team" of historic interest in this recital—the span that drew the plains hearse. Silas and Drusilla were attracted to the main road south of the big Keil house by an unusual racket that brought others to the scene. Queen and Kate were running away. They had been frightened and were beyond the control of the driver, excepting to keep them in the road on their wild career eastward down the hill past the house of the chairman of the board of trustees—the latter house still standing and in good repair. The chairman rushed toward the road as Aaron and Queen and Kate flew past.

"Guten morgen, Herr Präsident; it is a fine day," Aaron called to the chairman as he raised his hat and bowed in his customary greeting. Aaron, true to the colony spirit, could not think of forgetting his manners even while desperately sawing on the lines trying to stop the mules. He would have essayed the gesture and the bow and the word of greeting had he been sure he was to be dashed to his death for taking the time for them.

While that was an amusing episode in the sagas of colony life, and aroused the risibilities of the members in the frequent rehearsing of the true story of it, there was nothing of strangeness in the incident. Their very training taught members of the colony the rules of politeness. They caught the spirit of it as a matter of course whether to the manor born or coming into the community late in life. They felt politeness, breathed an atmosphere of gentleness of spirit.

Their good manners carried the colonists far in the esteem of their neighbors, and it made them a peculiar people in their dealings one with another. They would have missed their meals rather than forget their manners.

Queen and Kate pass into the limbo of forgetfulness

after this event. They headed the first and only covered wagon funeral procession that crossed the plains, were "a mule team" of the compact of 1866 reserved to Dr. Keil by the terms of that historic agreement, did good service all the days of their hybrid pilgrimage, from the end of their coltship till the curtain dropped on the colony stage. Dependable above the average of their tribe of the Missouri mules that helped conquer a continent and fight the wars of their country, and all "without pride of ancestry or hope of posterity," according to their kind, were Queen and Kate. They never ran away before or afterward, nor did they run far this time. Soon winded in their mad career, they plodded on their course as good mules should, after furnishing a thrill to half the people of the town.

By the usual law of natural selection that largely ruled in all such colonies, Silas soon had his place in the general merchandise store and Amos was given the work of finding markets for community products and looking after the deliveries and making necessary purchases. Houses were provided in the town for the two families, and they were eased into and oriented with the colony life as if they had been members from the beginning or had not broken off those relations.

Silas and Drusilla were to have other surprises. Politeness in colony life was not polish, nor assumed for outward show. It was felt. There was no quarreling; no bickering. No breath of scandal. No violent language, one to another. A survivor testifies that in all the time he spent at Bethel and Aurora, extending over a third of a century, he heard no harsh words of blame or abuse among the members. Can this be truthfully told of a like number of people who lived together as long in any other time or country?

CHAPTER 28

FACT AND FICTION

THE closing years of the life of the colony were quiet ones, marked by steady progress in material things and the usual routine of social activities and celebrations of the great days. All the members worked and all played. During that period Charles Nordhoff, historian, preparing his book, "The Communistic Societies of the United States," visited Bethel and Aurora. He related a number of things upon which, for some reason, he secured misinformation or "got the wrong slant"; for instance, that Dr. Keil in Pennsylvania "became a mystic and seems to have dealt in magnetism"; that "he professed to be the owner of a mysterious volume, written with human blood"; that near Pittsburgh "he gave himself out as a being to be worshiped, and later as one of the two witnesses in the Book of Revelation; and in this capacity he gave public notice that on a certain day, after a fast of forty days, he would be slain in the presence of his followers."

Men and women who knew and worked with Dr. Keil from his arrival at Pittsburgh till the day of his death declare that all these assertions are absolutely without foundation in fact. As to the beliefs of Dr. Keil and the members of the colony, Nordhoff was quite accurate in his statements. He found that among other things they held:

"That all government should be parental, to imitate the parental government of God.

"That societies should be formed upon the model of the family, having all interests and all property absolutely in common, and that all the members should labor for the general welfare and support, drawing the means of living from the general treasury.

"That, however, neither religion nor the harmony of nature teaches community in anything further than property; hence the family life is strictly maintained, and the Aurora Communists marry and are given in marriage and raise and train children precisely as do their neighbors. They reject absolutely all sexual irregularities, and inculcate marriage and support of the family relation as religious duties, as the outside world does. Each family has its own house.

"That Dr. Keil, president and preacher, holds the fundamental truth of Christianity to be, 'Love one another,' and interprets this in so broad and liberal a sense as requires a community of goods and effects.

"That while every man is expected to labor for the general good, there are no established hours of work, nor is any one compelled to labor at any special pursuit.

"That each workshop has its foreman, who comes by natural selection; the fittest man comes to the front. But it is a principle of their polity that men shall not be confined to one kind of labor. In some seasons a good many work on farms, at others most of them work in the shops."

"Dr. Keil, the president," said Nordhoff, "was the only person with whom I came in contact who was not very neat," and added: "He walked over the orchard with me in an untidy pair of carpet slippers."

Surviving members, themselves neat and good judges of neatness, cannot remember this as a conspicuous fault of Dr. Keil's, in many years of close association with him. Nordhoff related that he asked Dr. Keil about the 1872 division of the property:

"What, then, if you have divided all the property, will you do for the young people when they grow up?" (The property had not all been divided, and few, if any, of the

1872 deeds had been recorded and in the final division none of them was considered.)

Nordhoff reports Dr. Keil as replying:

"Dear me!—in the beginning we had nothing, now we have a good deal: where did it all come from? We earned and saved it. Very well; we are working just the same—we shall go on earning money and laying it by for those who are growing up; we shall have enough for all."

Nordhoff reported that Dr. Keil answered a question of his like this: "If one of our people wanted to train himself in some practical knowledge or skill for the service of the community, and if he were a proper person in stability of character and capacity, we would send him and support him while learning. This we have repeatedly done." Dr. Keil added that when such men returned they soon brought back more than the cost of their training. Nordhoff mentioned passing with Dr. Keil by the cemetery where several of the latter's children were buried, when the colony leader said:

"Here lie my children. One after another I laid them here. It was hard to bear; but now I can thank God for that too. He gave them, and I thanked Him; He took them, and now I can thank Him too. To bear all that comes upon us in silence, in quiet without noise, or outcry, or excitement, or useless repining—this is to be a man, and that can we do only with God's help."

Among Nordhoff's conclusions are these words: "Nor can it be safely asserted that there is no higher future for Aurora. If, when he (Dr. Keil) dies, the presidency should fall into the hands of a person who, with tact enough to keep the people together, should have intellectual culture enough to desire to lift them to a higher plane of living, I can see nothing to prevent his success. The difficulty is that Dr. Keil's system produces no such man. Moses was brought up at Pharaoh's court, and not among the Israelites whom he liberated, and who made his whole life miserable for him."

CHAPTER 29

"FEARS SHALL BE IN THE WAY"

NORDHOFF, casual visitor, and more or less unreliable reporter of what he found in his brief stay, could not have known what was taking place in the minds of the leaders of the colony. Dr. Keil foresaw the not distant finish of his earthly pilgrimage. The state of his health more than the approach of the end of his scripturally allotted time forewarned him. It is known that he talked of this with his intimates among the trustees. He counseled with the chairman of the board about the winding up of his earthly affairs in case he should be called to make the journey into the "country from whose bourne no traveler has yet returned."

He talked with Prof. Wolff. That staunch advocate of the community life wished to see the adventure carried on indefinitely. He had been pressing his ideas upon the leader for several years, so urgently as to cause a rift in the friendship of the two men, which was noted by the more observing among the colony members, and was resented by some of them who held their beloved leader in such affectionate regard as to border upon reverence, placed him on a plane above the common frailties of ordinary men, all but worshiped him as a person endowed with attributes of divinity.

"It is our duty," admonished Prof. Wolff, in urging his ideas upon Dr. Keil, "to prepare in advance for what the future must bring to all of us. We cannot live forever. Some of us may not last out this year. What if your time should come tomorrow? What, then, would happen to these people who have for years, some of them their whole lives, accustomed themselves to depend entirely upon your word in all difficulties?"

"I have thought of this," answered Dr. Keil, "and I have made provisions. Their lands and shops and homes and other properties were for the most part divided among them and deeded to them in 1872, and the rest would be easy to settle."

"By no means," protested Prof. Wolff. "A settlement would have to be made between the people here and those at Bethel. And the 1872 division would not stand, excepting with general or perhaps unanimous consent, and everything might be in an endless tangle, with law suits that would drag on for years and take all or a large part of the property from the people to whom it rightfully belongs."

Prof. Wolff had participated in the discussions that led to the agreement of April 5, 1866, when Dr. Keil covenanted with the trustees to transfer all the property to them, with the condition that they accept the trust and take it over and administer it as it had been administered by himself, to which they agreed. But that compact had not been carried out, excepting in its ratification by the signing of all the members.

"This was merely a gesture put in writing," Prof. Wolff told Dr. Keil, "giving recorded evidence of a trusteeship that already existed and had been a fact since the beginnings at Bethel; a trusteeship the faithful performance of which the court will decree in case of your death, and that will nullify and make invalid and of no effect every one of the 1872 deeds and transfers, insofar as this shall be necessary in apportioning all the colony property in both Missouri and Oregon. The trustees will be so ordered and directed by the court. They will have the duty of going back to the first act at Bethel and tracing the whole course of the community's life, in which all members acquired rights according as they labored or spent time in the community. It will all hinge on the fundamental rule, 'FROM EVERY MAN ACCORDING TO HIS CAPACITY TO EVERY MAN ACCORDING TO HIS NEEDS.' The least departure, on account of any deed or act or covenant or agreement, would be a violation of the rules of equity."

"I know this well," answered Dr. Keil. "It is in the nature of a promise given that it must be a promise performed, which alike is a fundamental rule with us—which we must defend to the uttermost, and without question. I expected to fully carry out the covenant made April 5, 1866. I proceeded to do this. It was my greatest wish. I only left the task uncompleted when I saw the alarm among the members."

"Yes, I know," said Prof. Wolff. "They feared they might be obliged to follow other leadership. 'After Dr. Keil, the deluge,' they reasoned. They had no one among them they were willing to trust, and much less would they have followed any outsider. That was beautiful. It was Utopia, Icaria. But who is to say it was not their weakness as well their strength? Who is to say that at your death it may not vanish into just another Utopian or Icarian dream, and thus go to prove again the impossibility of a long continuance of any perfect social system in a faulty world made up of people who ever are to be but never are blessed, because of the imperfections of their poor human nature?"

"I was powerless," sighed Dr. Keil. "I could organize and direct and control, but I could not prepare to perpetuate. My people themselves, wishing to have their society persist, made it impossible, by this very anxiety, to work out the rules and lay the only foundations of perpetuity."

"I understand, but I understood before, when my counsel was suspicioned and repudiated, and you and I were estranged largely without the fault of either of us," said Prof. Wolff. "They wanted you to lead. They would have none other. They did not want you supplanted. They had done well under your guidance. They reasoned that they might do ill under another leader. They had prospered. They thought they were secure. They were like the German proverb: 'Wen es zu wohl mit ein esal gahet, dan gehet er auf das eis danzen.' (When it goes too well with a donkey, then he goes onto the ice to dance.)

"They have been dancing on the ice, and it is thin ice and may break through and let them down. This can end in but one thing, and that is the dissolution of the colony and the distribution among the members of all the property, here and at Bethel, in the event of your death. Your end makes the colony's end. You will die together."

Dr. Keil said he feared that, and it made him sad, filled his days with heavy thoughts and robbed his nights of sleep.

"But," he added, "the court will act according to my wish, too. I want for members of my family only that to which they are entitled as members of the community. That is what I meant when I signed the agreement. That is what my wife meant when she signed it. We have talked this over between us, many times, though we have made no outward sign. We want no fears now and no repining hereafter on the part of our people we have loved and trusted and who have loved and trusted us all too much, perhaps, for their own good."

The leader and the teacher, who had been estranged, talked long. They reviewed their discussions at Bethel. Prof. Wolff reminded Dr. Keil, without arousing resentment, that if they could have counseled together more, in the early days of the community life at Aurora, they might have laid sure foundations of its perpetuity, for which both of them were concerned.

Prof. Wolff recited the fact that he had all along been for a greater stress upon the things that would have made for independence among all the members, so that they would be able and willing to carry on—more individuality and less satisfaction with the status quo. Larger undertakings in industrial life; more workers, even though many of them be hired workers at first and even permanently. More training for leadership in every department. More foremen and fewer followers. He reminded the good doctor—"the old doctor," as the colony members had begun to denominate him affectionately in conversations one with another or in groups—he reminded him that his own counsel, as he remembered, had been from the first for a greater stress upon higher education for the children of the colony, that they might have a keener pride in the finer things of life and thus knit them closer and more permanently to the community.

"I have dreamed, as you know," he told Dr. Keil, "of an Aurora that would lead in industries, in institutions of outlook and helpfulness, in all things, so that no one would think of going out into the world, because each one would have found his best opportunities and his greatest pride and satisfaction here. We could have made Aurora a Mecca for students everywhere looking for perfection or near perfection in the social order, an Athenian agora where might be discussed the problems of the ages, an idyllic dream place working out the questions of the future in the relations of all the members of the teeming and increasing individuals and societies of the human race. "It is not too late now, good doctor," he said, "if you will but give the word, and work to the ends you yourself now clearly see are wholly right, and for the lack of the attainment of which your own dreams will vanish into thin air with the flight of your spirit."

Dr. Keil was not unconvinced. His eyes flashed with the

fire of the crusader, with the look which some who had seen him in the periods of his greatest vigor and power mistook for an evidence of fanaticism. Had he lived, there would at least have been added chapters to the story. Who can say what chapters? But Dr. Keil unexpectedly died on December 30th, 1877, the next day but one before the beginning of a new year.

Followed the darkest days in the history of the community. The news cast a spell over its people that no words can describe. It was like an unexpected and sudden convulsion of nature, a total eclipse leaving the world in darkness, an earthquake seeming to cut the solid ground from under their very feet. Dr. Keil's taking off had an effect upon his followers something like that experienced by the people of the United States on receiving the news of the assassination of Abraham Lincoln, the chiefest of the martyrs of the struggle between the North and the South. Business was suspended. Strong men wept. Women cried out in their despair. In the words of the ancient preacher, it was as "In the day when the keepers of the house shall tremble, and the strong men shall bow themselves, and the grinders cease because they are few, and those that look out of the windows be darkened. And the doors shall be shut in the streets, when the sound of the grinding is low, and he shall rise up at the voice of the bird, and all the daughters of music shall be brought low; also when they shall be afraid of that which is high, and fears shall be in the way, and the almond tree shall flourish, and the grasshopper shall be a burden, and desire shall fail; because man goeth to his long home, and the mourners go about the streets: Or ever the silver cord be loosed, or the golden bowl be broken, or the pitcher be broken at the fountain, or the wheel be broken at the cistern. Then shall the dust return to the earth as it was; and the spirit shall return unto God who gave it."

Only the president of the board of trustees and some of his intimates had been informed by Dr. Keil of the seriousness of his last sickness. Even they and the leader himself hoped for early recovery. The greater was the shock for the suddenness of it. The first thoughts among the colony people were of their irreparable loss. They had no room for any other. From the time of the spreading of the dread news till the afternoon of the next day after the New Year his people spoke in whispers and went about as it were treading upon holy ground.

Then they all followed the body of their beloved leader to the family cemetery near the church and the park and reverently laid it to rest. Their neighbors from every direction came. The band headed the solemn procession with the music it had used on every such occasion. The Aurora flag designed by the leader was carried at half mast. The militia company in uniform marched. At the grave side Andrew Giesy took charge, in the place of the leader.

The people sang "Das Grab ist tief und stille" ("The Grave is Deep and Silent"), as they had not sung or had occasion to sing it before. It was as Dr. Keil himself would have ordered it, for this song, composed for the occasion of the funeral of Willie Keil, his son, whose body had led the covered wagon train of 1855 across the plains—composed and set to music by Dr. Keil himself—had been used since in every colony burial service, and was to continue long after community life was over. It is still used there, though it was never put into printed form till now. Its words and music were carried in the minds and hearts of the Aurora people. They are indelibly stamped in the memories of the survivors of colony times, and are written on the tablets of recollection by some of their children and children's children who have come after them.

CHAPTER 30

FOLLOWING the death of their beloved leader, the colony people were stunned into a state of inaction. Days and weeks passed in indecision as to what should be done next. After this period of depressing doldrums, Andrew Giesy began the Sunday services in the church, a little later alternating with Frederick Keil, son of the dead leader, who had been studying for the ministry. Andrew Giesy had been left in Dr. Keil's place as the leader at Bethel, but he had no ambition to attempt to fully assume the functions of Dr. Keil at Aurora. There was no one who could fill that place.

John Giesy was appointed administrator of the estate of Dr. Keil in the probate court of Marion County, and an appraisement was made, but the proceedings stopped there in this case. They were not resumed, excepting to make a final settlement and dismiss the matter, by referring the adjudication of the whole cause to the United States court. It was found that the settlement would have to be made in the federal tribunal and under a decree on a bill in equity, owing to the fact that the property was located in two states, and because of the intricate matters that would require adjustment and adjudication, the unraveling of a much tangled skein of circumstances and rights, covering a period of over thirty-three years till the death of the founder, and about thirty-seven years to the time of the beginning of the proceedings praying for the judicial arbitrament.

The trustees carried on the business affairs of the colony.

Even new members were taken in, signing the articles of agreement of April 5th, 1866. Signatures were attached throughout the years 1878 and 1879. In 1880 no new names were signed. It had been decided to wind up the affairs of the Aurora community and that at Bethel.

But it was not until March 15, 1881, more than three years after the death of Dr. Keil, that the bill in equity asking for the dissolution of the colony in the two states, and the distribution of the property, was filed. The case in Marion County was No. 829; in the U. S. Court, 752.

The Articles of Agreement, signed by all the members of the colony at Aurora read as follows:

Whereas Dr. William Keil at Aurora Mills in the County of Marion and State of Oregon has made with us the undersigned trustees and aldermen of the community or cooperative association at Aurora Mills the annexed agreement:

Therefore, in virtue of the authority vested in us, and in execution of our trust, we, the said trustees and aldermen, of the first part, do herewith covenant and agree to and with the undersigned members of the Aurora community or cooperative association, of the second part, in consideration of the covenants hereinafter contained:

1. That all persons, with or without families, so long as they remain in said community, shall receive free lodging, board, clothing and washing and in case of sickness free medical attendance, medicines and nursing.

2. That there shall exist no preference in disposing of the necessaries of life; on the contrary, all shall be treated alike, as far as circumstances allow it, and there shall be made no discrimination on that account between the first and last members of the community.

3. That all taxes and necessary expenses, to which the single members may be subjected, shall promptly be paid for them.

4. That all members of the community shall be free of expenses with reference to church and school purposes.

5. That all sick, disabled or indigent persons, *outside the com-*

munity, who ask and merit our assistance, shall be relieved, as far as the means of our community can afford it.

6. That all members of the community who, by accident, sickness or old age, may become disabled or incapable to perform their daily labor any more, shall receive their substance and all other necessary accommodations out of the means of the whole community for the remaining part of their natural life, provided that they remain in the community, but not otherwise. In like manner, proper care will be taken for the surviving widow and orphan children of a deceased member, as long as they remain in the community.

7. That every member of the Aurora community shall in no wise be restrained in the full enjoyment of his personal rights as a citizen of the United States, and therefore, if he chooses to dissolve his connection with the said community, he is at full liberty to do so, without objection of any one, provided, that before his leaving he deliver up to the trustees all the implements, tools and other property of the community which have been confided to him in particular. As for the rest, the understanding is, that the enjoyment of the above enumerated benefits and privileges during his membership is mutually regarded as a full compensation of all his labor for the community, and that he has no right to claim any other payment for his labor, except the sum of 25 dollars, which every person who has stayed one or more years in the Aurora community shall receive before his leaving as extra compensation or present from said community.

8. That every person joining the Aurora community must be full 21 years of age and of good moral character, that is, he must conduct himself in all his dealings with honesty, faithfulness and diligence; besides, he must faithfully perform the daily labor assigned to him by the trustees or foremen of the community according to his trade or ability, and if a work of common interest is to be done, whereby more as (than) the usual hands are necessary, then every member or shopman is bound to follow the call for temporary help of the trustees or foremen. In particular, every member must take good care of the tools and implements confided to him and not suffer or allow that any of them should be injured or wasted.

9. That whereas the seven trustees are made responsible for the proper management of all business branches in the community, therefore every member is bound to follow their advice or direction; and in case of difficulties or disputes among the single members, the board of trustees has to decide the matter amicably; and if a member should refuse to obey or to acknowledge their decisions or admonitions, then the trustees shall have a right to exclude such member from the community. Furthermore, the trustees have the right to appoint a member as treasurer of all the income of the community, and every foreman or single member who receives money belonging to the community is bound to make a monthly settlement of his account with the appointed treasurer, and pay over all moneys in their hands.

10. That no person is allowed to join the Aurora community, by subscribing his name to this agreement, who has not previously considered maturely the importance and consequences of this step, and who does not sincerely approve all the regulations and principles laid down in this agreement.

And the undersigned parties of the second part, in consideration of the covenants on the part of the first party, do herewith covenant and agree to and with the said trustees and aldermen of the first party, that they accept freely and without persuasion, fear or compulsion of any one, the membership of the Aurora community or cooperative association, and that they pledge themselves to comply faithfully with all and singular the regulations and conditions contained in this agreement, as long as they remain in the Aurora community. In witness whereof we have hereunto set our hands and seals this 5th day of April, 1866.

This document was signed by John Giesy, Samuel Miller, Jacob König, Fr. Scholl, Andrew Vogt, Adam Steinbock and G. Frederich Koch, trustees. On that date and other dates of that year, and the following years, names of all the qualified members of the colony were signed. A number signed "with this condition, to act under Dr. Keil's control." Several others, "Dr. Keil's control." Dr. Keil himself and his wife signed it May 23, 1868.

CHAPTER 31

THE BILL IN EQUITY

THE Bill in Equity in the United States Court for the District of Oregon, dated March 15, 1881, follows, the attorney for the complainants being W. H. Effinger, Portland, Oregon, the complainants the members of the colony at Aurora, Oregon, and the defendants the members of the colony at Bethel, Missouri; and there are no departures excepting the elimination of the legal verbiage and some omissions for the sake of brevity:

In the year 1845 (should be 1844) in the town of Bethel in the State of Missouri some of the complainants with the defendants and others by mutual and common consent and agreement, associated themselves together in a cooperative community and in a species of general partnership: at the time they selected as their head man the late Dr. Wm. Keil who controlled and directed their operations: the business upon which they entered was of general and varied character. They bought land for the purposes of cultivation and improvement, erected houses, stores and shops, nurtured and developed the manual arts and dealt and traded in real and personal property of various kinds. The agreement between them was not at the time reduced to writing, nor were the terms and conditions upon which their association was formed ever accurately or exactly fixed. They took and held titles now in one name and again in another—but always held everything in common. Their work and its fruits, their dealing and its results, were carried into one general fund—though no proper account thereof was ever kept, and from this common source each and every member of the association drew as he or she had need, for keep, maintenance and support.

They were of common nationality, were friends, and many of

them of kindred blood. They had faith in each other and implicit trust in their chosen leader—so that they never felt obliged to reduce to writing their contract and agreement, nor to keep—as in ordinary business—correct books of account.

At the time this association was organized many of its members brought in money or other property—withal a goodly number brought nothing—but whether they came full or empty handed they were all put upon a common basis and worked as equal sharers to a common end. From time to time the association drew to itself accessions, until it grew in numbers, and by prudent and careful management it gradually gained considerable property, which has always been held in trust for the benefit of all.

Inasmuch as the character of this association was and has been so much out of the usual and ordinary course of business transactions, it is necessary for them to trace their history more circumstantially than otherwise it would be.

As the association enlarged and its property increased, many of its members conceived the idea of planting a branch somewhere upon the Pacific Coast, and ultimately, in the year 1856, it was determined to locate in the State of Oregon. By this time the community at Bethel owned property in amount about $100,000, and as members made up their minds to come here they were supplied not alone with outfits but also with such money as was necessary, so that in the year last named a number came from Bethel and the counties of Marion and Clackamas were here selected and lands bought.

The land bought in this state was conveyed to Dr. Keil, who carried on in his own name all the external business of the society for some years. Subsequently he placed the control and management of personal property in the name of "Wm. Keil & Co.," committing the direct management thereof to a number of members selected by himself. The land and all other property bought or acquired here was paid for out of the funds belonging to the association or partnership, and the real estate so bought has been made cultivable and has been improved by buildings and otherwise entirely by the work and labor of members of the community.

The association which located here for convenience we will

hereafter designate as the "Aurora Community" and that at Bethel as the "Bethel Community."

They have prospered here in Oregon. They have built up the town of Aurora, have a store containing general merchandise, and various shops, and have improved their lands.

Up to the 5th of April, 1866, there had never been any written articles of association between them, nor between them and Dr. Keil, but on that day Dr. Keil prepared or caused to be prepared a paper in writing as follows:

"This agreement made this 5th day of April, 1866, between Dr. Wm. Keil at Aurora Mills, Marion County, Oregon, of the first part, and Samuel Miller, Jacob Köenig, John Giesy, Fred Scholl, Andrew Vogt, Adam Steinbach and Fred Koch, trustees and aldermen of the Aurora community or cooperative association of the second part, witnesseth: That the said Dr. Wm. Keil, in consideration of the covenants of the party of the second part, does covenant and agree to and with the above named trustees and aldermen, to convey and transfer to them all of his real and personal estates situated in the counties of Marion and Clackamas, to-wit: all and singular his lands, dwelling houses, grist and saw mills, stores, stage restaurant, workshops, livestock, farming implements, tools, and other appurtenances thereunto belonging, with the only exception of his two dwelling houses, garden AND A MULE TEAM; all in accordance with an inventory to be taken up of the property thus entrusted to them; to have and to hold the same under the following conditions: 1. That they keep all the properties thus entrusted to them in as good condition as they receive them. 2. That they make no burdening debts thereon. 3. That they pay all state and county taxes for persons and said property. 4. That they use all the income and net proceeds of the whole property with particular care to the sustenance and comfort of the families and persons who constitute the Aurora community. 5. That they take care of the erection of necessary buildings for families, workshops and machinery. But if the income should not be sufficient for such purposes, they must limit themselves to the preservation of the property they have received and act in all things in the same provident sense and manner as the party of the first part has done up to the present time. And the parties of the second part, in consideration of the covenants of the party of the first part do for themselves and in the name of the Aurora community gratefully accept the munificent gift thus conferred on them, and pledge themselves to comply with all the conditions under which the administration of said property is confided to them, to the best of their ability, especially in following the praiseworthy example which is set them by their beloved leader and protector"—

Which paper was signed and sealed by all the parties named in the first part thereof, and in the presence of witnesses.

On the day the said paper was made, Dr. Keil caused to be prepared another agreement setting out the terms and conditions upon which the property should be used by the persons designated as "trustees or aldermen" for the community—the same to be signed by all the members. This paper was so signed, though a goodly number signed upon the express condition that they were still to be under the leadership of Dr. Keil, though he himself signed it. There never was conveyed to said persons designated as "trustees" any of the said realty, so that the business of the community went on practically as before, until in the year 1872, Dr. Keil distributed to various members of the association real and personal property—the title to which he had continuously held. At this distribution a large amount of property was divided, and each distributee gave to Dr. Keil a receipt on account of property "held by Dr. Keil for the Aurora community." Though a large property real and personal was thus distributed in 1872, a considerable amount remained undistributed and now so remains.

Although it was the purpose of Dr. Keil to make a second and final distribution of the remaining property, he did not do so, but held the same until the 30th of December, 1877, at which time after a short illness he departed this life. The suddenness of his taking off is the sole and only reason why he did not make provision by will or otherwise for the division of the property held by him to those thereunto entitled. Dr. Keil died intestate and left surviving him as his only heirs at law his widow, Mrs. Louise Keil, Dr. August Keil, Frederick and Emanuel.

Shortly after his death it was necessary that letters of administration should be taken, whereupon John Giesy, at the request of the heirs and his fellow members of the community, applied for such letters, which were issued by the probate court of the county of Marion. Dr. August Keil then being a resident of Missouri, the widow and the two sons, Emanuel and Frederick made formal renunciation of their right, requested the appointment of the said John Giesy, and in addition declared upon solemn oath that the property, real and personal, owned by Dr. Keil was really and in truth held by him in trust for the sole benefit of the members of the Aurora community. Subsequently Mrs. Louise Keil died, so that there were now no legal heirs to Dr. Keil save his three sons before named. Prior, however, to Mrs. Keil's death she and her sons Frederick and Emanuel made and executed an agreement with Samuel Miller, John Giesy, Wm. Fry, Stephen Smith, Henry Ehlen, George Kraus and Henry Will, whereby, after reciting that the Dr. held all property in his name for the members of the community, it was agreed that the seven parties last named act as managers and control the entire property left by Dr. Keil, whether held in his individual name or in the name of "Wm. Keil & Co." Later, in the month of February on the 19th day, Dr. August Keil, then being in this state, he, in order to enable the members of the community to acquire the property of which his father died seized and possessed, released and conveyed unto the afore-named seven managers, for the benefit of the members of the community, and unto his mother and Frederick and Emanuel, his two brothers, all of his right, title and interest to and in the entire estate held by his father . . . and subsequently, along with his wife, he made another and confirmatory deed of the same property to the same grantees, . . . and Mrs. Keil having since died Frederick and Emanuel are the only heirs at law of Dr. Wm. Keil. At the time of Dr. Keil's death he was seized of the following realty: (Long list, omitted.) The managers before named have continuously from their appointment acted as such managers, except that in August, 1879, Samuel Miller resigned and Israel Snyder was elected in his place, who has since acted.

It is further shown that though they were here in Oregon there had always existed between the Bethel community and the Aurora community a community of ownership—that is, equitable ownership and interest—in the property owned in both states; that the Aurora community with the Bethel community owned in common the property held in the two states. So that after the death of Dr. Keil, and when it became desirable to divide the property and distribute the same, it was first requisite to have a separation between the two communities. To this end this community was called into a general meeting and duly elected Samuel Miller, Henry Will and Stephen Smith as a committee of three to visit the State of Missouri and to agree with some similar committee from the Bethel community upon the terms of separation. In order to empower the three said persons to accomplish this work of dividing the two communities and segregating to them their respective shares of the whole property, the members of the Aurora community, all of them save the chosen three, signed a power of attorney and delivered it to the said Samuel Miller, Henry Will and Stephen Smith, by which they were authorized to divide the joint property between the two communities. Shortly after this was done here, the Bethel community by a paper or letter of attorney of the same import, appointed Philip Miller, Philip Steinbach, John Shafer, John G. Bauer and Henry Will as their attorneys in fact to act with the attorneys in fact appointed by the Aurora community, so that on the 20th of June, 1879, the attorneys in fact representing respectively the two communities met and agreed upon a plan and basis of agreement, which was reduced to writing, signed, sealed, witnessed and acknowledged. That by this agreement it was agreed that the Aurora community should have and retain all the real and personal property then and now owned in Oregon, and that in addition thereto the Bethel community should convey to the Aurora community town lots in Shelby County, Missouri, of the appraised value of $7601.00; real estate in Adair County, Missouri, of the appraised value of $2790.00; real estate in Shelby County of the appraised value of $5836.25, and in cash and notes $887.85 —of the aggregate value of $17,115.10—which said conveyances and transfers were made. (Over $20,000 was realized by the Aurora community from the property thus transferred.)

The committee of managers as before named were directed to find out and report some plan by which the real and personal property could be equitably distributed among all the members of the community. They have encountered almost unsurmountable difficulties in reaching any conclusion. They have, however, reported a plan and method of division, in the carrying out of which their attorney, W. H. Effinger, is under obligation to represent the interest of all. They show the community is indebted to various persons and on various accounts in about the sum of $30,000, and inasmuch as some of the members of the community have already had repaid to them the money originally brought into the community, while some have not yet been so repaid, it has been thought advisable that before any distribution as such should be attempted, there should be reserved in property and in money enough to pay the entire indebtedness, and also to repay or to return—but without interest—to each of the members who brought in money or its equivalent the amount so brought in.

Along with the plan of division to be suggested, there are brought in the books and papers showing the amount and kind of property heretofore distributed and the list of distributees, and while this in one view makes a distribution, now, more difficult than it would be were the whole property still owned jointly, yet the books and papers, examined along with the plan suggested, will make it appear that the committee and the members of the community have only sought, and by faithful and conscientious work, to have a fair and equitable allotment of said property to each and every member of this community.

They have already converted into money some of the realty assigned to them in Missouri, and they are selling the rest as fast as possible; they have in the plan recommended by their committee made provision for the debts of the community and for the repayment of amounts originally brought in by members and unpaid— there may remain a small proportion of property which may be sold and the proceeds applied to such members as *may seem to have received less than some of their fellow members*.

The members of the Aurora community now show the division recommended by the committee, remarking that to some is allotted realty and to others personality—the description having been furnished by a surveyor who attended the committee as they were engaged in assigning the lands and personality; families or groups being directed to take—that being the desire of the members.

[Here follows a list of the selections. Some were allotted land; some land or money; some land and money; most retaining live stock and implements—but in numerous cases such being taken from one group and given to another.]

The committee now reports that they have made distribution of all the real and personal property which in the judgment of the members ought to be divided.

They show that in addition to all the property reported for division there is real and personal property left over which they ask direction to sell, and to apply the proceeds to pay the debts of the community, and to the return or repayment of the amounts originally brought into the community by members—that is, to all such members as have not yet been so repaid, and that the committee shall have the power to apply whatever amount shall remain to such members as shall seem to have received smaller shares than their fellows—or if none such there be—then to those whose *need* shall seem greatest.

[Here follows a list of the undivided property, including grist and saw mill, drug store, etc., etc., and wares and merchandise in their store, kitchen and household property IN STATE FAIR GROUNDS RESTAURANT, Aurora restaurant, etc., etc.]

It is shown that there will be ample for paying all debts and repaying originally contributed funds, with a balance left over to be divided as asked.

It was shown that the bill in equity had been read in the presence of all members of the community, and explained to them, and that they had selected one member, C. H. Ehlen, to verify it, reserving only the right, before final decree, of any member to be heard, in case he should so desire. (There was not a single objection urged.) It was shown also that the Bethel and Aurora communities had mutually released each other from all further claims.

A decree was asked in this *friendly* suit adjudging and pronouncing that the late Dr. Wm. Keil held all real and personal property in trust "for the sole use, benefit and behoof" of the two communities, also that no charge be made against the Bethel community for their portion of the costs of the proceedings, the Aurora community assuming the whole thereof. Also, that the decree ratify all the agreements and engagements made in the division of the property; also that it dissolve the community and partnership; also that deeds be issued according to the division.

There were three decrees, by Judge M. P. Deady. The settlement or adjustment was declared a just and equitable one and it was ratified and confirmed. Dr. Keil was declared to have held all the property in trust for the sole benefit, use and behoof of all the members of the two communities; and the same applied to all the property in whatever name it was held; that deeds be made by Emanuel and Frederick Keil, legal owners of all the property of the late Dr. Wm. Keil, and that the managers report under oath a full account of their doings since the death of Dr. Keil. The first decree was dated July 27, 1881.

The second decree was dated September 19, 1881, accepting and approving the report of the trustees and managers, John Giesy, George Kraus, William Fry, E. H. Ehlen, Israel Snyder, Stephen Smith and Henry Will, and they were directed to divide the surplus funds "in such manner as in their judgment will tend to equalize the shares of each—having regard to . . . errors or mistakes . . . and also the loss and depreciation of any shares, or from failures of crops or any other cause whatever. . . . Emanuel and Frederick Keil to receive any residue or balance of any land, by virtue of being heirs of Wm. Keil; the shares now allotted to them being only such as they are authorized to take in right of their membership."

The third and final decree, made on January 22, 1883, declared that the report of the committee or trustees was "in all things ratified, confirmed and approved," and the distribution of the assets of the Aurora community "declared to be a just and final settlement of the affairs of said community."

In the museum of the Oregon Historical Society, Portland, is a handsome sterling silver bowl, beautifully engraved: "Wise in counsel, just in judgment and fearless in administration. To Hon. Matthew P. Deady, from the Aurora Community, September 17, 1881, Aurora, Oregon." The reader will note that this was after the first decree and notice of the dissolution. The bowl was given by Dr. Henderson P. Deady, a son of the Judge, on November 23, 1932.

In effect, the gift is now owned by the people of Oregon. It is a fitting symbol of the breaking of new ground in judicial procedure in America, if not in the world, by a man capable of thus setting a precedent that may in the fullness of time prove epochal.

CHAPTER 32

ON THEIR OWN

IN THE first decree, the reader has noted, time was given for any member dissatisfied with the division to make formal complaint in writing to the clerk of the court, when his objections would be heard. On the first day of August, 1881, following immediately after the making of the first decree, the trustees of the colony notified all members that beginning on that date they were "on their own." At the same time they were all told that if any one had the least objection to the division of the property, he had the right to file it.

Not an objection was filed. There was no thought of making any complaint in court. All were satisfied. A few members thought they had been treated more liberally than they deserved, and made suggestions for payments out of the undivided funds left over, to some of their brothers and sisters who were more *needy* than themselves. It was a remarkable settlement of so intricate a matter having so many angles. Those people ran true to form. There had been no lawsuit in all their colony days, and there was none at the end, unless the reader may call the equitable adjudication of their affairs in the United States court a lawsuit—a necessary proceeding to fix their individual titles, the same as must be had at the death of any person holding property of any kind.

How did they make the distribution?

There was a long series of letters between the trustees at Aurora and those at Bethel. A chest full of this correspondence still exists. Number of days served in community life was the chief consideration in the division. This was the rule that made it appear, at the conclusion of the correspondence, and in the negotiations of the two committees with power to act, that there was due a balance from the Bethel community to that at Aurora, notwithstanding the large expenses of the covered wagon trains and the sea journeys by way of the Panama route, for most of the colonists who went from Bethel to Aurora had been members from the first or the early days; and the population was greater at Aurora than at Bethel after the arrival of the large train in 1863.

As indicated in the bill in equity, a surveyor attended the committee making the division, so that proper lines might be established in allotments of land. There were three members of the committee making the distribution, and they started each morning on their mounts, a deep bay, a white and what the colony members called a blue horse, and the three soon became known as the Uncle Sam trio— the "red, white and blue," as it had been with the Hobab quartette who were as eyes for the 1855 covered wagon train across the plains.

Families were grouped together in the allotments, according to their desires. Heads of families now owned their homes in fee simple, individually, severally, in their own names—though some of the deeds were not recorded for years. There was scarcely any difference of feeling in this status after the dissolution of the colony, for no one had ever been made to feel that he did not have full right to the home he occupied. But there was a great difference of feeling when it was realized that no longer could any member go to the colony store and get without question any necessary thing; any tool or implement required; or have his measure taken for a suit of clothes or a pair of boots or shoes, or a woman or girl take a dress pattern and have it worked up, or get any needed household or other article.

It was a strange feeling. They would have to bring money for what they bought at the general store, or establish a credit. The personal property as well as the land and the lots had all been distributed, or sold and the money distributed, though it was not until nearly eighteen months later that the final decree was made and the distribution of the assets of the colony "declared to be a just and final settlement of the affairs of said community." In that eighteen months there were opportunities to lend aid to those needing it in the way of divisions of money on hand, in conformance with the spirit of the second degree. The *need* was the main password, and the trustees observed it with the true old colony spirit of brotherhood.

No one was poor. Every one had a home or a roof over his head. Those who had shops generally owned also homes and small or large parcels of land. The general store after the division was owned in partnership by several members, most of whom also had homes and parcels of land. All had good credit, and they went on working and saving as before, and the community has been ever since a wealthy one, comparing in this respect more than favorably with the general run of town and rural neighborhoods in Oregon or elsewhere.

The colony spirit, however, was missed in several notable ways. The church was neglected and finally went to decay. One bell of the chimes is on the public school building. Another is used by the town's fire department. The other has been misplaced. The furniture is scattered. The fine park reverted to the forest primeval. Weeds choked the flowers. The men who devoted their labor of love to protecting and promoting the things of order and beauty turned to other employments. There was no more drilling of the militia company. The regular training of the bands fell into desuetude. The celebration of high days and holidays was neglected and then all but dropped.

The Aurora restaurant and hotel building has become a shell. For a long time the business was kept up by Jacob Giesy, who had charge in the colony days and to whom the property was given in the division. For several years, while practically the same colony help was available, this establishment maintained its popularity, and meals were served to railroad train passengers and business flourished. After Giesy was gathered to his fathers, new owners came, who could not command the services of the wonderful colony cooks and attendants, and business fell away. The good old days are a memory.

But the spirit of brotherhood and neighborliness remains among the survivors and their numerous descendants who make up a large part of the population of the town and the surrounding country, and this extends to the new comers. The welfare of each is the concern of all. Stark poverty is unknown there. Aurora has never had a severe unemployment problem. In all the concerns of life, there is mutual interest and quick response to the least call for aid—a heritage of the colony days that renders Aurora a singular community in the observance of the amenities of life, free from class distinctions or feelings of any kind. It is a model community as it was a model colony.

This chapter might be extended indefinitely with the sagas of community life; in relating incidents and giving illustrations of the observance of colony ideals, and the peculiar qualities of leadership of Dr. Keil. There are survivors who attribute the safety of the 1855 colony covered wagon train in its trip across the plains to his captainship and to his wise and kind treatment of the hostile Indian tribes. Some will tell you he prayed his people across. The reader of these pages knows of the plains hearse, of the music and singing. Perhaps prayer helped. That the colonists came through hundreds—thousands—of miles of danger at a time when many thousands turned back or feared to start is a historic fact, an incident akin to the sacred story of the escape of the three Israelites of old from the fiery furnace or that of Daniel in the lions' den. The reader may have his own guess concerning the modern miracle. The writer is convinced that the spell of superstition played the major part in turning the savage Indian mind from thoughts of scalps to the attitude of awe and respect that averted a massacre.

Dr. Keil was a praying man. But he was not accustomed to pray as the "hypocrites." He often talked of prayer, and quoted from the injunctions of the Master, like this: "And when ye pray, ye shall not be as hypocrites; for they love to stand and pray in the synagogues and in the corners of the streets, that they may be seen of men. Verily I say unto you, they have received their reward. (Their reward was from the advertising they got.) But thou, when thou prayest, enter into thine inner chamber, and having shut thy door, pray to thy Father who is in secret, and thy Father who seeth in secret shall recompense thee." Dr. Keil prayed both in public and in secret, and asked his followers to make their petitions not in the way of the hypocrites of old Judea.

William ("Cap") Miley, former county commissioner, was a very young man whose people had been with the colony from the first, at Bethel and Aurora, when in 1865 Dr. Keil called him and told him he was to make a dangerous trip. He had just celebrated his 21st birthday. The covered wagon train of that year was on the plains, under John Vogt as captain. They were bringing a large band of mules, and the leader had heard there was a better sale for these animals east of the mountains than in the Willamette Valley. Dr. Keil told young Miley that he was to set forth at once on Queen, of the celebrated mule team, and intercept the colony train at Fort Boise. When the young man pleaded inexperience, Dr. Keil said:

"Never mind; go. You will be safe. You carry my charge. You know I would not send you unless I knew you would get through."

Mr. Miley remembered throughout his life the flash of the eyes of the leader as he charged him, and the piercing look.

"The 'old doctor,' " he told the writer in his last years, "had a way of looking into your very soul, or clear through you; and no one ever questioned a request that was accompanied by that piercing and, as it were, prophetic gaze."

Young Miley did not fear after that. Cautioned by the leader that he was to talk little and give no confidences, but was to go on regardless of what he saw or heard, he mounted the faithful Queen and, with only a roll of two blankets, departed. The first day he reached Portland, the next The Dalles, by boat. In nine and a half days more in which Queen had carried him over 450 miles, he was at Fort Boise.

"You must stay with us; you must not go further," cautioned the captain of a company of United States troops on Burnt River, where there was a blacksmith shop. But the lone rider of the faithful mule pushed on, though the Indians had killed a man there the previous day. At the Farewell Bend he was ferried over the Snake River. Young Miley was warned of Indian danger at several points, but he recalled the assurance and the look of Dr. Keil in giving him his charge, and halted not, nor feared any harm.

He reached Fort Boise several days before the colony train arrived, and returned with it to the valley. They found no good market for the surplus mules east of the mountains, and so brought them through to Aurora. "Cap" Miley passed to his rest November 24, 1930, in his 87th year. He drove a three yoke ox team with the 1863 colony train, at nineteen. He was a member of the famous

Aurora band of the old days, playing the cornet, and being a wonderful performer in whistling parts.

A word should be added concerning the Diamond Rule as practiced at Bethel and Aurora: "Be kindly affectioned one to another with brotherly love; in honor preferring one another," given by Paul to the first church at Rome, which was the especial charge of the Apostle to the Gentiles. This the leader called the Diamond Rule of colony life, "in honor preferring one another." He enjoined its observance in all things; with respect to the trustees, the foremen, the preferred tasks. As to himself, it was not needed, for as a matter of course the members sought to give him the preference; but he practiced the rule, too, in all his contacts with his people. This built an Arcadia. Some readers will say an Arcadia is ephemeral, that it has not the qualities of permanence. If so, does it not lead to the conclusion that war is the natural state of society, brought down from the jungle? And that the tooth and the claw are the true signs manual of private dealings? And that the millennium or an approximation of it is as impossible as the building of a railroad to the planet Mars? And that the shibboleth of service above self is a business formula as far from possible realization in actual practice in this faulty world as the distance between the poles?

Does it not imply, too, that Oriental idealism approaches nearer to the highest precepts of the Founder of the Christian religion than does our own? For do we not see that Gandhi of India and Kagawa of Japan (and perhaps a baker's dozen others who are mostly of the so-called "heathen" nations), are among the very few who take literally—and live—the Sermon on the Mount? By no means overlooking Albert Schweitzer, the self-denying German scholar serving the lowly black people in French equatorial Africa.

Dwight L. Moody, the great preacher, was passing with a friend through an old time slum section of New York City.

"This is one place where Christianity has failed," remarked the friend.

"No," countered Moody, "this is a place where Christianity has never been tried."

Has Christianity been tried anywhere, for long, by a considerable body of people? Does the reader know of a larger or longer or more successful trial of it than was had in the Keil colony?

CHAPTER 33

THOUGHTS BY THE WAY

ON LABOR DAY, September 1, 1930, William Green, president of the American Federation of Labor, said at Syracuse, New York: "Those who manage and own industry, those who control and administer the affairs of government and those who work and are represented by men of their own choosing will be well nigh guilty of CRIMINAL NEGLIGENCE if they permit society to be intermittently exposed to the deadening and destroying effects of cyclical periods of unemployment. No serious effort has been made to deal with the problem of technological unemployment or to extend assistance to victims of mechanical displacement, and only by meeting this problem can the nation hope to maintain every human being as a consuming unit."

What will be the ultimate social order? Every person who asks this question is a Socialist. Every one who thinks socially, every man who wishes for his brother a state of well being equal to his own is a Socialist.

The first hypothesis of our Declaration of Independence is "that all men are created equal." They are not. They are as different as their finger prints; as their environment; as their training.

Former President Coolidge, not long before his death, in a syndicated article wrote: "Some day a sufficient organization, balancing productive output and consumptive need, will give us economic emancipation, but we have not yet perfected the formula." In another he wrote: "Our property must support our population." In speaking of the vast total of life insurance in the United States, he said: "It is a long step toward abolishing poverty."

One found him saying in his series: "The yearly damage from crime is estimated at $7,500,000,000. . . . This amount is more than half the entire agricultural production; . . . about eight per cent of the national income—goes on constantly, ought to be largely preventable, and represents a moral delinquency. . . . But law is not enough. We need a change of heart."

Also he said: "Considerable investigation is being made of the problem of old-age pensions. Some governments and some industries have adopted such a system and it appeals to your sympathies. Only the experimental state has been reached, so that its soundness has not been demonstrated. We are constantly trying to adopt reforms of such artificial nature as to save ourselves from suffering from the defects of human nature as it is now constituted. No doubt some of our efforts are helpful and the fact that we realize our deficiencies and are intent on remedying them is most encouraging. Our failures lie in attempting to reach the goal by some shortcut without really removing the cause of the difficulty. We try to reform ourselves on the outside when the only effective remedy is to reform ourselves on the inside. What a self-respecting people really needs is not a system of old-age pensions but a population made sufficiently self-controlled and well-disposed by the help of religion so that old-age pensions would be a superfluity. UNLESS REAL REFORM COMES FROM WITHIN, THE PROBLEM WILL NEVER BE SOLVED."

We heard eloquent words in the 1928 and 1932 national campaigns about equality of opportunity and the need of attaining it, with the inference that a favorable decision at the polls might lead toward that highly desir-

able goal. But economic emancipation, even in our rich nation, is far off, and the ideal demanding that our property
must support our population is a long way from attainment. Before life insurance could abolish poverty it would
have to cover every individual and be made compulsory.
How could this be done without assuring every one an income, and requiring the conservation of a portion of it, with
which to pay his or her premiums?

Equality of opportunity, in our country, and in every
other, is an iridescent dream. It is the pot of gold at the end
of the rainbow. In our machine age, we see the pitiful ranks
of the unemployed growing. We see men and women,
weary and heartworn, walking the streets and tramping
the highways in increasing numbers, seeking for something
to do that body and soul may be held together. Machines
and more and more and better and better and still better
machines, have set them adrift. The dollar urge of efficiency is weeding them out; elbowing gray hairs aside,
junking the helpless victims of "mechanical displacement."

Our prisons are overcrowded, with the tasks of modern
penology only half begun, and understood by one man in
a million—and that man all but hopeless against the mass
psychology harking back to the cruel, ignorant and musty
past. The money cost of it is appalling. But the cost in tears
of men, women and children bulks infinitely larger. Crime
is the cause of the world's greatest heartbreak. The innocent suffer with the guilty—far more than the guilty. The
yearly damage from crime, given by Mr. Coolidge at
seven and a half billions, is estimated by other authorities
at more than sixteen billions. More recent estimates make
the total eighteen billions. The total in tears and heart-
breaks is far beyond the power of words to portray or fig-
ures to estimate.

How old is old age? A babe in arms, or one at any time

of life before the state the world calls old age, may be as helpless or hungry or cold or nearly naked as the man or woman of eighty or ninety or a hundred. Stark poverty has no age limit. There is no time in life when an empty stomach reaches its majority. The panacea of old age pensions, the soundness of which Mr. Coolidge avers "has not been demonstrated," overlooks the hordes of men, women and children left out and set adrift by reason of not having attained that indefinite state.

We have a multiplicity of laws, made only to be broken or evaded, mounting in number.

We see a horde of lawyers busy at the task of misinterpreting the meaning of fair contracts. We witness the racketeers of our cities making bargains with men sworn to interpret, administer and enforce the laws, and taking pitiless toll from the grinding miseries of the submerged millions. We have hordes of human hyenas who out-Shylock Shylock with their thieving and jughandled installment loan agreements, compared with which ravening packs the highway robber risking life in his precarious and predacious trade is a tall and shining angel. And this carrion crew with its weasel worded indentures is protected by the majesty and mandates of statutory enactments, and by interpretations of parrot repeating judicial decisions and decrees.

Overriding the constitutional guarantees in the bills of rights of our states and our nation, daily are practiced the devilish devices of the third degree, as cruel and perversive of the rules of justice and the dictates of humanity as was the ancient use of the thumbscrew and the rack. We have hardboiled law enforcing methods far worse than the crimes against which they are directed. Suicide is on the increase. Hamlet's soliloquy points the way out of our social labyrinth for a trooping procession of desperation that mounts as the complexity of the present order thickens. And all this in our "civilized" country, our so-called Christian nation—Christian only in grossly misapplied name. Conditions are worse in all other lands.

> "So much to do,
> So little done,"

Sighed Cecil Rhodes on his deathbed, after he had conquered in a brief life span the better part of a continent.

"New occasions teach new duties, time makes ancient good uncouth.

They must upward still and onward who would keep abreast of truth, . . .

Nor attempt the future's portal with the past's blood-rusted key,"

Wrote Lowell in "The Present Crisis."

In the light of all that has transpired in the world since they reasoned together, can one wonder at the conclusions of the leaders at Bethel and Aurora, seeking for a better social order for their people? The slogan, "No cake for anyone till everyone has bread," would have had no special appeal to them. They all had both bread and cake, along with the essentials and refinements of comfortable life in their day.

For that community their way of living, founded on the words of the Master at Jacob's Well and in the Sermon on the Mount, and the Diamond Rule of Paul, brought a better and happier state than the average of their time, or before, or since, in this country or elsewhere. Did they find, in the fundamental rule, FROM EVERY MAN ACCORDING TO HIS CAPACITY TO EVERY MAN ACCORDING TO HIS NEEDS, the formula that will stand the test of the big world? How near are we to or how far are we from the dawn of the day of economic emancipation?

If the great mass of humanity is not tending in the direction of the law of love, groping after the correct answer to the first recorded social question of history, following the gleam of the principle of the parable of the Good Samaritan, looking, however vainly and feebly, to the universal adoption of the Golden Rule, and the Diamond Rule, whither is it speeding?

And will perhaps some reader suggest that, since we are seeking to perfect the formula of "a sufficient organization" for "economic emancipation," we are as yet in a state of economic slavery?

Many people fail to distinguish between our system of government in the United States and our economic system. They seem to think that our system of government is inextricably linked with the private property scheme of economics. Therefore they immediately brand as traitors to the government any who agitate for a different system of the control of wealth. Some of our patriotic organizations for instance have been vigilant in defending the government but sometimes it would appear that their defense also goes to the protection and support of our economic system.

Now it is quite conceivable that a republican form of government might operate under a socialist system of distribution of wealth. And it is quite conceivable that such a change in our economic system might be brought about through peaceful alteration of the Constitution. Government must naturally protect itself against violent overthrow; but there is no justification for government to extend its sanction over our economic system and protect the capitalist economy. What government should do and does do is to protect the person in his property, so long as the Constitution upholds the right of private property, against violence, theft or fraud. And private property under our form of government may be held cooperatively by all sorts of business and social organizations, such as lodges, foundations, trusts, churches which have brotherhoods and sister-hoods that are communistic in their living; communistic colonies having all property and the usufruct of it in com-mon, which may or may not increase amazingly in size and numbers—and so on through a long and lengthening list. This idea was recently expressed by Vice Chancellor John O. Bigelow of New Jersey, who declared:

"A man has as much right to be a Communist as a Democrat, and a Communist ought to have as much freedom as a Democrat. I say, however mistaken in his views a Communist might be, he should have an equal right to persuade others as long as it is done peaceably."

Commenting on the above, the editor of the *Oregon Statesman*, Salem, Oregon, recently said: "This is sound judicial doctrine; and should be learned by the people. The form of government should not be tied up with an economic system; and the right to work or plead for changes by constitutional means either in our government or economic system should not be molested. The country makes a serious mistake to try to ruthlessly bottle up or root out those whose political or economic ideas may be at variance with those of the majority."

The sanctions of law protect such a form of property holding and community living as brought the Keil colony together and under which it achieved remarkable success in material as in other ways. There is no doubt that, in any section of the United States, a body of people similarly associated, and as ably led, might now have as great suc-cess. Organized with better rules of permanency, and still as ably led, it might last for many decades, or generations, or even indefinitely, with higher ideals realized, such as the leaders at Bethel and Aurora dreamed, as outlined in these pages, and might have made their dreams come true had their founder lived a much longer span of years, and had prepared more carefully for permanency. And it is conceivable that the United States might have a multitude of such communities, perhaps pointing the way, quietly and peaceably, to the ultimate goal of "equality of opportunity" and "economic emancipation." There are in this country thousands of discouraged rural settlements, with neglected and abandoned farms, that might thus be made highly solvent, prosperous and happy centers, fostering and radiating American ideals, culture and patriotism, and rendering trustworthy and loyal service to every worthy cause. And this would hold true for any country with a system of laws like that of the United States.

(NOTE: The appendices of this book touching the teachings of Saint-Simon, Fourier, Baboeuf and Cabet were taken largely from "French and German Socialism in Modern Times," by Prof. Richard T. Ely of Johns Hopkins University, Baltimore, published in 1883. "To Every Man" was the title first chosen for this book, taken from the fundamental law of colony living, "From every man according to his capacity to every man according to his needs.")

CHAPTER 34

WHAT MIGHT HAVE BEEN—VISION,
A LINEN KINGDOM

IN THE opening chapters of this book there is reference to the broken engagement of John A. Roebling and Helena Giesy. Under the heading, "What Might Have Been," the *Daily Oregon Statesman* of Salem, Oregon, under date of January 24, 1924, printed the following editorial article:

Who is a great man? Milton said:

"He alone is worthy of the appellation who either does great things, or teaches how they may be done, or describes them with a suitable majesty when they have been done; but those only are great things which tend to render life more happy, which increase the innocent enjoyments and comforts of existence, or which pave the way to a state of future bliss more permanent and more pure."

And Swift said:

"Whoever could make two ears of corn or two blades of grass grow on a spot of ground where only one grew before would deserve better of mankind and do more essential service than the whole race of politicians put together."

There was printed in the *American Economist* of last week the following tribute:

"The Pioneer"

"The Pioneer" is the title of a painting by Peter Marcus of New York. It represents a portion of New York's picturesque skyline and includes such skyscrapers as the Singer building, the Woolworth building, the Municipal building near the New York terminal of Brooklyn Bridge, as well as the terminal of that bridge, the pioneer bridge of its class.

Brooklyn Bridge represents the realization of the dreams of a "practical idealist," John A. Roebling, the great engineer. Without the magic strength of untold miles of wire rope, Brooklyn Bridge would have remained but a dream, and the greatness of New York would never have been developed as has been the case. After forty-one years the dream that came true still stands as the monument to a man's ideal.

A reproduction of the picture, "The Pioneer," adorns the 1924 calendar issued by John A. Roebling's Sons Company of New Jersey, manufacturers of wire and wire rope, the company founded by the idealist who planned and built Brooklyn Bridge, and whose last days were passed in a building overlooking that bridge, so that he might behold daily with his own eyes the completion of his life's ideal. The picture is a fitting tribute to the greatness of John A. Roebling, and the bridge itself is his most fitting monument.*

In the forties, John A. Roebling was a young man residing in Pennsylvania, near what is now the great city of Pittsburgh. He was engaged to be married to a young woman who was a member of the company of people who were on the point of going to Bethel, Missouri, where they were to have their property in common. The young woman persisted. John A. Roebling hesitated, and finally drew back. He remained in Pennsylvania and she went to Missouri and joined the colony—

And from that colony, and the same colony charter, grew the colony that founded Aurora, Oregon, and, under the leadership of Dr. Keil and its seven trustees, one of whom was a brother of the then young woman, secured about 10,000 acres (it was actually over 18,000 acres) of land in Marion and Clackamas counties, and conducted one of the most successful community property enterprises the world has ever known; and one that again proved what had been proved so many times before, and since, that every such enterprise contains the seeds of failure—for when Dr. Keil died there was no other leader whom all members, about 1000 members then, would trust implicitly in all things, material, moral and spiritual. And so the Aurora colony was dissolved, and the property divided, and every one had a competence from what they had worked in common to create—about a million dollars' worth of property. The young woman lived a saintly (single) life in the Aurora colony, and died there.

What might have been? Had such a genius, such a "practical genius" as John A. Roebling chosen a different course in his youth in Pennsylvania, and had he become a member of the Aurora colony, and had he with his vision made an industrial colony there, instead of an agricultural, what a different history might not this part of Oregon have had!

In the early days of the Aurora colony, flax was grown on a small scale, and homespun made, spun with a distaff and woven on hand looms. What a future Aurora might have had with the full development of the linen and lace industries there, under the leadership of such a master as John A. Roebling! Aurora would have become the Belfast of America. Aurora might have become a greater city than Portland is now. The makings were all there, in that colony.

Several days later, under the heading, "Reverting to Roebling," the *Oregon Statesman* printed the following in its editorial columns:

A good deal of attention has been attracted by an editorial article in this corner of *The Statesman* of January 24, under the heading, "What Might Have Been," containing a clipping from the *American Economist* referring to a painting entitled "The Pioneer," by Peter Marcus of New York, referring to John A. Roebling, the great engineer who planned the Brooklyn Bridge—

And, the *American Economist* said, who built it. But *The Statesman* of yesterday contained a letter from Washington A. Roebling, the oldest son of John A. Roebling, showing that he himself was the builder of the bridge, his father having met with an accident which caused his death, after planning the bridge. The rest of the story in the editorial article, outside of the mistake made by the writer in the *American Economist*, and not by the writer in *The Statesman*, was correct.

The vision was this:

John A. Roebling, when he was a young man near Pittsburgh, Pa., was engaged to be married to a young woman. But she wished to remain with her people who went to Bethel, Mo., and then came to Oregon and founded the Aurora colony. Mr. Roebling decided against joining the colonists. He turned back. The wedding outfit of the young lady had been arranged for. She went with her people to Missouri and came to Oregon and never married. She led a helpful and saintly life. She lavished her great love upon her people; upon the Oregon colonists—

And the vision: What a different history might have been written of Aurora had the "practical dreamer," the great engineer and man of genius, married the young woman and gone to Bethel and come to Oregon; and taken up the manufacturing of flax products into fine linens! The Aurora colonists raised flax and made it into fiber and spun the fiber into yarn and wove the yarn into home-spun for wearing apparel and household use—the same as most pioneer Americans did, from colonial times. Washington's troops wore this home-spun clothing.

They did not realize that they were producing fiber fit for the making of fine linens—the finest in the world. The genius of John A. Roebling might have led him to this knowledge. He would have had the willing help necessary for developing a great industry. All the natural conditions were there in perfection. So Aurora might have become the Belfast of America. It might have been the chief manufacturing city of Oregon. It might have extended its limits as far as Salem, and reaching out to the suburbs of Portland. Millions might have poured into its lap, from all corners of the earth.

That is what Salem needs now—

A man with the genius of John A. Roebling, and with the vision of James J. Hill. The beginnings of a great linen industry are here. . . . The opportunities now are greater than they were in the time when the Aurora colony was in its most flourishing condition.

Why?

Because Congressman Fordney worked with flax when he was a boy on his father's farm, and when he became chairman of the Ways and Means Committee of the House, and came to frame the present protective tariff law, he saw to it that the flax industry should have a chance—

He gave it high protective rates; especially the manufactures of flax; and still more especially the fine linens that may be made with Salem district flax fiber.

The full development of the flax industry in the Salem district will be a bigger thing than the Brooklyn Bridge. It will mean the bringing to this valley each year of $100,000,000, from all sections of the United States, and from all the countries bordering on the seven seas. And it will never run out. It will last as long as grass grows and water runs.

---

* Titled, "Still a Masterpiece," the *New York Times* of May 24, 1933, contained this masterly editorial:

"When opened fifty years ago the Brooklyn Bridge was the engineering wonder of the world. Other suspension bridges now have longer spans and higher towers, yet it still stands as a technical and architectural masterpiece, a monument to the courage and tenacity of John A. Roebling, and to the iron will and directive ability of his son Washington, who built it and almost died in the process. Newspaper accounts of the dedicatory ceremonies make it plain that the public was impressed not only by granite towers 276 feet high and a central span of almost 1600 feet, but by 'lines of delicate and aerial grace combined with strength more enduring than marble.'

"In the Brooklyn Bridge an engineer dared for the first time to let steel stand nakedly against stone, proclaiming its right to exist as architectural material. This was in a day when the Bessemer process was only beginning to supply the world with steel in unlimited tons. America then caught a glimpse of its architectural future—of lace-like webs of steel towering to heights that still evoke astonishment. There is also something symbolic in this weather-worn bridge of many fine strands collected to form cables stout enough to bear the traffic of two cities—something that suggests a nation that owes its strength to the union of many feeble states. Dr. Storrs, who delivered one of the orations fifty years ago, must have felt this when he hailed the bridge as a triumph of democracy:

" 'It will show to those who shall succeed us of what largeness of enterprise, what patience of purpose, what liberal wisdom the populations now ruling these associated cities were competent in their time. It takes the aspect, so regarded, of a durable monument to democracy itself.'

"It was not a happy accident that made the Brooklyn Bridge what it is. Something of the two Roeblings went into these Gothic towers, the caissons, the delicate tracery of steel threads. Perhaps if John Roebling had never been a favorite pupil of Hegel's, had never buried himself in Emerson, had never written a highly intricate 'Theory of the Universe,' the span would have been just another collossal engineering achievement. What made him a first-class architect without being aware of it was a passion for utilizing his cables rationally. If an engineering enterprise is right, it usually looks right. That may be the explanation of a design which is a delight both to the eye and the engineering sense."

CHAPTER 35

WHAT MIGHT HAVE BEEN—VISION, A SUGAR EMPIRE

IN 1875 there appeared at Aurora a man speaking German who presented to the colony people the idea of establishing a beet sugar factory. He remained for several weeks, a guest of Dr. Keil, and there was much discussion of the matter with the colony leaders. The visitor "sold" Dr. Keil on the idea, after much persuasion, and the leader of the community became a strong advocate of the undertaking. But it involved a large investment, in an untrodden field, and all the members of the community were consulted, as was the case with every proposal of magnitude.

They had the land. They had the labor. The man who brought the idea painted the possibilities of large profits and great benefits in glowing colors. It almost "went over." But the trustees finally decided in the negative. They drew back, even against the urging of their leader, whom they followed and whose judgment they trusted in most matters, in nearly all things.

That might have been the first successful beet sugar factory in the United States. It might have led to vast developments there and throughout the state and the Pacific Northwest. Aurora might have become known as the sugar city, with the innumerable indirect benefits that come from the growing and processing of sugar beets and the use of the by-products in dairying, swine breeding, poultry raising and other industries on the land, with the help that such a crop gives in renovating the soil, providing a cultivated crop and one that leads to the kind of rotation that is desirable.

The first beet sugar factory of any consequence in America was erected in 1870 in Alvorado, California. Not being successful, the machinery was moved to Soquel, Santa Cruz County, and run for a short time there, when the enterprise was given up. E. H. Dyer, the father of the beet sugar industry in America, bought the buildings and real estate and moved a plant from Brighton, near Sacramento, onto the old site in 1879, and that proved to be the only successful plant in the United States at the time. In 1890 a factory was built at Grand Island, Nebraska, which was successful. Also in 1890 one was built at Lehi, Utah, backed by Mormon interests, which led to the far-flung Utah-Idaho Sugar Company, for a long time the largest concern of the kind in the country, and now the second largest.

During those early years of the beet sugar industry in the United States, William Kuhlburg and Thomas Gennert were engaged in the enterprises started at Fond du Lac, Wis., and in California. One informant believes it was Mr. Gennert or Mr. Kuhlburg who was at Aurora; but another authority thinks it could not have been one of these. However, the man who made the proposal at Aurora spoke good German and was evidently qualified to assist in establishing the enterprise. The point is, had this been done, and had Dr. Keil lived or left a qualified successor, or trustees who were willing to carry on the community life vigorously, there might have been a different story to tell.

Compared to the original capital invested, and the time it lasted, the Keil experiment was the most successful one in communal life ever launched, considering the fact, also, that it had no peculiar practice or belief to hold the people to their purposes, any different from its neighbors with individual holdings, outside of the one peculiarity of having its property in common and carrying on its operations under rules of common ownership of the increments and fruits of the labors of all its members.

CHAPTER 36

WHAT MIGHT HAVE BEEN—
A VISION OF PERMANENCY

TWO years before the beginnings at Bethel, the Amana Society was started. It is still going, and in a flourishing condition, at Amana, Iowa. Basing most of the facts upon an account written by Bertha M. H. Shambaugh, wife of Prof. Benjamin F. Shambaugh, superintendent of the State Historical Society of Iowa, the following, very briefly, is the story of Amana:

In one of the garden spots of Iowa there is a charming valley through which the Iowa River flows. That is Amana, seven villages, about which stretch 26,000 goodly acres well cultivated. It is the Community of True Inspiration. The name was taken from the Song of Solomon, chapter four, verse 8: "Come with me from Lebanon, my spouse, with me from Lebanon: look from the top of Amana, from the top of Shenir and Hermon, from the lions' dens, from the mountains of the leopards." The seven villages are Amana, East Amana, Middle Amana, High Amana, West Amana, South Amana, and Homestead. Born of religious enthusiasm and disciplined by persecution, it has ever remained primarily a church. And so the real Amana is Amana the church. In the eighteenth century the Inspirationists paid the penalty in the Old World for their nonconformity to established customs by imprisonment and exile.

"There is much in the life of the people of Amana that seems plain and monotonous to the outside world," says Mrs. Shambaugh, "and yet we are compelled to acknowledge that in many respects theirs is a more rational and ideal life than that which is found in the average country village. It is more genuine and uniform. There is less extravagance; no living beyond one's means; no keeping up of 'appearances;' and fewer attempts to pass for more than one is worth."

Throughout its history the Community of True Inspiration has been dominated by a spiritual ideal and a determined purpose to realize that ideal. To this end they have persevered, suffered and sacrificed for more than 200 years. "And finally," says Mrs. Shambaugh, "that their ideal of a simple religious life might prevail, they substituted a system of brotherly cooperation for one of individual competition."

The railroad and airplane, telephone and telegraph, newspaper and magazine and many inventions have come, and an intelligent adjustment of the life of the community to the new order explains the "blessed continuation" of Amana in this day and generation.

The Community of True Inspiration became a distinct religious sect about 1714. From time to time spiritual leaders arose and "prophesied like the prophets of old." There were many great leaders. But to the genius of Christian Metz, a young carpenter of Ronneburg, the community owes its greatest debt. There were many communities of these people around Ronneburg, not far from Hamburg, Germany, where "all that believed were together and had all things in common." Persecutions there caused them to cast abroad for a new home. In 1842 a committee of four led by Christian Metz set out to find a new home in America, in a devout belief that the journey had been "ordained and directed by divine revelation." In the end they purchased the Seneca Indian reservation, 5000 acres near Buffalo, New York. The tract was laid out and peopled. There were six villages. They called themselves the "Ebenezer

Society." Twelve years later another committee of four, with Christian Metz as its leader, was "ordained and directed" to go forth to "find a new home in the Far West." Finally the present home in Iowa was selected. The transfer from near Buffalo to Iowa extended over a period of ten years. While one detail of members prepared the new home in Iowa, the other looked to the profitable sale of the old estate in New York. When the decision to move was made there were 8000 acres in New York. The whole property was finally disposed of without loss. What had been a forest was encroached upon by the growing city of Buffalo, hence the move to Iowa.

The first village in the Iowa purchase was laid out during the summer of 1855, the year the first Bethel colony train under Dr. Keil went to the Oregon Country. Homestead was a town built on the first railroad, in 1861. The Amana people bought the whole town.

The community is incorporated as the "Amana Society" under the laws of Iowa. It lives under its constitution which went into effect the first day of January, 1860, which has received the signature of every member since its adoption in December, 1859. The assessed valuation of the property of the Amana community was listed in 1920 at $2,102,984. The Amana Society is simply a voluntary association depending on the general good will and good faith of its members.

It has a board of trustees that settles all things and is the high court of appeal. There are no lawyers in Amana. Each village is governed by a group of elders. The highest authority in each village is the head elder; in matters temporal, the resident trustee. Each village manages its own affairs; but all accounts are finally sent to the headquarters at Amana. The system is a federation. Local affairs have local control, general affairs general control.

Tender care is given the aged and infirm; all are on an

equality. There is much individual freedom; homes, separate rooms and the like. But there is in the private home no kitchen. At more or less regular intervals in each village there is a kitchen house, where the meals for the families in the immediate neighborhood are prepared and served, 16 to 50 persons eating in one kitchen. The kitchen houses are models of order and convenience. There is absolute system; work, but no hard work. There are hotel kitchens for visitors; but hired help is employed in these, in order to shield the young women of Amana from the rude conduct of the tourists who leave their manners at home.

The Amanans are good livers, enjoying three meals a day, and a lunch in the middle of each half day. The woman with children under two is required to do no work, and her meals are brought to her home. There is a nursery in each village. There are flowers everywhere in Amana. There is a lake formed by the mill race, of 200 acres, filled with the American lotus or yellow nelumbo. There is floral beauty everywhere.

There have been no "instruments" and no new revelations for a number of years; but the inspired literature of the society takes 42 printed volumes to hold it, to say nothing of many collections of community poetry and songs. There is much of worship, and many prayer meetings, for the Amanans are a devout people.

There is no outward mourning for the dead. The faith of the community teaches that death is but "the blessed release of the spirit" from the pain and suffering which is the lot of man during his "pilgrimage on earth," and that the unencumbered spirit passes beyond into a "blissful eternity" where other souls will join it as they in turn are "freed from their burdens." And Amana's simple doctrine of "brothers all as God's children" is maintained even in death. In the cemetery there are no family plots, no monuments. The departed members of each village are buried side by side in the order of their death in rows of military precision, regardless of birth, family, or spiritual rank. Some men of wealth came early to the community. They sleep beside their brothers who had naught to give but the labor of their hands; and beyond, resting beside the least among them, lies the great hearted Christian Metz, whose headstone reads simply: "Christian Metz 24 Juli 1867." The rest—the loving tribute of his followers—is graven upon the heart of every member of the community.

Says Mrs. Shambaugh: "The history of mankind teaches that 'religion often makes practicable that which else were impossible, and divine love triumphs when human science is baffled.' "

A letter from Dr. Charles F. Noe of the Amana Society, under date of August 28, 1930, says:

In 1923 we had a very disastrous fire which destroyed one woolen mill and the flour mill and grain elevator. As it has always been the policy of the society not to insure, there was a very great loss amounting to several hundred thousand dollars. The woolen mill was rebuilt immediately in a more modern and fireproof manner and equipped with electric power. Of the other buildings, only the grain elevator was rebuilt as it had long been found that the flour mill could not successfully compete with the large mills in the north. Also the print works has not been resumed as the markets for the blue prints have practically disappeared since the great war. Agriculture and the woolen mill, which at present is running overtime, form the principal sources of sustenance at this time.

Another and more recent letter from Dr. Noe furnishes these interesting particulars:

The amount of land (of the Amana Society) is about 26,000 acres, and the membership remains at about 1400. Our industries at present are very much depressed in connection with the quite general industrial depression throughout the country. Agricul-

turally our section has not suffered greatly from drouth. Although
the rainfall has been below normal there has been enough to insure
average crops. There are no new inspired leaders and no new industries have been founded. Speaking of Communistic societies,
have you learned of the changes of the Hutterische Societies of
South Dakota? I understand that they have mostly sold and are
moving to Canada. Are you familiar with the Llano Society at
New Llano, Louisiana? They seem to be fairly successful.

The children of the Amana community generally remain
when they grow up. One of the interesting things about
Amana is the fact that its experiences disprove two universally prevalent ideas: First, that no such community
can outlive the leadership of its founder, or be governed by
a board. Second, that no such community can exist for long
under modern conditions, and surrounded by people having individual property. Having disproved these ideas,
Amana still flourishes and is strong.

The writer having noted recent news reports to the effect
that some members of the Amana Society had agitated for
a change to the corporation form of ownership and management, and, subsequently, that the press carried matter
alleging such consummation, the full text of a letter from
Dr. Noe, written at Amana, January 26, 1933, answering
one of a few days before, will interest studious minds. It
follows:

Replying to your inquiry, can say that your information is correct
as to our reorganization on a semi-capitalistic plan. We changed
into a joint-stock company on June 1st, which, however, is quite
unique in its organization. We issued shares of stock of a non-voting
character to the members in proportion to the length of time spent
as a member. Also one share of voting stock to each member which
made the organization completely democratic. The non-voting
stock carries a dividend of 7% and any earnings above that are
distributed to the voting stock share and share alike, thus retaining
a communistic feature. We also retain free medical care as well as

care in old age and free burial. We give preferential rights as to employment to members and aim to avoid unemployment by distribution of labor and shortening of hours. We pay quite moderate wages to our members. So far we have had no unemployment and are operating without loss under our new plan.

The careful, thoughtful reader has already noted that number of days in colony life was the chief basis for the conclusions by the two committees with power to act when considering the historic settlement between members of the colony at Bethel and Aurora. Inveigling is the fact that this rule was used when the leaders at Amana, over a half century later, had under consideration the problems of a readjustment designed to satisfy the urge of new ideas and at the same time preserve and perpetuate the cherished ideals of the founders of their society.

The Llano Cooperative Colony was established in 1914 in California by Jacob Harriman and others, and moved in 1917 to Louisiana. Two years ago it owned 16,000 acres of land. George T. Pickett had been in the colony some thirteen years and was general manager. He was president of the company, the Llano Del Rio Company, incorporated under the laws of Nevada, because the corporation laws of that state were "liberal, safe and well construed;" there was "no disposition on the part of state officials to interfere." Of the 16,000 acres of land owned by the Llano colony, free of mortgage, 12,000 were of hardwood and pine timber. It was a sawmill tract when purchased with its buildings and machinery.

The colony conducted gardens and farming operations, including dairy, rice farm and orchards; had horses, mules, hogs, poultry; tractors, wagons and trucks and farm implements, shoemaking and tailor shops, laundry, sewing room, bakery, brick factory, building construction department, hospital and visiting nurses, kid kolony, kindergarten, schools, and night classes for young and old. Also, for its own service and the public's, a printing establishment, saw and planing mill, shingle mill and cabinet shop, garage and repair shop, engineering consulting and painting departments, steam, Diesel and electric plant, large ice and cold storage plant; candy peanut butter making and canning plants, a crate factory and store, and, for the entertainment of the colonists and their friends, a theater, roof garden, open forum and swimming pool.

Very briefly: They claimed that in society in general the heart plays no part; the powerful and crafty succeed, the good and humane too frequently go down before them. "It is a survival of the unfit." They had Jews, all kinds of Protestants, Catholics, atheists, agnostics and Christian Scientists, living and working together in harmony. They held that competition is the root of all wars and strife. Said one of their writers: "We know there is no need to live in this (competitive) way, if we would only agree to live by mutual service. Then why is it not done? We may say we are compelled by circumstances; that while every one else is competing we are compelled to do so too. Then we cannot complain if others do the same, for by competing ourselves we are helping to make the circumstances that compel them to do so. The obvious thing to do, if we really wish to get away from this un-Christian competition, is for those who have sufficient faith in the principles they profess to join together and live in accordance with them, and show the world that they really can be practiced. There is nothing to prevent us doing this, except our want of faith in each other. Surely, we stand condemned as 'Ye of little faith.'" This writer was an Australian, converted to the Llano colony way by a visit. He claimed Jesus taught the right way; that the principles have been written in plain language for nearly two thousand years; that "it seems strange that Christian people are still living in enmity and strife toward one another" after so long a time. Failures? He admitted them, but added: "This is no excuse for not making other trials. Any one might as well say it is useless to try to overcome a bad habit today because he failed yesterday."

The Llano colonists are ambitious: working for "a world cooperative commonwealth;" and declaring that "this implies eventually a world state of common ownership, a universal medium of exchange, a world-scale production and distribution for use and not for profit." But in some of their literature they call their association the Llano Integral Cooperative Colony, meaning or at least inferring that they are in themselves self sufficient, self contained, a perfect whole. The colony is located in the western highlands of Louisiana; 110 miles from Shreveport, and the same distance from Beaumont, Texas; on the main line of the Kansas City Southern railroad. New Llano is in Vernon Parish: healthful location, good soil, and a variety of crops.

The foregoing information was gleaned from printed matter sent with a letter, under date of August 27, 1930, from a man in charge of the colony office, in the temporary absence on a lecturing tour of the general manager. The words that follow are taken from a letter to the writer dated at New Llano, February 9, 1933:

Your letter of January 29th came to hand, inquiring with regard to the present status of the Llano Co-operative Colony. You will note by this letterhead that Mr. Pickett is still the general manager of the colony; and we may add that although there has always been a dissenting minority in the history of the colony, the present prospects are that the policies which have been established, during Mr. Pickett's management of over 12 years, have no likelihood of discontinuance.

The additional buildings completed during the period including 1930 have been: a two-story apartment building, mule barn, dairy barn, farm house, brooder house, residence for General Manager Pickett, saw mill at home unit, and a number of new dwellings. This year there has been a beginning of development of the gas and oil field underlying the colony lands, which has gone far enough to demonstrate the existence of gas, and the probability of oil. Since June, 1930, the population has practically doubled, and is now approximately 500. Many of these have been received as refugees from the Great Depression: in other words, the Unemployed. But our limitations of housing, equipment and operating funds have compelled us to call a halt in this.

Perhaps the most significant development has been along the line of expansion, in the program of opening new units in other locations. This was begun in the Rice Ranch, about 75 miles from New Llano. We have a unit at Premont, in southwestern Texas, in the citrus fruit and winter garden district, which is well under way and will doubtless grow in extent. We have been trying for a location in the Sugar Bowl district of Louisiana, but have been handicapped by lack of equipment. We are now trying to secure a 3500 acre ranch in southwestern New Mexico, with full equipment for cattle and dairy and other stock. You will receive a few copies of *The Llano Colonist.*

The Llano Colonist is a weekly newspaper, well edited, arranged and printed; much above the average in this country: under the main heading the line: "From the Pine Clad Western Highlands." It is 10 cents a copy, $1.50 a year. It claims to be "the only paper of its kind in the world telling how co-operation applies to the whole economic life." In the issue of February 11, 1933, numbering sixteen pages, a front page article by George T. Pickett, contains this statement: "Do you realize that units such as we have here at Llano and other places and such as are going to be organized BY THE THOUSANDS within the next twelve months, are the real safeguard of civilization?" He is reported as saying in a meeting of his colonists that week: "The wonderful write-ups of the colony by Editor Coad in the *New Orleans Item* and the *New York Times* have started an avalanche of correspondence from interested people who either want to come here, start new enterprises of their own or corroborate their ideas as to the soundness of co-operative colonies. Co-operation, the integral type, as found in Llano, is making a hit and the plan will be adopted IN A THOUSAND PLACES." The reporter at the meeting added: "It is this idea that he wants to spread, and he is very happy that the minds of TENS OF THOUSANDS are centered on the idea." Mention was made of a movement along the line in the Canal Zone; "that there might not be a man or woman in the Zone without work or the assurance of being taken care of for the rest of their days." There was also reference to "two splendid propositions in Arkansas, each of 800 acres," offered to the Llano people, and of "one of 230,000 acres in Colorado," the latter pending for some time; and urgent calls were reported from Washington, New York, Philadelphia, Boston, Cleveland, Chicago and Milwaukee—where "a world of good could be accomplished"—in spreading the ideals of co-operative living.

These items are taken from a statement in *The Colonist* of the issue named: "There are no laws in the community, other than the Golden Rule of doing only what you expect your neighbor to do unto you." "A centralized form of administration is employed, adopted after other forms had failed. . . . All business affairs are directed by one head and the working out of details . . . is left to men in charge of the various departments." "New members have no vote in the colony's affairs for one year." "If you are a single man or woman, . . . membership costs you $1000. For each adult member $200 additional (over 21); for those between 12 and 21, $150; for children under 12, $100.)" But many are taken without money, and allowed to work out their membership dues. In a question and answer section of the paper, these words appear: "Why are members being taken in without payment of cash while your literature quotes a cash payment? Answer: By reason of special need here in the colony, on account of certain qualifications, and because of lack of funds on the part of the applicant, and his needs, often members are taken in without the usual $1000 membership or a start thereon. . . . Such members always leave a residue of work even if they soon depart, and very frequently such have made the best colonists. Those who have the money or other resources are expected to pay. Were it otherwise, it would be unfair to those who have put in cash memberships."

One unit, No. 4, is operated as a "co-operative Christian community." A physician member, Dr. Walter Siegmeister, conducts a page in the *Colonist* on "Scientific Living," with dietary rules and all the rest; object, "The creation of a superior mankind." Much is said of the warm, healthful climate, allowing a great deal of outdoor work. A printed pamphlet giving detailed information for inquirers carries a declaration of principles, standing for a constitution. Two paragraphs: "Talent and intelligence are gifts which should rightly be used in the service of others. The development of these by education is the gift of the community to the individual, and the exercise of greater ability entitles none to the false reward of greater possessions, but only the joy of greater service to others." "Only by identifying his interests and pleasures with those of others can man find real happiness."

The banner above the head of *The Colonist:* "And in the dim chaos of a restless and joyless life, like a glittering, cheerful star, like a guiding flame of the Future, there shimmered a simple word, deep as the Heart: COMRADE!"

The pamphlet says: "Leesville, the parish seat of Vernon Parish, is about two miles north of New Llano. It is the usual small country town, with court house, excellent high school, stores, railroad round house, and all other industries which go with a town of its size. The population is about 3500, predominantly white."

On the back cover page of the pamphlet is printed "A Vision of the Future," by Robert G. Ingersoll, reading:

"I see a country filled with happy homes, with firesides of content—the foremost land of all the earth.

"I see a world where thrones have crumbled and where kings are dust. The aristocracy of idleness has perished from the earth.

"I see a world without a slave. Man at last is free. Nature's forces have by science been enslaved. Lightning and light, wind and wave, frost and flame, and all the secret subtle powers of earth and air are the tireless toilers for the human race.

"I see a world at peace, adorned with every form of art, with music's myriad voices thrilled, while lips are rich with words of love and truth; a world in which no exile sighs, no prisoner mourns; a world on which the gibbet's shadow does not fall; a world where labor reaps its full reward, where work and worth go hand in hand, where the poor girl trying to win bread with the needle—the needle that has been called 'the asp for the breast of the poor'—is not driven to the desperate choice of crime or death, or suicide or shame.

"I see a world without the beggar's outstretched hand, the miser's heartless, stony stare, the piteous wail of want, the livid lips of lies, the cruel eyes of scorn.

"I see a race without disease of flesh or brain—shapely and fair—the married harmony of form and function—

and, as I look, life lengthens, joy deepens, love canopies the earth; and over all, in the great dome, shines the eternal star of human hope."

Organized August 1, 1931, at Eugene, Oregon, by nine people, three married couples and three single men, mostly University of Oregon students and ex-students who had become interested in the co-operative movement as discussed at the campus Y.M.C.A. open forums, their organization patterned after a p'an originating in England and later spread in the United States, the Co-operative Farm, near that city, has functioned, grown and prospered, reports a writer of the *Eugene Register-Guard*, in three articles in the issues of that journal for Jan. 22, 23 and 24, 1933. Two members are talented musicians, one a civil engineer of international experience, several have been engaged in educational work, two in social work, several in the study of agriculture. All are American citizens. Their incomes are pooled. Ownership of property is in common and its usufruct flows to a common treasury. The enterprise is purely co-operative. There is a common table, and if a member is employed away from the community home he contributes his earnings, less the amount required for his maintenance. There is a monthly allowance to each member for picture shows and other forms of entertainment. The enterprise is a paying one, solvent and making steady progress. It has 185 acres; 85 owned, 100 leased; plans on acquiring more, with increase of membership. A new member puts in all his property. A valuation is arrived at, and if he later wishes to withdraw and get his money out, the association agrees to reimburse him as soon as finances permit; also his share in the common property. There is a truck garden, a growing dairy and swine industry, bakery, and a stall for sales of products in the Eugene public market. Grain is grown, ground, baked and the products sold. The talents of the engineer are applied to the installation of an irrigation system on the farm. A regular business procedure is followed, each member being in charge of work for which he is best qualified, with a labor program chairman—to secure efficiency. New members will be taken in—but for the present one must bring enough to care for additional housing and establish him (or her) at some type of productive work. The applicant must believe in co-operation, and existing members reserve the right of election, to guard against misfits. All nine founders were between the ages of 20 and 30. Some drew out. There were fourteen members January 24, 1933; satisfied, hopeful, buoyant. The series in the *Register-Guard* concluded: "The Co-operative Farm . . . appears to be 'making a go' of it. It is an experiment which is being followed with interest here. The members welcome investigation and visitors are always received cordially." A. Bristol, the secretary, and one of the original organizers, told the reporter that no prediction of failure, of which a variety have been advanced by outsiders, has come true. He commented: "As a matter of fact, all co-operative farms of this type are economically sound. The reduced per capita expense of the individuals through the use of a common kitchen, common homes, and so on, makes it profitable from a financial standpoint." A mimeographed Bulletin is published monthly, at 25 cents a year to subscribers, copies of which are sent to other co-operative farms in the United States and to interested outsiders. The Bulletin for August, 1932, celebrating the completion of the first year of the association, said the original nine members, "becoming aware of the inevitable destruction of both ourselves and society, that will be the result of our competitive order, wanted to do something to change the underlying principles that are wrecking our society," and organized their Co-operative Farm "in order to serve as a living example of a larger way of life than our capitalistic system; to assure its members the necessities of life, and to allow its members an opportunity to live in an unselfish way, practicing the ethical principles of Jesus and living the socialistic, co-operative life."

"The co-operative era will be characterized by co-operative living, nothing less," are words in the November Bulletin. "We must give of our all without stint—nothing less," is quoted from the December Bulletin. "We have never demanded a definite membership fee; whenever we have the means to put people to producing we invite them to become one of us, regardless of their economic circumstances"; these words from the January, 1833, Bulletin. Farm land near by, rich, capable of producing highly profitable crops, may now be had for mortgaged prices, low interest, 30 years to pay principal, and the January, 1933, Bulletin asks for persons able to finance such deals, and believing in community living, to correspond: Address Co-operative Farm, Rural Route 2, Eugene, Oregon. Successive issues of the Bulletin quote many letters from near and far places, showing a wide and growing interest, and indicating that many new ventures in co-operative living may be launched soon. "There are numerous living co-operative colonies and societies in the United States. Each, however, is of a unique type, and has no affiliation with the others," writes A. Bristol, of the Eugene Co-operative Farm. A partial list follows:

Brotherhood House, Gerald Geraldson, director, 324 Pleasant Ave., New York City.

Commonwealth Co-operators, Waldo, Florida.

Concord Springs Colony, John McBride, secretary, Concord Springs, Madison County, Arkansas.

Co-operative League, 107 West 12th street, New York City.

Garden Homes Community, Transylvania, Louisiana.

Golden West Co-operative Brotherhood, 3214 Fair View Ave., Alameda, California.

Kristenstad Colony, Kristenstad, Texas.

Los Angeles Co-operative Exchange, 233 South Broadway, Los Angeles, California.

Mittelbuscher, Wm., Federated Co-op. Council, 611 Coronado Street, Los Angeles, California.

New Hope Colony, Sam Rule, manager, State Line, Missouri.

United Co-op. Industries, 11251 South New Hampshire Avenue, Los Angeles, California.

The Llano colony was in the above list, but is omitted because of the more extended description the reader has found in preceding pages. There is added, from the first letter mentioned therein: "The [Llano] colony is on a substantial basis with great potential possibilities, and under proper management it can become not merely a COLONY but 'a MOVEMENT that will solve unemployment and all social and economic problems.'"

The American Colony in Jerusalem is similar in its fundamentals to the Keil colony; has been in existence some forty-eight years, and, a friend tells the writer, "is very successful."

The Doukhobors, meaning spirit fighters, so named in derision by the Russian Orthodox clergy, and the title assumed by the non conforming peasants as an honored one, appeared in the middle of the eighteenth century. By that period of the nineteenth, there was fierce persecution by the state church. In the Caucasus, the Doukhobors, men, women and children, were subjected to horrible outrages and indignities. Tolstoy was aroused, secured help from the Society of Friends in England—and the Russian government, through influences thus elicited, allowed members of the sect to emigrate. Some went to Cyprus. In January, 1899, 4000 arrived in Canada, later nearly 2000 of the Cyprus party, followed by about 2000 more from the

Caucasus. More than 8000 are now in Saskatchewan near Yorktown, and around the Nelson, Trail, Brilliant, Grand Forks and McCloud districts in British Columbia and Alberta. Their property is worth over $7,000,000; around $1000 per capita. They ban meats, wines and tobacco. They seek to live the law of love; regard all men as equals; brothers. In worship, each bows to each, regarding every human being, with the divine spirit, in a bond of brotherhood. They use only passive resistance, going to extremes that seem to outsiders ridiculous. Their ideas carry equality to government officials, and they refuse to obey laws which they hold to be subversive to their religious beliefs—hence occasional conflicts with the authorities. Doukhobor children are taught to strip themselves naked in case truant officers seek to hale them to public schools. The Doukhobors are peasants and they plan to remain peasants. They have no books. They sing much—five tone folk songs from memory—and their folk lore comes down, mouth to ear, from ancestral tradition. Their official name in Canada is Christian Community of United Brotherhood, Limited, and titles are in chosen trustees, held in common, as its uses and usufructs, intended to be perpetual. They fight for only one thing: their contest is with the soil for their living and that of their posterity. A British writer says their beliefs are similar to those of the first Quakers, and that they are nearest to the original Christian ideals of any people in the world. If the reader—any reader—were to go into one of their churches in Canada, every member would bow to the floor, recognizing a brother with the divine spirit.

As these pages pass to the printer, Senate Bill 1142, by Morris Sheppard, member of the upper house of Congress from Texas, is under consideration in the Committee on Agriculture and Forestry; it is intended to aid experiments in common ownership enterprises, with a view to solving unemployment problems by putting the idle millions to useful production. George T. Pickett, head of the Llano colony, who appeared before the committee, thinks the bill will pass. An amendment in committee prohibits the paying of salaries. This would have met the approval of the Keil colony sages, as a matter of course, as a condition precedent, the least departure from which, whether on a great scale, as in Russia, or in the smallest unit any where, would be the thin entering wedge destined to wreck the whole—a sop to selfishness necessarily tabu and anathema maranatha if the cardinal sin in that form of living is to be banished for the sake of success and the security of enduring life.

Later: The June, 1933, Bulletin of the Cooperative Farm, Eugene, contains this paragraph: "May 10 a meeting was called to rearrange the work program. The question, 'How long do you expect to remain on Cooperative Farm and what work do you prefer?' was asked each member. Only two members stated that they propose to remain on the farm. The rest were leaving as soon as they could arrange their affairs. The group unanimously gave the remaining members a vote of confidence. The organization continues to exist in spite of the loss of membership, although the future of Cooperative Farm lies largely with two people. . . . The action of the associate members in regards to their relation to the farm will probably depend largely on the manner in which these two manage the affairs of the Cooperative Farm."

Later, No. 2: The Llano colony, many crises in its checkered career passed, has been going through another, in the form of troubles originating from the attacks of seceded members, but it is apparently emerging, stronger and more firmly organized than ever. The Gila, New Mexico, unit has been added. The outlook for Llano, largest and leading colony of its kind in America, appears good, with ambitions for great expansion.

The Llano colony people are just now offering special

terms to new members, hoping to double their number within ninety days.

At various other points in the United States in recent months more or less feeble or ambitious beginnings have been made in common ownership of property and communistic living. In several localities elaborate programs of a similar kind are promulgated, some of them vaulting in prospect. At least one has a vision of financial and other support of the state and a number of the federal government. It is conceivable that the movement which attained its height in America around the middle of the last century may soon have a vigorous resurgence, perhaps taking leaves from the book of experiences of that period, and essaying improvements upon them, in the light of changed conditions in material things, through science and invention—

And of new mental, moral, social and spiritual attitudes unfolding with amazing rapidity, variety and complexity throughout the United States—

And which are often more rapid, or fantastic and phantasmagoric, in other countries—as witness the tidal wave that is Russia, the seething caldron that is India, the continental Chinese puzzle that is the ancient-modern Orient, the volcano that is Italy, the earthquake that is Central and Southern Europe, and the seismic disturbances, major and minor, and the siroccos, hurricanes, euroclydons, cyclones, geysers and calderas that are the big and little nations and their varied possessions under tenures strong or weak around the earth—

With their 57 varieties and 57 times 57 cross currents of tradition, religion, class and caste, and of race prejudices and ambitions, yellow, brown, red, black and white and all the in-betweens, invoking the spectre a recent writer called "the rising tide of color," which he might perhaps

more aptly have named the unceasing undertow of fusion—
the ever warm and often hot human melting pot—that
slowly though probably no less surely will endlessly
undergird the restless waves, as the wand of destiny rolls
humanity into one mass, one neighborhood, realizing
Tennyson's cosmic vision as he mused,

"For I dipt into the future, far as human eye could see, . . .
　Till the war-drums throbb'd no longer, and the battle-flags were
　　furl'd,
　In the Parliament of man, the Federation of the world."

THERE is mention in these pages of the Oneida Community. This was the most remarkable in some respects of all the American societies having property in common. It was founded by J. H. Noyes, son of a banker, graduate of Dartmouth, student of law, then of theology, first at Dartmouth and then at Yale. Noyes fitted himself for foreign missionary service, but under the preaching of a revivalist "landed in a new experience and new views of the way of salvation, which took the name of Perfectionism." His wife was a granddaughter of a member of Congress. She had become a convert to his doctrines.

He gathered a company of believers. In 1847 they numbered forty, with others reached by correspondence calling themselves Perfectionists, willing to follow his leadership. In that year Noyes made known to his followers his peculiar views of the relations of the sexes. In 1846 the society had begun at Putney, Vermont, an experiment in communal living. They were mobbed and driven out of the state. In the spring of 1848 they went to Oneida, New York, and began community life anew. The members were nearly all Americans. They had hard early struggles, but later prospered greatly, bought land, built shops and became an industrial community, manufacturing many articles. Among the members were lawyers, clergymen, merchants, physicians, teachers. They took religious experience as their cornerstone. Their code concluded: "Perfectionists hold that intercourse with God may proceed so far as to destroy selfishness in the heart, and to make an end of sin. This is the special phase of religious experience which we profess, and for which we are called Perfectionists."

They held communism to be "the social state of the resurrection."

The community system, which they held to have been divinely commanded, they extended beyond property—to persons; and thus they justified their extraordinary social system, in which there was no marriage; or, as they put it, "complex marriage takes the place of simple." They surrounded this singular combination of polygamy and polyandry with certain social and religious restraints; but affirmed that there was "no intrinsic difference between property in persons and property in things; and that the same spirit which abolished exclusiveness in regard to money would abolish, if circumstances allowed full scope to it, exclusiveness in regard to women and children."

They had no preaching and did not observe Sunday, because they held that with them every day was a Sabbath. They did not pray aloud and avoided with care all set forms, but they read the Bible and constantly quoted it.

For the time in which they were in community life, and compared to their numbers, they were the most prosperous of all American communities, in the matter of worldly goods. They employed much outside labor in their industries; themselves became largely superintendents and foremen, and forewomen. They treated their employees well and paid them good wages, and were well respected by them and their neighbors. J. H. Noyes, founder and leader, was highly intellectual and a man of exalted character. They printed much literature. Mr. Noyes was the author of the book, "History of American Socialisms." They published a newspaper, called the "Circular." In a "Home Talk" reported in the "Circular" of February 2, 1874, Noyes said: "We have got into the position of com-

munism, where without genuine salvation from sin our
passions will overwhelm us, and nothing but confusion and
misery can be expected. On the other hand, we have got
into a position where, if we do have the grace of God
triumphant in our hearts and flowing through our nature,
there is an opportunity for harmony and happiness beyond
all that imagination has conceived. So it is hell behind us,
and heaven before us, and a necessity that we should
march!"

"Complex marriage" meant, in their practice: that within
the limits of the community membership, any man or
woman might freely cohabit, having first gained each
other's consent, not by private conversation or courtship,
but through the intervention of some third person or persons, and that the propagation of children was controlled
by the society. They practiced what they called "scientific
propagation." They reverted to the common wives and
husbands idea of Plato's Republic for his guardians of the
state, but took their authority from what they thought
the Bible taught.

The Oneida Community lasted in its original form over
thirty years but was finally dissolved in 1880. The great
Mansion House of the old community still stands, in the
center of the town of Kenwood, New York, and is still
occupied. J. H. Noyes, founder and leader of the community, died in 1886. The division of the property was
effected by forming a stock company, and issuing the stock
to the members. It is now the Oneida Community,
Limited; the O.C.L., as they call it. They long led in
the field of trap and chain manufacturing, and manufactured among other things plated silverware. After Pierrepont B. Noyes, born in the Mansion House in 1870, son
of the founder, had received his education and taken time
to cast about for ways to lead a useful life, he returned to
Kenwood in 1894 and became the president and head of
the Oneida Community, Limited. The community was

then making $200,000 worth of silverware a year. Under his leadership, they devoted their energies to this one specialty, and the business increased before long, to over $14,000,000 a year. They make Community silver and have the largest business in their special line in the world. No one person is allowed to hold more than three per cent of the whole stock. Their original holdings had, a few years ago, been multiplied in value five times. But the percentage of distribution remains the same. Their people own their own homes and every family has an automobile.

There is a social creed like the original one, but adapted to new times and conditions—every man has his chance. They are literary. They write. They have a magazine; and old and young contribute to it. They travel and devote much time to music and play. They are still like one big family, but under all the social conditions of their neighbors.

During the World War, Pierrepont B. Noyes, the moving spirit of the metamorphosed community, was first assistant fuel administrator.

Community of goods and complex marriage went out over fifty years ago, but the stamp of brotherhood has been handed down from the oldtime and extends to the children's children.

All this is given here for the purpose of showing another way out, another method of unscrambling the eggs, unraveling the tangled skeins of community ownership of property held in common.

[*Continued from page 50*]

Community of wives and husbands does not mean indiscriminate mating; rather there is to be strict eugenic supervision of all reproductive relations; for it is not enough to educate the child properly; he must be properly born, of select and healthy ancestry. "Education should begin before birth." Another philosopher has said the edu-

cation of the child should begin a thousand years before
it is born.

"Now men engrossed in the pursuit of money are unfit
to govern a state; and our entire plan rests on the hope
that if the guardians rule well and live simply, the economic
man will be willing to let them monopolize administration
if they permit him to monopolize luxury. In short, the perfect society would be that in which each class and each unit
would be doing the work to which its nature and aptitude
best adapted it; in which no class or individual shall interfere with others, but all would cooperate in difference to
produce an efficient and harmonious whole. That would be
a just state."

That, in short, was Plato's Republic; rather, his dream
of a near perfect republic. What is a just state? What is
justice? There are only three things worth while in this
world—justice, beauty and truth; and none of them can
be defined. Four hundred years after Plato, a Roman pro-
curator of Judea, Pilate, asked, helplessly, of Jesus of
Nazareth, "What is truth?"—and philosophers have not
yet answered, nor told us what is beauty. But for justice
Plato ventured a definition. "Justice," he says, "is the having and doing what is one's own."

"This," says Durant, "has a disappointing sound." What
does the definition mean? "Simply that each man should
receive the equivalent of what he produces, and perform
the function for which he is best fit. A just man is a man in
just the right place, doing his best, and giving the full
equivalent of what he receives. A society of just men would
be therefore a highly harmonious and efficient group; for
every element would be in its place, fulfilling its appropriate function like the pieces of a perfect orchestra. Justice in
a society would be like that harmony of relationships
whereby the planets are held together in their orderly (or,
as Pythagoras would have said, their musical) movement."

Or as in Job, 38:7: "When the morning stars sang together, and all the sons of man shouted for joy." So organized, a society is fit for survival. "Where men are out of their natural places, where the business man subordinates the statesman, or the soldier usurps the place of the king—there the coordination of parts is destroyed, the joints decay, the society disintegrates and dissolves. Justice is effective coordination. All evil is disharmony: between man and nature, or man and men, or man and himself. Justice is not mere strength, but harmonious strength; justice is not the right of the stronger, but the effective harmony of the whole. Morality, said Jesus, is kindness to the weak; morality, said Nietzsche, is the bravery of the strong; morality, says Plato, is the effective harmony of the whole."

Plato must have felt that in propounding his plan he was not making an impossible advance on realities which his eyes had seen in his twelve years of wandering; in Egypt, in Sparta where a small ruling class lived a hard and simple life in common in the midst of a subject population; eating together, restricting mating for eugenic ends. He had stayed for a time in Italy with a Pythagorean community, vegetarian and communist, which had for generations controlled the Greek colony in which it lived.

Plato answered all the stock arguments that were hurled against his plan, that have come down to this day, that "when everything belongs to everybody nobody will take care of anything." And Plato was bold enough to risk himself when a chance offered to realize his plan. In 387 B.C. he received an invitation from Dionysius, ruler of the then flourishing and powerful Syracuse, capital of Sicily, to come and turn his kingdom into Utopia; to set up his Republic. But when Dionysius found that the plan required that he should become a philosopher or cease to be a king, he balked; and the upshot was a bitter quarrel.

BORN in London in 1480, at 24 Sir Thomas More was a member of the House of Commons. In the year 1509, when More was 29, King Henry VII died, and King Henry VIII, then a youth of 18, succeeded him. In 1529 More was made chancellor, at 49. He was the first lay chancellor for a considerable period who had been raised to that dignity. He succeeded Cardinal Wolsey, who in *King Henry the Eighth* is made by Shakespeare to say upon receiving the news of the succession:

> "That's somewhat sudden:
> But he's a learned man. May he continue
> Long in his Highness' favour, and do justice
> For truth's sake and his conscience; that his bones,
> When he has run his course and sleeps in blessings,
> May have a tomb of orphans' tears wept on 'em!"

And Wolsey, expecting no such fortune as he hoped for his successor, is made by Shakespeare to say to his good servant:

> "Cromwell, I charge thee, fling away ambition;
> By that sin fell the angels; how can man, then,
> The image of his Maker, hope to win by't?
> Love thyself last; cherish those hearts that hate thee:
> Corruption wins not more than honesty.
> Still in thy right hand carry gentle peace,
> To silence envious tongues. Be just, and fear not:
> Let all the ends thou aim'st at be thy country's,
> Thy God's, and truth's: then, if thou fall'st, O Cromwell,
> Thou fall'st a blessed martyr. . . .
> Had I served my God with half the zeal
> I served my King, He would not in mine age
> Have left me naked to mine enemies."

In the reign of Henry VIII, 12,000 human beings were put to death for theft. Soldiers home from the wars in an impoverished country without chance of employment stole to live and were hanged for their hunger. Cruelty and crime fattened and increased on cruelty and oppression. How much has the world improved since in such periods of stress and readjustment?

Sir Thomas More, out of favor and in prison and brooding on the wrongs of an oppressive system of government, dreamed of a fanciful and better form for society. Utopia is a Greek compound, and means, literally, the Country of Nowhere. It is a portraiture of an imaginary republic, and embodies the conception of the author, partly sound and partly fanciful, as to an ideal excellence of laws and institutions existing among ideal people. Such a conception has been a favorite topic among speculative thinkers, from Plato downwards.

Some of More's conclusions, put into brief form and in modern English were:

"Now I have declared and described unto you, as truly as I could, the form and order of that commonwealth, which verily in my judgment is not only the best, but also which alone of good right may claim and take upon it the name of a commonwealth or public weal. For in other places they speak still of the common wealth. But every man procures his own private gain. Here where nothing is private, the common affairs are earnestly looked upon. And truly on both parts they have good cause to do as they do. For in other countries who knows not that he shall starve for hunger, unless he make some several provision for himself, though the common wealth flourish never so much in riches? And therefore he is compelled in very necessity to have regard to himself, rather than to the people, that is to say, to others. Contrariwise there where all things are common to every man, it is not to be doubted that any man shall lack anything necessary for his private use: so that the common store houses and barns be sufficiently stored. For there nothing is distributed after a niggardly sort, neither is there any poor man or beggar. And though no man has anything, yet every man is rich. For what can be more rich than to live joyfully and merrily, without all grief and pensiveness; not caring for his own living, nor vexed and troubled with his wife's importunate complaints, nor dreading poverty to his son, nor sorrowing for his

daughter's dowry? Nay, they take no care at all for the living and
wealth of themselves and all theirs, of their wives, their children,
their nephews, their children's children, and all the succession that
shall ever follow in their posterity. And yet besides this there is no
less provision for them that were once laborers and are now weak
and impotent, than for them that do now labor and take pains.
Here now would I see, if any man dare be so bold as to compare
with this equity the justice of other nations. Among whom, I forsake God if I can find any sign or token of equity and justice. For
what justice is this if a rich goldsmith, or an usurer, or to be short
any of them, that which either do nothing at all, or that which they
do is such that it is not very necessary to the common wealth, should
have a pleasant and wealthy living, either by idleness, or by unnecessary business: when in the mean time poor laborers, carters,
ironsmiths, carpenters, and plowmen, by so great and continual toil
as drawing beasts be scant liable to sustain, and again so necessary
toil that without it no commonwealth were able to continue and
endure one year, should yet get so hard and poor a living, and live
so wretched and miserable a life that the state and condition of
the laboring beasts may seem much better and wealthier? For they
are not put to so continual labor, and their living is not much worse,
yea to them much pleasanter, taking no thought of the mean season
for the time to come. But these poor wretches are presently tormented with barren and unfruitful labor. And the remembrance
of their poor indigent and beggarly old age kills them up. For their
daily wages is so little that it will not suffice for the same day, much
less does it yield any overplus that may daily be laid up for the relief of old age. Is this not an injust and unkind public weal, which
gives great fees and rewards for gentlemen, as they call them, and
to goldsmiths, and to such others, which are either idle persons, or
else only flatterers and devisers of vain pleasures? And of the contrary part makes no provision for poor plowmen, colliers, laborers,
carters, ironsmiths and carpenters: without whom no commonwealth can continue? But after it has abused the laborers of their
lusty and flowering age, at the last when they be oppressed with
old age and sickness, being needy, poor and indigent of all things,
then forgetting that their so many painful watchings, not remem-

bering their so many and so great benefits, recompenses and ac-
quires them most unkindly with miserable death. And yet besides
this the rich men not only by private fraud but also by common
laws do every day pluck and snatch away from the poor some part
of their daily living. So whereas it seemed before unjust to recompense with unkindness their pains that have been beneficial to the
public weal, now they have to this their wrong and unjust dealing
(which is yet a much worse point) given the name of justice, yea
and that by force of a law. Therefore when I consider and weigh
in my mind all these commonwealths, which nowadays any where
do flourish, so God help me, I can perceive nothing but a certain
conspiracy of rich men procuring their own commodities under the
name and title of the common wealth. They invent and devise all
means and crafts, first how to keep safely, without fear of losing,
what they have unjustly gathered together, and next how to hire
and abuse the work and labor of the poor for as little money as may
be. These devices, which the rich men have decreed to be kept and
observed under color of the commonality, that is to say, also of the
poor people, then they are made laws.

"But these most wicked and vicious men, when they have by their
unsatiable covetousness divided among themselves all those things
which would have sufficed all men, yet how far are they from the
wealth and felicity of the Utopian common wealth? Out of the
which, in that all desire of money with the use thereof is utterly
secluded and banished, how great a heap of cares is cut away! How
great an occasion of wickedness and mischief is plucked up by the
roots! For who knows not that fraud, theft, rapine, brawling,
quarreling, bribing, strife, chiding, contention, murder, treason,
poisoning, which by daily punishments are rather revenged than
refrained, do die when money dieth? And also that fear, grief, care,
labors and watchings do perish even the same moment that money
perishes? Yea poverty itself, which only seemed to lack money, if
money were gone, it also would decrease and vanish away. And
that you may perceive this more plainly, consider with yourselves
some barren and unfruitful year, wherein many thousands of people
have starved with hunger: I dare be bold to say that in the end of
that penury so much more corn or grain might have been found in

the rich men's barns, if they had been searched, as being divided among them whom famine and pestilence then consumed, no man at all should have felt that plague and penury. So easily might men get their living, if that same worthy princess lady, money, did not alone stop up the ways between us and our living, which in God's name was very excellently devised and invented, that by her the way thereto should be opened. I am sure the rich men perceive this, nor are they ignorant how much better it were to lack no necessary thing, than to abound with overmuch superfluity; to be rid out of innumerable cares and troubles, than to be besieged and encumbered with great riches. And I doubt not that either the respect of every man's private commodity, or else the authority of our savior Christ (which his great wisdom could not but know what were best, and for his inestimable goodness could not but counsel to that which he knew to be best) would have brought all the world long ago into the laws of this weal public, if it were not that one only beast, the princess and mother of all mischief, Pride, doth withstand and let it. She measures not wealth and prosperity of her own commodities, but by the miseries and incommodities of others; she would not by her good will be made a goddess, if there were no wretches left, over whom she might, like a scornful lady, rule and triumph, over whose miseries her felicities might shine, whose poverty she might vex, torment and increase by gorgeously setting forth her riches. This hellhound creeps into men's hearts: and plucks them back from entering into the right path of life, and is so deeply rooted in men's breasts that she cannot be plucked out.

"This form and fashion of a weal public, which I would gladly wish unto all nations, I am glad yet that it chanced to the Utopians, which have followed those institutions of life, whereby they have laid such foundations of their common wealth, as shall continue and last not only wealthy, but also, as far as man's wit may judge and conjecture, shall endure forever. For, since the chief causes of ambition and sedition, with other vices, is plucked up by the roots, and abandoned at home, there can be no jeopardy of domestic dissension, which alone has cast under foot and brought to nought the well fortified and strongly defended wealth and riches of many cities. But forasmuch as perfect concord remains, and wholesome laws are executed at home, the envy of all foreign princes is not able to shake or move the empire, though they have many times long ago gone about to do it, being evermore driven back."

In More's Utopia of his dream all property was in common. All worked for the good of all. But gold and silver were used only among the people of More's dream country for making toys for children and chains for binding prisoners, and the meaner vessels, so that they were thought of only with contempt. Excepting only that hoards of gold and silver were kept to loan to outside peoples, in order to earn more gold and silver in interest, and to pile up stores of it against wars of aggression, when soldiers of the other nations were hired to fight their wars of aggression, of which there were not likely to be any, or many, because these hoards of gold and silver were employed also in hiring their enemies to fight against one another, in case the Utopians themselves were threatened, and in employing internal agents in any country plotting against them (the Utopians) to procure peaceful measures instead of armed conflict.

Once, More says in his *Utopia*, ambassadors came to treat with the Utopians. They came wearing uniforms bedecked with gold and silver, and as they passed among the people of Utopia, these thought they were poor prisoners, wearing the disgraceful signs of servitude.

APPENDIX B

TWO HUNDRED years after Sir Thomas More had dreamed of his Utopia, Jonathan Swift ventured into the same land of dreams, with a country he found in the journeyings he called *Gulliver's Travels*, when he was cast by accident upon the island of the Houyhnhnms. This part of the travels of Gulliver he called "A Voyage to the Houyhnhnms." Jonathan Swift was born in Dublin March 30, 1667, and died in October, 1745. His training and environment gave him singular facility as a critic of the injustices and inharmonies of the period in which he lived and was a part.

The Houyhnhnms inhabit an imaginary country where a superior race of horses rule, with an inferior race of men, the Yahoos, their servants. The Houyhnhnms are vegetarians, of course. This book is a satire on European governments and the habits and morals of their peoples, with their wars for trivial causes or no cause above a whim; their injustices, diseases, follies, vices; where there are beggars and robbers and cheating, flattering, suborning, forging, gaming, lying, drunkenness, gluttony, poverty and starvation; where doctors charge high fees for curing imaginary diseases; where there is a society of men bred up from their youth in the art of proving by words multiplied for the purpose that white is black and black is white, according as they are paid (lawyers); to which society all the rest of the people are slaves. The visitor tells the Houyhnhnms that the chief minister of state in the country he came from (England) gets office by knowing how with prudence to get ride of a wife, daughter or sister; or by betraying or undermining his predecessor; or through furious zeal in public assemblies against the corruptors of the court; that these ministers, having all employments at their disposal, preserve themselves in power by bribing and all sorts of dishonest practices; and at last by an act of indemnity they secure themselves from after reckonings and retire from the public laden with the spoils of the nation.

Compared with the race of humans in Europe is this race of the Houyhnhnms who have not in their language a name for lying but can only describe it as saying the thing which is not. They are endowed by nature with a general disposition to all virtues, and have no conceptions or ideas of what is evil in a "rational" creature, so their grand maxim is to cultivate reason and be wholly governed by it. Friendship and benevolence are their prime virtues; and these are not confined to particular objects, but are universal to the whole race. They preserve civility and decency in the highest degrees, but are altogether ignorant of ceremony; they believe nature teaches them to love the whole species. They have no word to express anything that is evil, except what they borrow of the deformities and ill qualities of the Yahoos. "Wherever there is any want (which is but seldom), it is immediately supplied by unanimous consent and contribution." They have no money, nor do they need any.

APPENDIX C

THE pioneer of modern socialism was Saint-Simon, who was responsible for the founding of a new sect, called the Saint-Simonians, which flourished in France for a considerable period; was carried to other countries by its disciples there, and for a time commanded the attention of intellectual classes. The leaders held a large place in the world of thought and were numbered among the men who projected and carried out some of the great undertakings of their time.

Count Henry de Saint-Simon was born in Paris in 1760. He belonged to a noble family of France, which traced its origin to Charlemagne. He entered the army at sixteen and the year after came to America and fought in the War of the Revolution under Washington. He took part in the siege of Yorktown and witnessed the surrender of Cornwallis. He distinguished himself for bravery on this occasion, and received honorable recognition of his gallant conduct from the Society of the Cincinnati. On his return to France, in speaking of his sojourn in the United States, he said: "I occupied myself much more with political science than military tactics. The war in itself did not interest me, but the purpose of the war interested me exceedingly, and this interest enabled me to endure its hardships without repugnance. I desire the attainment of the purpose, I was accustomed to say to myself, and I ought not to rebel against the means thereto. . . . My vocation was not that of a soldier; I was drawn towards a very different, indeed, I may say, diametrically opposite, kind of activity. The life purpose which I set before me was to study the movements of the human mind, in order that I might then labor for the perfection of civilization. From that time forward I devoted myself to this work without reserve; to it I consecrated my entire life."

Saint-Simon was taken prisoner by the British when returning to France in the Ville de Paris, and carried to Jamaica, where he was detained until the close of the war. In returning to Europe he visited Mexico, and there made an attempt to carry out one of the magnificent plans for the advancement of mankind which he had been revolving in his mind. He endeavored to interest the viceroy in a project for building a canal to unite the Atlantic with the Pacific.

(While his exertions were unsuccessful, it is interesting to note that De Lesseps drew his inspiration largely from him. Viscount Ferdinand De Lesseps was born in Versailles; entered the consular service of France; was consul at Cairo, Rotterdam, Malaga and Barcelona, and in 1848-49 minister to Spain. In 1832, in Egypt, the idea of a canal at Suez occurred to him, as it had to Napoleon. He became a friend of Said Pasha, who was later viceroy. In 1854 De Lesseps was in Egypt again. The viceroy granted him a concession and gave him the assistance of the Egyption government, to connect the Mediterranean and the Red Sea. English engineers were skeptical and the English government opposed the project. But De Lesseps secured the favor of Emperor Napoleon III and Empress Eugenie, to whom he was related. Work on the canal began in 1859 and was finished in ten years. The formal opening was November 16-20 in 1869. De Lesseps conceived the reclaiming of the Sahara Desert; a canal through the Isthmus of Corinth; a railroad from Europe to India. Backed by 200,000 investors, in 1881 he undertook the building of the Panama Canal; failed largely on account of the ravages of tropic diseases; but pointed the way to the consummation of this gigantic project.)

A few years later Saint-Simon formed designs for a canal to connect Madrid with the sea, and might possibly have succeeded in realizing them, had not the French Revolution recalled him to France. He sided with the people, was elected president of the commune in which his property was situated, in 1789, and in an address to the electors proclaimed his intention to renounce the title of count, since he regarded it as inferior to that of citizen. He likewise refused another office lest it should be supposed he owed it to his rank. All this, however, did not prevent his imprisonment on account of his nobility, which rendered him in the eyes of the terrorists a dangerous character. It was at this time that he believed his ancestor Charlemagne appeared to him and encouraged him with a prophecy of future greatness. "Charlemagne appeared to me and said: 'Since the world has existed, no family has enjoyed the honor of producing a hero and a philosopher of the first rank: this honor has been reserved for my house. My son, thy success as a philosopher will equal mine as a warrior and politician.' "

Saint-Simon upon his release from prison speculated in the confiscated national lands, realized 144,000 francs from his investments, and then retired from business and devoted the following seven years to preparatory study in the universities. Physiology and the physical sciences interested him chiefly.

He concluded that the crisis of society was due to the fact that it was experiencing a transitional period; came to believe that a restoration of harmony was dependent upon the advancement of science, and that social regeneration must be physico-political, the subordination of knowledge to feeling. Finally, he concluded that religion of some kind is indispensable to social progress, and that the priests of this religion must be the rulers of the world.

Saint-Simon then decided that it was necessary to add an experimental training to his theoretical one in order to prepare him for his mission, and accomplished this by living every kind of life, from that of the wealthy entertainer of savants to one of poverty and dissipation. This attempt to pass through the experiences and feelings of a lifetime in a few years made him prematurely old.

He began his career as an author and reformer at 43, in 1803, and never abandoned it until his death in 1825. He taught that the golden age of humanity was not behind us; that it was to come, and will be found in the perfection of the social order. "Our fathers have not seen it; our children will one day behold it. It is our duty to prepare the way for them."

He became poverty stricken, almost starved as he worked on. Afterwards his disciples were proud of his appeals for financial help at this stage, to enable him to carry on his labors and publish and proclaim his doctrines. One of them wrote to accompany a copy of a book on his doctrines: "Children of Saint-Simon! generations of the future; guard as a religious memorial these lines which your father has left you as a sacred legacy. When his word shall have renewed the face of the earth, when the doctrine of RECOMPENSE ACCORDING TO WORKS shall have been realized among men, when the last of the living shall obtain from the solicitude of society a guaranteed subsistence, a remuneration in proportion to merits, children of Saint-Simon, you will then love to repeat how, in order to accomplish his mission of regeneration, your father was reduced to begging."

In a state of loneliness, when past 60, Saint-Simon was filled with despair by the thought that his life had been a failure, and he resolved to put an end to his own wretched existence. Fortunately, however, he succeeded in inflicting only severe but not fatal injuries upon himself. His pitiable condition moved some kind hearts, and he was cared for tenderly and until he recovered, when he regained his faith in his mission and worked more diligently than ever. In the same year he finished one of his most important works, and in 1825, the year of his death, he completed *The New Christianity*. (*Nouveau Christianisme*.) It was from this that his disciples chiefly drew their inspiration.

On his death bed he told his favorite scholar, Rodrigues: "All my life is comprised in this one thought: to guarantee to all men the freest development of their faculties. Forty-eight hours after our second publication the party of the laborers will be formed; the future is ours." These were his last words. In very brief, this is an epitome of his doctrines:

The time is ripe for a new social system based on universal association. Belief, faith, having lost its power, must be replaced by knowledge. Knowledge and industry are to be united and govern the world. They are to furnish to men the guidance and leadership they need and desire.

Universal peace was first to be guaranteed. A European parliament composed of true leaders must now arbitrate between nations.

Equality is to be avoided, as involving greater injustice than our present economical life. RECOMPENSE IN PROPORTION TO MERIT is the true maxim. But all are to be guaranteed work; all must work either mentally or physically. In a socially regenerated state there is no room left for idlers. An idler is a parasite; he devours what others produce and makes no return. Wealthy idlers are thieves; another class of idlers consists of beggars, and this last class of do-nothings is scarcely less contemptible and dangerous than the first. The abolition of inheritance was proposed. Flesh and spirit both had their rights, and their harmonious union and development alone formed the perfect man. Everything that was good and true and beautiful was to be encouraged. Luther is even accused of heresy because he rejected art as a handmaid of religion. The new society is religious and holy, and its chiefs are its priests.

Revolution is injurious and is not to be looked to as a means of social regeneration. It is destructive, whereas a constructive power is sought. Reform must be brought about by public opinion, and public opinion is to be enlightened by the printed and spoken word.

An appeal is made to royalty to assist in this noble work, as its interests are at one with the industrials, and opposed to those of the do-nothings. In the new state the king is to take the title of the "First Industrial of his kingdom."

"In the New Christianity," said Saint-Simon, "all morality will be derived immediately from this principle: men ought to regard each other as brothers. This principle, which belongs to primitive Christianity, will receive a glorification, and in its new form will read: Religion must aid society in its chief purpose, which is the most rapid improvement in the lot of the poor."

It is thus that the social question becomes the essence of religion. This was the starting point of Saint-Simon's disciples, and led to the formation of a Saint-Simon sect with a priesthood.

They established missions and bishoprics in all parts of France, and also carried the new gospel to foreign lands, as Belgium and Algeria. Paris was divided into twelve districts and a male and a female missionary sent into each part. They propagated their faith by numerous lectures and by the press. One of their organs was called *The Globe*. Its mottoes were: "Religion, Science, Industry, Universal Association." The purpose of all social institutions ought to be the intellectual, moral and physical amelioration of the poorest and most numerous class, they said, and all privileges of birth are abolished, they declared.

"TO EACH ONE ACCORDING TO HIS CAPACITY; TO EACH CA-
PACITY ACCORDING TO ITS WORKS," was their motto. They
adopted a peculiar costume. They retired to a sort of monastery.

There came a schism. One branch advocated views which can
fairly be called free-love. The other adopted a life of severe as-
ceticism, with husbands separated from their wives. They employed
no servants, as they held the performance of labor to be a religious
act. They stressed mental development; gave instruction in astronomy, geology, physical geography, and engineering. De Lesseps
was connected with them. They projected the Suez Canal, and
De Lesseps finally built it. "The initiation of that gigantic enterprise
was taken by those whom the Old World could recognize only as
Utopists, dreamers, or fools," wrote one of their leaders. The
learned and expert among the Saint-Simonians occupied many great
positions in France and other countries.

Saint-Simonism is the first example of pure socialism, which in
its definition is an economic system in which production is carried
on in common, and the fruits of labor distributed according to some
ideal standard, which appears just to the promoters of the scheme.
This standard has varied according to the subjective ideals of different socialists. The Saint-Simonians were led to socialism by observing the ill regulated distribution of economic goods under our present social regime. They found the idle surfeited in luxuries and the
diligent without the comforts and often without even the necessaries of life, the former enjoying the right to live as parasites on
the fruits of the toil of the busy, the latter enjoying the right to
choose between hard and ill paid labor and death by starvation. The
world appeared in a state of disharmony, and they proposed to
restore harmony by a new economic system.

The Saint-Simonians believed it only possible to remedy these evils
of distribution by the substitution of state property for private
property. They held that men were by nature unequal, and that it
was right to reward superior power, when exerted for the general
good. Their idea was that EACH ONE SHOULD LABOR ACCORDING
TO HIS CAPACITY AND BE REWARDED ACCORDING TO THE SERVICE
RENDERED.

They wished to organize civil society on the plan of an army.

They rejected inheritance. Christ's command was "Away with slavery!" Saint-Simon's, "Away with inheritance." Property now inherited would naturally become common property in the new society.

The Saint-Simonians were accused in the Chamber of Deputies of advocating community of goods and community of wives. They defended themselves in a brochure dated October 1, 1830. "The Saint-Simonians reject this equal division of property," the brochure said, after an introductory statement, "which would constitute in their eyes a more reprehensible act of violence, a more revolting injustice, than the present unequal division, which was effected in the first place by force of arms, by conquest. . . . They believe in the natural inequality of men, and regard this inequality as the very basis of association, as the indispensable condition of social order. They reject the system of community of goods, for this would be a manifest violation of the first of all the moral laws which it is their mission to teach—that in the future each one should LABOR ACCORDING TO HIS CAPACITY AND BE REWARDED ACCORDING TO HIS WORKS. But in virtue of this law they demand the abolition of all privileges of birth, without exception, and consequently the destruction of inheritance, the chief of these privileges, which today comprehends all the others, and the effect of which is to leave to chance the distribution of social privileges among a small number, and to condemn the most numerous class to deprivation, to ignorance, to misery. . . . Christianity has released woman from servitude but has condemned her to religious, political and civil inferiority. The Saint-Simonians have announced her emancipation, but they have not abolished the sacred law of marriage, proclaimed by Christianity. On the contrary, they give a new sanctity to this law. . . . They demand that one man should be united to one woman, but they teach that the wife should be the equal of the husband."

After the Revolution of July, 1830, the faith gained a large number of adherents, and among men of distinction and learning. De Lesseps, builder of the Suez Canal, as before stated, was among them. So were many authors of books and writers of plays.

At one period, they adopted a peculiar costume embracing a

waistcoat so contrived that no one could either put it on or take it off without assistance; this symbolized the dependence of man upon his fellow-man.

Saint-Simon left his impress upon history. A writer has said of him that "he first taught us to consider the history of labor and property as an essential element of human development; he first discerned clearly the two great classes of industrial society, and implanted bitter hatred in the consciousness of the lower classes. He first represented social reform as the only true function of government. He first brought forward the question of inheritance, the question upon which the entire future of the social form will rest. He is the boundary of a new era. He left the beaten track and laid down his life in discovering and opening for society a new path. In it we have as yet taken only a few steps, and no human eye is able to discern the goal whither we are tending."

APPENDIX D

FRANCOIS NOEL BABOEUF was born in St. Quentin, in the Department of Aisne, France, in 1764. He appears to have come of good family, for his father was a major in the French army and devoted much attention to his son's education. He became a land surveyor and was elected an administrator of the Department of the Somme. He was soon arrested on a charge of forgery, condemned, and sentenced to 20 years imprisonment. He escaped to Paris and joined the revolutionary movement. Like Mably and numerous speculative thinkers at that time, he was filled with admiration for the socialistic institutions of the Greeks and Romans. He founded a paper which he named *Tribune of the People*, and which was the first socialistic newspaper ever published. His violent abuse of those in authority and his revolutionary projects led to his imprisonment for a few months in 1795. He improved the opportunity to establish a connection with Darthe, Buonarroti and other Jacobins and terrorists of whom there were nearly 2000 in the same prison. Upon their release they formed a conspiracy, called, after its leader, "the conspiracy of Baboeuf." Its object was to overthrow the Directory and introduce the communistic millennium, which they had begun to evolve while in prison. The members of the band called themselves The Equals. The activity of the leaders was remarkable, and met with considerable success in winning adherents. In April, 1796, 17,000 men were prepared to join them in an insurrection against the Directory and for the establishment of a communistic republic. Discovery of their plot was followed by arrests and a long trial. Baboeuf and Darthe were condemned to death the following year and guillotined on May 24, 1797.

Baboeuf's theoretical development of communism is comparatively simple. Its leading idea is thus expressed: "The aim of society is the happiness of all, and happiness consists in equality."

It is emphasized again and again that this equality must be perfect and absolute. It is officially proclaimed that the harmony of the system would be broken by having a single man in all the world richer or more powerful than his fellows.

"Nature has given to every man an equal right to the enjoyment of all goods," the followers of Baboeuf said. They maintained that all public and private wrongs, as oppressions, tyrannies, wars and crimes, take their origin in disobedience to this natural law.

"In a true society there ought to be neither poor nor rich," they declared. Baboeuf proposed to attain equality by degrees. He desired that a large national and common property should be at once formed out of the property of corporations and public institutions. The property of individuals was to be added to this upon their death, as inheritance was to be abolished. All property would thus become nationalized in the course of fifty years. The earth must belong to all, and its fruits must be common property. Officers were to receive no more than those under them, and a rapid rotation in office was to prevent the acquirement of habits and thoughts consequent upon superior position. No one would become accustomed to command, no one accustomed to obey. All differences save those relating to age and sex being abolished, equality is interpreted to mean uniformity. All must be dressed alike, save that distinctions are made for sex and age; all must eat the same quantity of the same kind of food, and all must be educated alike. Comfortable mediocrity in everything is the openly expressed ideal. Children are removed from the family at an early age, and brought up together, to train them in principles of communism, and to prevent the growth of differences and inequalities. The most cheerless of all communistic schemes fitly took its origin among those sunk in the most degraded materialism of the French Revolution.

IDEALS OF FOURIERISM

CHARLES FOURIER, born in 1772 in France, at an early age inherited 100,000 francs upon the death of his father, invested the money in foreign trade and lost it in the siege of Lyons in 1793, during the Reign of Terror, when his bales of cotton were used to form barricades and his provisions to feed the soldiers. He was taken prisoner and kept in confinement, expecting daily to be led forth to execution. Release, however, enabled him to join the army, for which he had some taste. He was able to make suggestions which were followed to advantage by his superiors, but ill health obliged him to retire from the army after two years. Events of his early life led him to a train of thought which ended in his condemnation of the economic organization of society as a disastrous failure, and he began to elaborate a social scheme which should promote truth, honesty, economy of resources, and the development of our natural propensities. This became the one aim of his life. He constructed an ideal world, and in this he ever lived. Association with its imaginary creatures was his company; the fancy that he had benefited them was his consolation in adversity, and the unwavering belief that the creations of his brain were good enabled him to persevere to the end. In 1808 he published a prospectus and an outline of his system, but it was five years before he found even one supporter. His was the case of a reformer who presents to mankind plans which he knows will save men from poverty, selfishness, hypocrisy, corruption, intrigue, deceit, crime and all manner of misfortune and wickedness, and for five years his projects are not so much as noticed. Like Luther, Fourier offered to maintain his theses against all comers, and no one thought it worth while to engage in the controversy. He wrote to Robert Owen, the English communist, but received no encouragement. The Saint-Simonians treated him with contempt. He did not desire so much the adherence of personal disciples as men of property, who could enable him to make a trial of his scheme; for he thought the practical workings of one experiment would convince the world. He announced publicly that he would be at home every day at noon to meet any one disposed to furnish a million francs for an establishment based on the principles which he had published, and for twelve years repaired to his house daily at the appointed hour. The philanthropist whom he awaited never came. Only one experiment was made in his lifetime. In 1832 a member of the Chamber of Deputies offered an estate near Versailles as the basis of an association, and the offer was accepted by a few converts. Fourier was never satisfied with the management, which seems to have been defective, and the experiment soon failed.

"A social organization must be formed which will allow free play to our passions, so that they may combine harmoniously. Our present society, called civilization, does not, and cannot, do this. It is a system of oppression and repression, and is necessarily a frightful discord. Harmony can be found only in combinations of suitable numbers in communities known as phalanxes, and occupying buildings called phalansteries. Each phalanx is a unit, a great family, and dwells in a single building, a phalanstery. What is it that determines the proper number for a single phalanx? It is the twelve passions of man. They are seeing, hearing, smelling, feeling, tasting —passions tending to luxury; and amity, love, paternity, ambition —passions tending to groups; and cabiliste, alternate, and composite—passions tending to series. These can be combined in 820 different ways in as many individuals, and no possible combination ought to be unrepresented in the workers of any phalanx, or there will be a lack of perfect harmony. But in every community there will be found old men, infants, and those disabled on account of illness or accident. Provision must also be made for absences. There ought not, then, to be less than 1500 or 1600 members in a phalanx, though 400 is mentioned as a possible but desirable minimum; and 1800 to 2000 members are recommended. A larger number would produce discord, and is, therefore, inadmissible. But a further arrangement is necessary. These different characters thrown together helter-skelter would no more produce harmony

than it would for one blindfolded to draw from a bag two thousand combinations of notes for the piano and play them in the
order in which they are drawn. On the contrary, they must be
ordered intelligently in series, the series combined into groups, and
the groups united into the phalanx. Those having similar tastes form
series, which must consist of some seven, eight, or nine members.
Several series having related tastes and desires unite in a group. A
group undertakes some kind of labor, such as the care of fruit trees.

"All labor becomes pleasant to man, as nature meant it should
be. It is only when he is forced to do a kind which he does not like,
or is obliged to overwork, that productive exertion becomes repul-
sive. This is avoided in the phalanxes, as each one is allowed to follow his own bent, being at perfect liberty to join any group of
laborers or to change from group to group as he may see fit.

"Work of this character becomes play, and children like it, while
men are as fond of it as of athletic sports. We now discover men
undergoing severe physical exertion for the sake of excellence in
running, swimming, wrestling, and rowing. There will spring
up a similar rivalry between groups of cultivators in the phalanxes.
One set of laborers will endeavor to obtain more useful products
from ten or a hundred acres than another similar group from the
same extent of land of like quality."

Fourier held that a man could produce enough under this social
regime from his 18th to 28th year, so that he could pass the remainder of his life in leisure.

He held that the socialistic phalanx will avoid the waste of goods
caused by industrial and commercial competition. "Think of the
enormous loss to society of labor and capital due to a superfluity of
shops all over a great country like the United States.

"Whenever capital, consisting of economic goods, like houses
and implements, is not fully employed, or whenever men are waiting for work, economic power is being wasted. Competition often
makes it cost far more to do a given amount of business than it
would otherwise.

"Every square league of land has its one phalanstery occupied by
a phalanx, consisting of some four hundred families. It costs no
more to build a palace for all these families than it would to con-

struct four hundred separate and comfortable cottages. While each family has its separate rooms, cooking is carried on in common, and great saving is thereby secured. A fire to cook four hundred dinners may not cost ten times as much as a fire to cook two, while it costs scarcely a greater exertion to watch a large roast than a small one. A large number working together afford every opportunity for fruitful combination and division of labor. Other economies will be effected by the suppression of useless classes. In the new society there will be no soldiers of destruction, no policemen, no criminals, or lawyers.

"Products are conveniently exchanged among members of a commune, while phalanx exchanges superfluities with phalanx and nation with nation in the most economical manner."

Fourier retained private capital, and, temporarily, at least, inheritance. A very generous minimum is set apart for each member of the commune, and the enormous surplus is divided between labor, capital and talent—five twelfths going to labor, four twelfths to capital, and three twelfths to talent. The division is made by the phalanxes through the agency of officers whom they elect. The maxim is not LABOR ACCORDING TO CAPACITY AND REWARD ACCORDING TO SERVICES, as with the Saint-Simonians and others, but LABOR ACCORDING TO CAPACITY AND REWARD IN PROPORTION TO EXERTION, TALENT AND CAPITAL. Labor is divided into three classes—necessary, useful, and agreeable—the highest reward accruing to the first and the smallest to the last division, in accordance with the principles of equity.

Government, for which there is little need, is republican. Officers are elected. The chief of a phalanx is a unarch. The next highest officer is at the head of three or four phalanxes, and is called a duarch. Triarchs, tetrarchs, and pentarchs follow: while the highest officer of the world is the ominarch, who dwells at Constantinople, the capital of the world.

While there are grades of society, the rich and powerful are so animated by the spirit of association that the differences give no offense. Holding that a single experiment would convince the world that his system of phalanxes was the only correct organization, Fourier believed the millennium was to dawn in a few years, even within a shorter period than ten years! Once he advised his followers to not purchase real property, as the progress of Fourierism would soon cause it to depreciate in value.

Fourier's first adherent was Just Murion, who attached himself to the master in 1813, and remained a faithful follower for many years. He wrote two books, explaining Fourierism. One of them, first in three volumes and a second edition in two volumes, is the ablest presentation of the doctrine, and became the text book of the school. Wealthy and talented and titled people fell in line. When the Saint-Simonians separated, a considerable number of them passed over to Fourierism. After the death of Fourier the school received large accessions of adherents. The disciples published a paper, even a daily, then a weekly and monthly, and they formed a society, with a capital of seven hundred thousand francs.

Fourierism was brought to America about 1840, and soon found numerous advocates, including, many names of which America is proud. Thirty-four experiments were made by Fourierists in this country, all of which failed for some reason or other. The most remarkable of these experiments was Brook Farm.

APPENDIX F

ETIENNE CABET was born in 1788 in Dijon, France. He received a good education, became a lawyer and practiced first in his native city, then in Paris. He was appointed attorney-general of Corsica in 1830, but lost his place the following year on account of his opposition to government. He was elected to the Chamber of Deputies after his return to Paris. He devoted the remainder of his life to literature, politics, and communism. One of his principal works was a "Popular History of the French Revolution from 1789 to 1830." In a journal which he published at that time, *La Populaire,* he advocated moderate communistic principles, as they were afterwards called. He was condemned to two years' imprisonment for an article in this paper, in which he attacked the king personally, but he was fortunate enough to escape imprisonment by flight to London. It was here he became acquainted with Sir Thomas More's "Utopia," from which he received a large part of his inspiration. He returned to France in 1839, and published his "Voyage to Icaria." He describes in this book a previously unknown country. Peace, wisdom, joy, pleasures and happiness reign there. Crimes are unknown. It is Icaria; "a second Promised Land, an Eden, an Elysium, a new terrestrial Paradise."

The object of the book is to show that communism is practicable and the solution of all social problems. It contains an account of an ideal society, but one Cabet thought he was able to establish. He made the attempt, choosing Texas as a place in which his ideals were to be realized. He secured a grant of land on the Red River, and in 1848 sent out several advance guards of Icarians, who were, however, attacked by yellow fever and had disbanded before he arrived in New Orleans with a later detachment. He learned on his arrival that the Mormons had abandoned their settlement in

Nauvoo, Illinois, and set out for that place with his followers. While the Icarians were in Nauvoo they numbered, all told, at one time 1500. They met with some success in cultivating their land, established shops, pursued trades, and set up a printing office, but instead of rejoicing in his prosperity, and laboring to increase it, Cabet was dreaming what he might do if he had half a million, the theater and fine houses he would build, the parks he would lay out.

A division took place among the Icarians. The colony at Nauvoo was broken up, and the members scattered. Cabet and his followers went to St. Louis, where he died in 1856. Some members went to Iowa from Nauvoo and founded a settlement near Corning, which they called Icaria.

Cabet's principles were quite simple, and all centered in the beneficent effects of equality, to which fraternity, as understood by him, necessarily leads. But how are people to be taught to practice Communism? how induce the aristocracy to renounce their privileges? This was to be accomplished by peaceful means alone. The apostles of Icarianism should, like Christ, whose principles they were only carrying out, convert the world by teaching, preaching, writing, discussing, persuading, and by setting good examples. Cabet allowed only fifty years for a peaceful transition from our present economic life to Communism. In the interval, various measures were to be introduced by legislation to pave the way to the new system, among them communistic training of children, a minimum of wages, exemption of the poor from all taxes, and progressive taxation for the rich. But "the system of absolute equality, of community of goods and of labor, will not be obliged to be applied completely, perfectly, universally, and definitely until the expiration of fifty years."

This is, it is said, a fast age, and in not a few respects the saying is true. But man's nature and society are not changing so rapidly. It is the mere externals of our life which change speedily. The economies of common production, thought Cabet, enable all to enjoy every comfort and many luxuries. Elegance and beauty are encouraged. The only choice allowed in one's clothes concerns their color; otherwise all are dressed alike, save that distinctions are made for age and sex.

Marriage and family are held sacred. Celibacy is prohibited. Cabet's views concerning the elevated position due woman were influential in drawing to him the large number of sympathizers he found among the ladies of Paris, who encouraged him with kind words and frequent floral gifts. Work was common, but young men and women were allowed to choose their own careers. If there existed a disproportionate number of applicants for any trade or profession, competitive examination decided who should be selected for it. The others were obliged to make another choice. Diligence and thrift were enjoined on all. Men worked till 65; women till 50. A day's labor was seven hours in summer and five in winter; for women, however, only four. All labor ceased at 1 P.M. Dirty and disagreeable work was performed by machines. Science and literature were held in esteem.

The Icarians had no religion. Communism was their religion, and Cabet its prophet and interpreter and preacher. They had no outstanding leader, but undertook each year to elect a new leader, whose powers were strictly limited to carrying out the commands of the society. They held a meeting every Saturday evening for the discussion of all their affairs. The conclusions ruled the president during the week. He could not sell a bushel of wheat without the instructions of the society. They struggled on bravely, at times with a measure of comfort and success. They had an interesting history, but they failed because of too much government and too little religion, among other faults. Icaria is a memory. The Icarian dream did not come true. Or, reverting to the symbolism suggested by the name, it did come true.

Another Platonian or Utopian or Icarian dream should be mentioned here. It was shaped two years before his death in 1873 by Lord Lytton, who had published at least fifty books and near the end of his labors tried his hand at a volume suggesting the working out of better social conditions. He embraced these in "The Coming Race," in which the author represents an American by accident coming into the regions underneath the earth inhabited by a race of people calling themselves the Vril-ya, who had perfected forms of government far more just and orderly than are found in the outer world. They unite "the greatest degree of happiness with the highest degree of intellectual attainment." The females do the courting. They fly with wings and travel in air boats. They have discovered a mysterious force, vril. This power can destroy like a flash of lighting; yet, differently applied, it can replenish or invigorate life, heal and preserve. By this agency they rend a way through the most solid substances, and open valleys for culture through the rocks. From it they extract light. It affects political polity. Wars between the vril-discoverers ceased, for they brought the art of destruction to such perfection as to annul all superiority in numbers, discipline or military skill. The force lodged in the hollow of a vril rod directed by the hand of a child could shatter the strongest fortress, or destroy a whole army. The age of war was therefore gone. All notions of government by force vanished. Theirs was an autocracy of learning. But the supreme magistrate was not distinguished from the rest by superior habitation or revenue. They had no armies or police, nor needed any; no crime or courts. All had plenty. They were vegetarians. All considered themselves as brothers in an affectionate family. Automatons propelled by vril force performed all the work of servants in the outer world.

"The exquisite politeness and refinement of manners among the Vril-ya, the generosity of their sentiments, the absolute leisure they enjoyed for following out their own private pursuits, the amenities of their domestic intercourse, in which they seemed as members of one noble order that can have no distrust of each other's word or deed, all combined to make the Vril-ya the most perfect nobility which a political disciple of Plato or Sidney could conceive for the ideal of an aristocratic republic."

"The poor man's need is the rich man's shame," was the red thread of the motive running through the pattern that made up the reason for the writing of Lord Lytton's book.

The Roman Catholic Church, while itself teaching individualism, has from the first allowed and encouraged a form of communism in its flourishing and far flung brotherhoods and sisterhoods—in fact has performed and is still doing some of its greatest works through these, with its hospitals, orphanages and similar institutions of mercy, wherever it serves humanity throughout the world. These orders, in the nature of an imperium in imperio, have pioneered in taking light and learning to backward races in ways that would have been impossible through selfish agencies of individualistic exploitation. They are still performing vast good throughout the world—unselfishly, self sacrificing to the last full measure of devotion. Credit this as a further item in the exhibit of historic dreams, with the names of St. Francis, St. Benedict, Junipero Serra and other heroes and martyrs of universal brotherhood shining down the ages. Add it as testimony in the case of Christian socialism or communism.

APPENDIX G

THE ROYAL LAW

THE founders of Bethel and Aurora knew of the experiment at Oneida, New York, where there was community of both property and persons as between the sexes, on the pure plane of eugenic reasons, such as was argued by Plato for his guardians of the state in the Republic of his dream country. They knew of the Shakers in all of whose communities celibacy was practiced; of the Rappists, who adopted and then adhered strictly to celibacy; of the Amana society, who held to the orders of what they believed to be direct revelations from God—and of all the rest.

They were acquainted with the Brook Farm experiment, which in its last years adopted Fourierism, brought to America from France by Albert Brisbane, who was responsible for infecting the shrewd Yankee intelligence with its allurements, and whose versatile and talented son, Arthur Brisbane, was to become perhaps the most prolific and highest paid newspaper editor and writer in America if not in the world, and with the greatest clientele of newspaper readers in history.

Emerson had said that Fourier "had skipped no fact save one, namely, life," and that he "carried a whole French Revolution in his head, and much more."

Horace Greeley was one of the easiest and ablest victims of the enthusiasm of Albert Brisbane for Fourierism. Brisbane had written his "Social Destiny of Man, or Association and Reorganization of Industry," followed by "A Concise Exposition of the Doctrine of Association," which were the American interpretations of the meaning of Fourierism, and of its application to the conditions of this country. Brisbane's vision was described by Emerson as embodying a system in which it took "1680 men to make one man", having reference to the proper number for the dwellers in a phalanstery, the idealistic home of a unit under the Fourieristic plan of the organization of society.

These men planning at Bethel for their greater community home in Oregon had found that in every communistic community so far developed in America there was some peculiar system proposed or practiced—every one but their own at Bethel and the proposed extension of it in Oregon. In several it was celibacy, in one it was community of wives and husbands, in a number it was a peculiarity of religious views; in most of them a peculiar dress; in some community dining and cooking houses.

In their own, they had just one peculiarity—community of goods. Nothing else. No other distinction from the regular order of society in the United States and most other countries.

"Every man and woman must be a brother or a sister to every other man and woman in our family under the fatherhood of God," insisted Dr. Keil, "and in a true Christian family there can be no distinction of persons or interests. Every one is a proprietor. Every one is a partner, and an equal partner. Every one is a boss; or rather there are no bosses at all excepting by mutual and unanimous consent. All own all. No man owns anything individually but every man owns everything as a full partner and with an equal voice in its use and its increase and the profits accruing from it.

"But in no other way do we differ from our neighbors. As a community we are one family. FROM EVERY MAN ACCORDING TO HIS CAPACITY TO EVERY MAN ACCORDING TO HIS NEEDS is the rule that runs through our law of love. As between ourselves we are many with one purpose. In contacts with outsiders we are as one dealing with many, but with justice and honesty and neighborliness, withholding no solicited or needed act of charity or mercy, and giving it without money and without price where there is any call for it, to the limit of our ability in money or food or clothing or service in sickness or in health."

Dr. Keil frequently quoted from Paul's letter to the Romans, giving rules of conduct to the first adherents of the Christian faith in that country, as these: "Owe no man anything, save to love one another: for he that loveth his neighbor hath fulfilled the law. For this, thou shalt not commit adultery, thou shalt not kill, thou shalt not steal, thou shalt not covet, and if there be any other commandment, it is summed up in this word, namely, thou shalt love thy neighbor as thyself. Love worketh no ill to his neighbor; love therefore is the fulfillment of the law. Let us walk becomingly, as in the day, not in reveling and drunkenness, not in chambering and wantonness, not in strife and jealousy."

These words of the apostle to the Gentiles and the first great missionary teacher were the flaming texts of many sermons by Dr. Keil, throughout his career, and of the other colony preachers.

"No man can love his neighbor as himself," expounded Dr. Keil, "without regarding his neighbor's good in all things with the same interest as his own, and that makes impossible any other life than the life in which there shall be community of goods, services, and their usufruct, if our world is to ever realize the dreams of universal and permanent peace and good will among men, with equality of opportunity and complete concord and justice between races and nations. 'Let us walk becomingly, as in the day,' meant, to the Roman Christians of that time, that each one should regiment himself like a faithful Roman soldier, whose participation in parades and drills was in the day time, because, on account of the scarcity of illumination, there was little parading or drilling at night. The Christian must be marked by uprightness in all things, comparable to a Roman soldier on dress parade."

ADDENDA

FINNISH residents of Brooklyn, New York, long maintained a sort of Communism in cooperative labor and property holding, with a resultant high degree of well being and prosperity.

Newly immigrated Jews in Palestine are being formed into like communities, with equally happy results, their cooperative endeavors rendering them soon self contained and presently solvent and able to accumulate surplus holdings above their current necessities.

An able writer, dissatisfied with the present general order and its trends, quotes the lines:

"Oh whereunto is money good?
Who has it not, lacks livelihood;
Who has it, has all trouble and care;
Who once has had it, has despair."

Then adds: "Nobody should 'have it not'; nobody should have a surplus to give him 'trouble and care'; nobody should be obsessed to the point of 'despair,' with the fear of losing his modest capital and income. In other words, (1) adequate incomes and enough of this world's 'goods' to make possible health and comfort, should be within the range of all; (2) an excess should be prohibited any; and (3) economic security with its attendant peace of mind should be the possession of mankind as a whole."

"But how," the colony sages would interpose, "in a society not governed by the Golden Rule, reinforced by the Diamond Rule, and made perfect by the law of love, can there be maintained such a state of well being as the writer visions?"

They would add: "No program ever devised by man can bring about a near approach to the millennium next Monday morning at 7 o'clock. But we can sow the mustard seed of the perfect parable, that by slow growth may become a great tree. Paul can plant, Apollos water, but God giveth the increase. We may vision: 'And every life shall be a song, when all the earth is paradise.' We have a present duty to plant the mustard seed. If we plant it not, we serve not our day and generation."

At a concluding session the colony sages reviewed these words on Communism from one of the latest writings of John Stuart Mill, the great English philosopher and political economist:

"The objection ordinarily made to a system of community property and equal distribution of the produce, that each person would be incessantly occupied in evading his fair share of the work, points, undoubtedly, to a real difficulty. But those who urge this objection forget to how great an extent the same difficulty exists under the system on which nine tenths of the business of society is now conducted. The objection supposes that honest and efficient labor is only to be had from those who are themselves individually to reap the benefit of their own exertions. But how small a part of all the labor performed in England, from the lowest paid to the highest, is done by persons working for their own benefit. From the Irish reaper or hodman to the chief justice or the minister of state, nearly all the work of society is remunerated by wages or fixed salaries. A factory operative has less personal interest in his work than a member of a Communist association, since he is not, like him, working for a partnership of which he is himself a member. It will no doubt be said that, though the laborers themselves have not, in most cases, a personal interest in their work, they are watched and superintended, and their labor directed, and the mental part of the labor performed, by persons who have. Even this, however, is far from being universally the fact. In all public, and many of the largest and most successful private undertakings, not only the labors of detail, but the control and superintendence are intrusted to salaried officers. And though the 'master's eye,' when the master is vigilant and intelligent, is of proverbial value, it must be remembered that in a Socialist farm or manufactory, each laborer would be under the eye, not of one master, but of the whole community. In the extreme case of obstinate perseverance in not performing the due share of work, the community would have the same recourse which society now has for compelling conformity to the necessary conditions of the association. Dismissal, the only remedy at present, is no remedy when any other laborer who may be engaged does no better than his predecessor: the power of dismissal only enables an employer to obtain from his workmen the customary amount of labor, but that customary labor may be of any degree of inefficiency. Even the laborer who loses his employment by idleness or negligence has nothing worse to suffer, in the most favorable case, than the discipline of a workhouse, and if the desire to avoid this be a sufficient motive in the one system, it would be sufficient in the other. I am not undervaluing the strength of the incitement given to labor when the whole or a large share of the benefit of extra exertion belongs to the laborer. But under the present system of industry this incitement, in the great majority of cases, does not exist. If Communistic labor might be less vigorous than that of a peasant proprietor, or a workman laboring on his own account, it would probably be more energetic than that of a laborer for hire, who has no personal interest in the matter at all. The neglect by the uneducated class of laborers for hire of the duties which they engage to perform is in the present state of society most flagrant. Now it is an admitted condition of the Communist scheme that all shall be educated; and this being supposed, the duties of the members of the association would doubtless be as diligently performed as those of the generality of salaried officers in the middle or higher classes; who are not supposed to be necessarily unfaithful to their trust, because so long as they are not dismissed their pay is the same in however lax a manner their duty is fulfilled. Undoubtedly, as a general rule, remuneration by fixed salaries does not in any class of functionaries produce the maximum of zeal; and this as much as can be reasonably alleged against Communistic labor.

"That even this inferiority would necessarily exist is by no means so certain as is assumed by those who are little used to carry their minds beyond the state of things with which they are familiar. . . .

"Another of the objections to Communism is similar to that so often urged against poor-laws; that if every member of the community were assured of subsistence for himself and any number of children, on the sole condition of willingness to work, prudential restraint on the multiplication of mankind would be at an end, and population would start forward at a rate which would reduce the community through successive stages of increasing discomfort to actual starvation. There would certainly be much ground for this apprehension if Communism provided no motives to restraint, equivalent to those which it would take away. But Communism is precisely the state of things in which opinion might be expected to declare itself with greatest intensity against this kind of selfish intemperance. Any augmentation of numbers which diminished the comfort or increased the toil of the mass would then cause (which now it does not) immediate and unmistakable inconvenience to every individual in the association—inconvenience which could not then be imputed to the avarice of employers or the unjust privileges of the rich. In such altered circumstances opinion could not fail to reprobate, and if reprobation did not suffice, to repress by penalties of some description, this or any other culpable self-indulgence at the expense of the community. The Communistic scheme, instead of being peculiarly open to the objection from the danger of over-population, has the recommendation of tending in an especial degree to the prevention of that evil."

Had the Keil colony sages lived to this day, and enjoyed the continued success their manner of life assured, they would have noted the theories of the growing group led by Karl Barth, German theologian, called Barthians, outlined in the words of their recent pronouncement, thus:

"We condemn the dreams of an earthly kingdom of peace and righteousness and general welfare for all. The party programs of various parties prove such dreams are still being dreamed. To dream of a commonwealth of peace, equality and justice and of a classless society in which hunger and misery will be abolished is to deny the limits set by God for earthly bliss and thus to deny the necessity of Christ's salvation. We believe and confess on the contrary that because of our sins there will never be an earthly state in which wages will be commensurate with human needs, in which peace will be attained and in which justice will really be justice. This perfection God has reserved for the new world which will come into being through the resurrected Lord. Until such time human life must stand under the cross which Christ suffered."

The answer of the Aurora philosophers would have been: "Go to the 25th chapter of Matthew. Read there almost the last message of Jesus, given two days before Gethsemane, containing these words:

" 'For I was an hungered, and ye gave me meat: I was thirsty and ye gave me drink: I was a stranger and ye took me in:

" 'Naked, and ye clothed me: I was sick and ye visited me: I was in prison, and ye came unto me. . . . Verily, I say unto you, inasmuch as ye have done it unto one of the least of these my brethren, ye have done it unto me.'

" 'Read on, in verse 41: 'Then shall he say unto them on the left hand, 'Depart from me, ye cursed.'

" 'Read on, in verse 46: 'But the righteous into life eternal.'

"This was the highest point in the teachings of Jesus," they would have concluded. "It proclaims active, unselfish service here the prerequisite of Christian life, and, inferentially, the saving rule for the whole of human society, and the only certain hope of blissful existence beyond the grave."

INDEX